SEXUAL LIBERATION

"...a lucid and masterful account of Christianity's shifting attitude toward sex from the positive valuation of its Jewish roots to the contemporary Church's obsessive hysteria about sex. For anyone who is seeking a clue to today's Christian sex wars, this book will provide it."

Rev. John M. Gessell, Ph.D.
Professor of Christian Ethics, emeritus
School of Theology, University of the South, Sewanne, TN

"...the author has the courage to restore Jesus the Jew to his own origins. In doing so he removes the false garments the Church has spun to make Jesus non-sexual and super-human."

Rev. Myron C. Madden
Retired clinical chaplain and professor in psychiatry
LSU Medical School

"Like the child in the fairy story who noted that 'the emperor has no clothes,' the author sees what others miss... This well-documented but easy to read volume is well recommended to thoughtful Christians, Jews befuddled by their Christian colleagues, and anyone trying to comprehend Western sexual ways."

Robert C. Powell
Psychiatrist and Historian

"A playful, big-hearted, thought-rattling exploration of how sexual pleasure has fared at the hands of Christianity through the ages. For those of us who have been appalled by the recent backlash against sexual liberation and the ensuing witch hunts, reading Lawrence is like drinking champagne at the successful re-election of common sense."

Susan Baur Ph.D.
The Intimate Hour, Love and Sex in Psychotherapy

"Ray Lawrence's new book is a cautionary tale for us all, but told with a light touch and fine pastoral sensitivity to our human nature as sexual beings. It will quickly become a top-tier candidate for adult studies in churches."

Rev. Dr. Wayne G. Boulton

SEXUAL LIBERATION

The Scandal of Christendom

Raymond J. Lawrence, Jr.

Psychology, Religion, and Spirituality
J. Harold Ellens, Series Editor

PRAEGER

Westport, Connecticut
London

Library of Congress Cataloging-in-Publication Data

Lawrence, Raymond J., Jr.
  Sexual liberation : the scandal of Christendom / Raymond J. Lawrence, Jr.
    p. cm. — (Psychology, religion, and spirituality, ISSN 1546–8070)
  Includes bibliographical references (p.) and index.
  ISBN 0–275–99373–6
  1. Sex—Religious aspects—Christianity—History of doctrines.   I. Title.
BT708.L43   2007
  261.8'357—dc22   2006035008

British Library Cataloguing in Publication Data is available.

Library of Congress Catalog Card Number: 2006035008
ISBN-10: 0–275–99373–6
ISBN-13: 978–0–275–99373–3
ISSN: 1546–8070

First published in 2007

Praeger Publishers, 88 Post Road West, Westport, CT 06881
An imprint of Greenwood Publishing Group, Inc.
www.praeger.com

Printed in the United States of America

The paper used in this book complies with the
Permanent Paper Standard issued by the National
Information Standards Organization (Z39.48–1984).

10 9 8 7 6 5 4 3 2 1

Dedicated to Kelly Michaels, Robert F. Kelly, Elizabeth Kelly, Kathryn Dawn Wilson, Scott Privott, Ray Buckey, Gerald Amirault, Kathy Dobie, Duane Parker, Sandra Beth Geisel, Charles Anderson, Gordon MacRae.

And to those countess others,
known and unknown,
who have been inappropriately shamed and penalized by a society profoundly befuddled by sexual pleasure.

Shall we never, never get rid of this Past? … It lies upon the Present like a giant dead body![1]

Nathaniel Hawthorne

A serious examination of sexuality is preferable to a eulogy of love.[2]

Paul Ricoeur

CONTENTS

Series Foreword

The interface between psychology, religion, and spirituality has been of great interest to scholars for a century. In the last three decades a broad popular appetite has developed for books that make practical sense of the complicated research on these three subjects. Freud had a negative outlook on the relationship between psychology, religion, and spirituality, and he thought the interaction between them was destructive. Jung, on the other hand, was quite sure that these three aspects of the human spirit were constructively linked, and one could not be separated from the others. Anton Boisen and Seward Hiltner derived much insight from both Freud and Jung, as well as from Adler and Reik, and fashioned a useful framework for understanding the interface between psychology, religion, spirituality, and human social development.[1] We are in their debt.

This series of General Interest Books, so wisely urged by Greenwood Press, and particularly by its acquisitions editors, Suzanne Staszak-Silva and Debbie Carvalko, intends to define the terms and explore the interface of psychology, religion, and spirituality at the operational level of daily human experience. Each volume of the series identifies, analyzes, describes, and evaluates the issues of both popular and professional interest that deal with the psychospiritual factors at play (a) in the way religion takes shape and is expressed, (b) in the way spirituality functions within human persons and shapes both religious formation and religious expression, and (c) in the ways that spirituality is shaped and expressed by religion.

The books in this series are written for the general reader, the local library, and the undergraduate university student. They are also of significant interest to the informed professional persons, particularly in fields somewhat related to religion, spirituality, and social psychology. They also have great value for clinical settings and ethical values. I have spent an entire professional lifetime focused specifically upon research into the interface of psychology, sociology, religion, and spirituality. These matters are of the highest urgency in human affairs today when religious motivation seems to be playing an increasing role, constructively and destructively, in the arena of social ethics, national politics, and world affairs.

The primary interest in this present volume by Raymond J. Lawrence, Jr. is spiritual, religious, and ethical. In terms of the field and science of theology and religious studies, this volume investigates the operational dynamics of religion and spirituality in their influence upon notions of human sexuality, within the sociohistorical context of the church's life. Lawrence's superb volume entitled, *Sexual Liberation: The Scandal of Christendom*, addresses issues that are of universal concern but at the same time very personal and close to home. The author has seen through the sham and superficiality of much of the Christian tradition's view of human sexuality throughout the twenty centuries of the developing church. He also has the objectivity to affirm in ringing terms the heroic strengths, insight, honesty, and courage of those insightful clerics and laypersons who have seen through the erroneous and unbiblical attitudes that so often prevailed in the Christian theology and ethics of sex.

Not all of the influences or expression of human sexuality and its relationship with spirituality throughout Christian history have been negative or harbored potentially negative consequences. Indeed, much of the impact of the great religions upon human life and culture, including sexual ethics, has been redemptive, and generative of great good, as this author implies. It is urgent, therefore, that we discover and understand better what the spiritual, theological, sociological, and psychological forces are that empower people of faith and genuine spirituality to give themselves to all the creative and constructive enterprises that, throughout the centuries, have made of human life the humane, ordered, prosperous, and beautiful experience it can be at its best, in the practice and celebration of spirituality and sexuality. Surely the forces for good in both religion and spirituality far exceed the powers and proclivities toward the destructiveness that we too often see in our world today.

Spirituality and sexuality are part of the essence of being human. They are two expressions of the same inner life force. If one is expressed in a distorted manner, that distorts the other one. When the Medieval Mystics repressed and sublimated their sexuality, their spirituality became psychotic. When in our day spirituality is truncated and ignored, sexuality has become insanely irresponsible, shearing off sexual gymnastics from meaningful emotion and relationship. When the central energy of our inherent vitality expresses itself in a transcendent reach for meaning and connection, through our psyches, toward God, we call it spirituality. When that same force expresses itself horizontally through our psyches and bodies toward another human, we call it sexuality. It is the same force. Healthy sexuality and spirituality are inseparable. When either sexuality or spirituality has been suppressed, manipulated, or erroneously controlled as a means of coercion, by the church or other authorities, the result has been monstrous and destructive of human wholeness.

Raymond Lawrence demonstrates with numerous detailed illustrations what went wrong with the church's perspective on human sexuality over the centuries. He suggests, as well, the concrete ways in which this outlook can and must be repaired for humans to enjoy the celebrated and wholesome sexuality God intended us to experience. This tightly argued, articulate, and highly readable volume is a worthy companion to another recently published Praeger imprint entitled, *Sex in the Bible*.[2]

J. Harold Ellens, Series Editor

FOREWORD

Donald Capps

A couple of decades ago, a colleague and I were having lunch in the seminary dining hall. We were talking about the historical development of Christianity, a subject on which he was an acknowledged expert and I—we would both agreed—was a rank amateur at best. At some point in the conversation, I asked him, "How do we know that the best views prevailed and the worst ones went down to defeat?" His look told me that he had heard dumb questions before, but this one was in a class by itself. "Do you seriously think that God would let that happen?" He didn't wait for an answer but instead signaled that he had to go to class. End of conversation.

Raymond J. Lawrence, Jr. believes that the worst views regarding human sexuality have generally prevailed throughout the history of Christianity. *Sexual Liberation* is mostly an account of how wrongheaded Christianity has been about sex. He tells a dismal and disquieting story. What makes his perspective especially so is the evidence he marshals that attitudes have not changed. From Saint Jerome in the fourth century to Marie Fortune in the late twentieth century, the enemies of human sexuality have carried the day. But if the story is dismal and disquieting, the book itself reads like a bracing tonic. I thought *Sexual Liberation* would make depressing reading, but this was not at all the case. One reason for this is that the sex-aversion of Christianity has provoked counter-reactions, and Lawrence shows that these counter-reactions have not always been effectively suppressed. There are bright spots, and some of the very brightest are those that couple an openness to sexual freedom with a lighthearted sense of humor. I especially appreciated the dinner table banter between Martin Luther and his wife Katy, and I imagined Marie Fortune listening to their repartee with horror and shock. The other reason is the desire that fuels Raymond's affirmation of healthy sexuality, which is the even deeper or stronger desire for a better way of being. I think that what galls him about the sex-aversion of Christianity is its negativity, its tendency to think the worst of humans, and to think mostly in terms of worst-case scenarios. Over and over again, he shows that what outsiders assume to be instances of human sexuality run amok may, in fact, be experienced by those involved as expressions of human affection. His penetrating insights into the sensual life of Paul and Hannah Tillich is exemplary in this regard.

I first became acquainted with Lawrence's work—I'd call it a lifetime crusade—when I read a review of his first book, *The Poisoning of Eros: Sexual Values in Conflict*.[1] The tone of the review was dismissive and supercilious. The reviewer's assumption that everyone would surely agree with him that Lawrence's book was wrongheaded and that he needn't even offer arguments to support his negative reaction was so irritating to me that I did something I hardly ever do. I wrote Lawrence to tell him that I thought he was the victim of unprofessional conduct. We have been friends ever since.

The reader of this new book will find a self-reflectiveness here that one wishes would also characterize the writings of those who take opposing views. I especially appreciated the author's personal stories about being the object of the sexual advances of lonely wives when he was a newly ordained minister in a well-to-do suburban congregation. His acknowledgement of his own subliminal attraction to them and his sense that there was no malicious intent behind their actions is utterly different in tone from much of what is written these days about ministers—and some parishioners—as sexual predators. I deeply appreciate the nonstrident tone of this book. I also applaud Lawrence's plea for churches to be named for that great pair of Christian lovers, Peter Abelard and Heloise. When that day arrives, Christianity will turn the corner and begin to walk down a very different street with the lighthearted gait reminiscent of its liberating founder.

Donald Capps
Professor of Pastoral Theology
Princeton Theological Seminary

FOREWORD

Don Jones

Raymond J. Lawrence, Jr. has written a valuable, illuminating, and invariably provocative book. *Sexual Liberation* is filled with perceptive biblical, historical, theological, and psychological analysis and is loaded with anecdotal evidence. Lawrence has written a polemical book with a clear point of view. It is a broadstroke survey of Christendom's startling history of negativity toward sexual pleasure. His thesis is that in the formative years of early Christianity, the Church turned its back on its biblical roots and with open arms embraced the Greco-Roman culture marked by the sex-negativity of the Stoic and Neoplatonic philosophy that permeated the Roman imperial world.

A major assumption underlying the Lawrence thesis is that Christianity and its moral code was shaped under the impact of Constantine's adoption of Christianity as the official religion of the empire in the fourth century. This political co-option of Christianity had a devastating negative impact on the Christian church's ethics and sexual morality. This historical event ensconced the early church in the Neoplatonic and Stoic sex-negative culture rooted in a philosophic mind–body dualism and away from a biblical sex-affirming moral view rooted in a spirit–body unity concept of the self. For instance, Lawrence contrasts the Roman religionists, who were fascinated with virginity and held it in high esteem, with the Apostle Paul, who seemed to know nothing of a virgin birth.

Especially valuable about this book is Lawrence's use of biblical and theological insights to contrast the lives and the teachings of both Jesus and Paul with the medieval church's obsessive negativity about sex. His treatment of biblical materials in the first four chapters makes for a compelling case that the life and work of Jesus was marked by acceptance and even permissiveness regarding sex. The chapter on "The Two Wives of Paul the Apostle" with scholarly support from Clement and Origen is persuasive in making the case that Paul was married and certainly not against licit sex in its various forms.

The 21 brief chapters of this book take the reader through an historical journey from the early church through the medieval era and the Protestant Reformation to the modern period right up to the close of the twentieth century. Particularly impressive about this journey is the scope of Lawrence's concern—including insightful profiles of such figures as Abelard, Martin Luther, Teresa of Avila, Paul Tillich, Karl Barth, and leaders of the current radical feminist movement. Impressive as well is his readable, lucid style, and his courageous refusal to accept common moral notions about sex, no matter how oft repeated, if they cannot stand the scrutiny of his critical mind.

Don Jones
Professor Emeritus of Social Ethics
Drew University

INTRODUCTION

Sexual Liberation is an account of the strange ways sexual pleasure has been profoundly devalued, even perversely demonized, in the so-called western world, meaning Europe and its sphere of influence. It is also an exploration of the likely motivations driving this process of demonization. Astonishingly, sexual pleasure has been, and continues to be, debauched by Christendom. This book tells the story and describes how such a situation evolved.

The reader may wonder why a Christian minister with almost half a century of religious service would write what is essentially an attack on Christendom. The answer is a simple one: truth begs to be told, and history shows us that it is often very elusive.

I take issue with the inimitable Edward Gibbon, who wrote in his *The Decline and Fall of the Roman Empire.*

> The theologian may indulge the pleasing task of describing Religion as descended from heaven, arrayed in her native purity. A more melancholy duty is imposed on the Historian. He must discover the inevitable mixture of error and corruption which she contracted in a long residency upon earth, among a weak and degenerate race of beings.[1]

For all his brilliance, Gibbon got it wrong, as the proper role of a theologian or any religious leader should be not propaganda but truth-telling. I propose to tell the truth about the odd posture of western religion toward sexual pleasure by delineating the strange evolution of sexual values in the West, the major twists and turns that occurred through twenty centuries, the last seventeen of which have been dominated by Christianity. Just as Gibbon described his own task as a melancholy undertaking, so, too, is my production of this small book. To make my task more melancholy, the winners of the numerous cultural wars throughout history have seldom, it seems to me, been those we might have wished to emerge victorious.

The purview of this book is the western world, as described above. I've focused on Christianity simply because this is the form of religion, in its various manifestations, that has most shaped the West. For good or ill, Christianity has been, since before the ebbing of the Roman Empire, the principal bearer of public values in the western world. As James Hillman, one of the most original of twentieth-century psychologists, says, we are all Christians, whether we like it or not.[2] This book traces the changes that have shaped and reshaped what is considered to be of value, as well as what is considered immoral, in the arena of sexual behavior. One does not have to be a Christian to be determined in large part by the Christian juggernaut.

This book will tell, in chronological order, the story of that evolving process. Special attention is given to individuals who made a significant impact on the public process of sexual value-making. While this is principally a study of religious history, I take the liberty at various points in the text of injecting autobiographical material.

Only people unread in history and anthropology could assume that the sexual values and mores of today are the same as those of yesterday. Change is the rule, not the exception. The evolution of values can be glacially slow or convulsively rapid, but change is the rule. Many divergent, conflicting forces and interests contribute to change. Matters that were critically important yesterday may be of little interest today, and vice versa. For someone like me, who entered puberty in the southern U.S. middle class in the 1940s, the change has been dramatic. For example, I recall that, in those not-too-distant days, virginity and sexual innocence were *de rigueur* requirements prior to the formal wedding ceremony, especially for females. Even if the rule was kept more in its violation than in its compliance, the matter was not something treated lightly for the vast majority of us in the middle class. (Upper and lower classes followed, then as today, somewhat different, more permissive moral codes.)

One of my high school classmates, a girl on whom I had a crush, got pregnant in her teens and then suffered the public humiliation of a hurried wedding. I vividly recall the profound shame permeating what should have been a joyful wedding. I have often wondered what became of her in the years since. Her suffering could not have been inconsequential. Today, hardly anyone blinks at the prospect of a pregnant bride. Such information would likely result merely in bawdy humor, benign, and perhaps *sotto voce*. My pregnant classmate, on the other hand, was not seen as an object of humor, but as someone who had toyed with dark and dangerous forces and lost. The shape of public sexual values has changed significantly in the half-century since my classmate's shotgun wedding, and not in all respects for the worse.

This brief account begins with the intersection of the early Jesus movement and the morality of the Greco-Roman culture and empire, shaped as it was by Platonism, Stoicism, and the imperial cult. Various points of miscommunication will be pointed out, as the biblical and the Roman worlds collided and converged in the early centuries of the so-called Common Era (C.E.). This book will point out the ways Christianity and its moral code was reshaped under the impact of Constantine's adoption of Christianity as the imperial religion. The roles of various key figures will be examined. I'll also analyze the impact of monasticism, a movement that in time won the heart of western religion. Key figures of the Middle Ages—those on the winning side—generally succeeded in promoting a religion whose chief ethic was the obliteration of sexual pleasure. Peter Abelard, Heloise, and Martin Luther, lonely voices of a return to common sense, are the principal heroes of this book. Their contributions to western religion were monumental, but their affirmation of the goodness of sexual pleasure was extraordinary and, in the context of their times, quite unprecedented. There have been no giants in the field of sexual ethics in the five hundred years since Luther.

This is far from an exhaustive survey. Many more stories remain to be told. This is merely a broadstroke survey of Christendom's unsettling history of negativity toward sexual pleasure.

This is a polemical book, with a particular point of view. As I do not pretend to offer all arguments, pro and con, I leave the readers to reach their own conclusions. Some, perhaps a great many, will demur from my conclusions. So be it. Contrary arguments can always be made; the trade in ideas is an open market. However, all the claims in this book have the best historical bona fides. This is no work of fiction or fantasy.

This book is a more accessible sequel to my earlier work, published in 1989, *The Poisoning of Eros: Sexual Values in Conflict.*[3] Readers who wish to explore additional source material may wish to refer to the previous work.

The western world has been shaped principally by two powerful and quite different cultures, the Jewish-biblical and the Greco-Roman. Neither tradition is monochrome or monolithic, but each has basic cohesive themes that inform its tradition. In the particular area of sexual values and practice, the Jewish-biblical tradition, in my judgment, is much more commendable than the Greco-Roman.

The central conclusion of this book is that Christianity made a catastrophic turn early in its development, a turn largely fixed in the fourth century C.E. and cemented in the eleventh, and adopted a sex-phobic Platonist posture toward sexual pleasure. In the process it jettisoned its Judeo-biblical origins. Christianity has been profoundly damaged by this radical reversal, a reversal from which the West has never recovered. Consequently, we Westerners are now part of a Christianity that is the most sex-negative of all the major world religions.

CHAPTER 1

The Sexual Life and Teachings of Jesus

The public fascination with Dan Brown's *The Da Vinci Code*, a story that begins with the premise that Jesus was married and fathered children, has been a surprise. *The Da Vinci Code* is properly classified as fiction, but the beginning premise of this fanciful tale is actually more than plausible. It is in fact the most likely conjecture among the various possibilities regarding Jesus' marital status. Nowhere do the biblical texts disclose any clear data on the subject. One of the noncanonical (extrabiblical) texts suggests that Jesus was paired with Mary Magdalene in a special way, a claim that cannot be dismissed out of hand as nonhistorical.[1]

Among the many collections of writings that appeared in the early years of the Christian Church—and many others were undoubtedly lost—only a few were selected for inclusion in the New Testament. Those included now have the label "the canonical texts." Whether a text is considered canonical—an arbitrary categorization devised by the church leadership in the fourth century—is not taken by historians, even Christian historians, as a measure of its historical reliability. The considerable quantity of noncanonical Christian literature that has survived tends, on the whole, to be of a fanciful sort but purports to be rooted in historical events of Jesus' life.

The later Christian Church made Jesus out to be a celibate and was passively abetted in this claim by the silence of the canonical texts on the subject. However, a celibate Jesus would have been so peculiar in the context of first century Palestinian Judaism that the absence of comment on the subject rather indicates he was not celibate. First and foremost, Jesus was a Jew, and not a syncretizing Jew, which is to say that he does not act and speak like a

Jewish version of Plato or one of the Stoic philosophers contemporaneous with Jesus. There were such Jews, but Jesus, on the other hand, acts and talks like the radical, Pharisaic-Talmudic rabbi he was.[2]

The Platonists and Stoics of Jesus' time, who were the mavens of morality in the empire at large, were highly negative toward sexual pleasure and relationships with women generally. Orgasm, they argued, disordered the mind's rationality and tainted the soul. They promoted sexual abstinence except for purposes of procreation. The Palestinian Jewish tradition, which is brought forward by the law, prophets, wisdom literature, and later the Talmud, has a radically different perspective on sexual pleasure, marriage, and women. It is exuberantly positive about sexual pleasure, which it considers to be a divine gift and even mitzvah—a meritorious act—in certain circumstances. We will find three things in heaven, the Talmud says, sunshine, Sabbath, and sex.[3] In Judaism, marriage and procreation are not options but religious obligations. Furthermore, monogamy is nowhere promoted as the organizing principle of sex and procreation, as it eventually came to be among the imperial Romans. Thus we should assume, without evidence to the contrary, that Jesus married at the typical age of about 19 to a girl of about 14 and that they probably had children.[4]

Some have argued, incorrectly, that Jesus' wife or children would have been mentioned in the texts had there been any. On the contrary, the Talmudic tradition reflecting Palestinian Judaism promotes the injunction that one should marry and procreate first, then study the Torah.[5] Jesus may well have followed that precept in his youth. Two or three decades later, when he was executed, his wife and children may have died, gone their separate ways, or simply become peripheral. The traditional notion that Jesus was 33 when he was executed is no more than a Platonist fantasy, 33 being considered the perfect age. In the sixth century, the western calendar was calculated on that erroneous assumption, with Jesus' birth arbitrarily fixed on the year 0. Historians agree that the actual year of his death was either 30 or 33 C.E. However, there is no consensus on his birth date. In fact, he was likely in his early 50s at his death, and certainly not as young as 33.

Historians do not agree on the question of Jesus' age at the time of his crucifixion. While Luke's Gospel seems to support an age of early 30s, Luke is not considered a credible chronologist. A preponderance of Christian historians argue for an age of late 30s, but the supporting data is anything but conclusive.[6] Furthermore, these historians discount, for unstated reasons, the single most credible piece of evidence on the subject. Irenaeus, a reliable second-century bishop, wrote that Polycarp, his mentor, had told him that the disciple John in Ephesus conveyed to him that Jesus was about 50 when he was executed.[7] This data is persuasive, third-hand though it may be, simply because it is the only direct answer given in any text to the specific question of Jesus' age at his death, and the particular sources are generally credible ones. All the other data concerning Jesus' age at his death are attempts to extrapolate tangentially from data to the main question.

In what may be biblical support for Irenaeus' claim, one of Jesus interlocutors is recorded in the Gospel of John saying, "You are not yet 50 ... "[8] suggesting that he was in fact near 50. Furthermore, if we take the intriguing statement by Jesus, or later put into his mouth by his followers, seeming to relate his age with the age of the temple in Jerusalem, the construction of which began about 20 B.C., we would have an age of about 50 at the time of his death.[9] In support of the parallel, we can see in the text that Jesus himself made the association between his body and the temple. Whether late 30s or 50s, Jesus at the time of his death would have been at least two and probably three decades from his marital year were he a typical Palestinian Jew. A lot of things can happen in two or three decades. The absence of any mention of a wife or children at age 50 is less significant than at age 33.

The story of Akiba ben Joseph, another first century rabbi, is instructive on this issue. Akiba married, raised a family, and then left home to study the Torah. When he returned after 24 years with numbers of disciples in tow, Akiba spotted his wife in the multitude and credited her with his success. The story describes a devoted and devout wife but also a wife who was far outside the inner circle of study and teaching. It is also a rare mention of a specific rabbi's wife.

Modern readers generally read the biblical texts—when they read them at all—with modern assumptions, not grasping the alien nature of the context from which the texts sprang. One of the major differences from today's context is the full acceptance of polygamy in first-century Palestinian Judaism. Monogamy had no moral or religious support in the religion and culture in which Jesus grew up. Monogamy was the law in late imperial Rome, but those laws did not penetrate significantly into Jewish law or practice. Even fairly well-read persons today are often taken aback to learn that neither Jesus nor anyone else in the biblical texts—Jewish or Christian—proposed that polygamy be supplanted by monogamy in Jewish or Christian law or morality.

The book of Ruth provides some perspective on marriage in the Jewish context. When the young widow Ruth slipped into Boaz' bed in an unambiguous sexual overture, Boaz restrained himself. He did not restrain himself because he was already married, which he likely was. That was morally irrelevant. The ethical question for Boaz was the status of Ruth's own male attachments and obligations. To whom was she accountable as a widow? She would normally be accountable to her deceased husband's brother. With a few exceptions, there are no unattached women in patriarchal Israel. Boaz thus went to the city gate, as was the custom, and got a release from Ruth's brother-in-law with whom she was mutually accountable and who would be obliged to marry her under the levirate law. Receiving the release, Boaz was free to take Ruth as a wife, probably one of his wives. From this story we can see something of the moral code in first-century Judaism as it pertains to sex and marriage. We may also note how alien it is to later Christendom.

Polygamy, in the view of modern enlightenment, is a dreadful form of exploitation of women, a judgment hardly subject even to debate. Even the establishment of the theocratic State of Israel in 1947 legislated monogamy as the only legal form of marriage. However, exemptions were put in place for already polygamous Jews, particularly those emigrating from cultures that tolerate polygamy. Polygamy has been countenanced throughout most of history by Judaism and has been in continuing practice among Sephardic Jews, who dwell mainly in Muslim-dominated cultures. Ashkenazi Jews of Europe, on the other hand, adopted monogamy, but did so only in the eleventh century C.E.

Rabbi Gershom ben Judah of Worms was the first authority to "legislate" monogamy. The fact that he did so at the height of the Gregorian Reform is not a coincidence. The Gregorian Reform was a powerful cooptation of power by the pope in the eleventh century, in which he moved to exercise absolute centralized power over the European church, and simultaneously—with a heavy hand—abolished clerical marriage. In the context of such centralization of power and repression of sexual freedom, polygamous Jews would have been extraordinarily conspicuous. To parade around medieval Europe with multiple wives, subsequent to the Gregorian reform, would have been an invitation to more vicious pogroms than the ones Jews already experienced. Hence, Gershom made his move on the chessboard of history and issued a judgment prohibiting polygamy for Jews, which was transparently a decision for survival. Gershom's ruling made no impact on Jews outside of Europe.

Monogamy was mandated in the late Roman Empire as the only proper form of sexual expression and family organization. The practice of monogamy gave Romans a reason to feel morally superior to Jews and other Eastern religions with their polygamous ways. Westerners since have generally assumed, for the most part unreflectively, that monogamy is the most ethical and humane system of family organization. However, on closer examination the picture is not so clear. In monogamous Rome any child born of illicit sexual congress was legally a bastard and outcast. The role of mistress was similarly tainted. The same holds true today, though with significantly less virulence since the Sexual Revolution of the 1960s. Illegitimate children are not, in legal terms, bastards any longer but still face certain social stigmas. In first-century Palestinian Judaism, there were no bastards, except in certain rare cases of incest. Every child was the full responsibility of the natural father. Any sexual union with an unattached woman was tantamount to marriage, in terms of obligations and responsibility. Even sex with a prostitute carried such moral obligations. Jewish polygamy, rather than abusing women, arguably provided better for the welfare of women and children than did the monogamy of Rome.

A definitive picture of Jesus' own ethical and religious posture toward sex and marriage may be undiscoverable, but the texts preserve quite a few tantalizing fragments. Jesus himself clearly had some notable conversations about marriage. In one instance he was asked a presumably trick question, "Whose wife will a woman be, in paradise, when she has been married successively to seven brothers?" Jesus replied, "The men and women of this world marry; but those who have been judged worthy of a place in the other world and of the resurrection from the dead, do not marry, for they are not subject to death any longer."[10] The woman in question who marries one brother after another is not a Hollywood starlet, jumping from bed to bed. She has married one brother after another because of spousal death and the implementation of the levirate law, the law that requires the brother-in-law to take his widowed sister-in-law into his family as a wife. These six brothers likely had wives already. Had Jesus been a proponent of either monogamy or celibacy, this would have been the place to make his case. He does not. The text shows that he levels an implicit critique against marriage—that there is no marriage in the resurrection—but beyond that leaves us in the dark.

In a similarly tantalizing saying, presented within a discussion of divorce, Jesus says, "There are eunuchs who have been so from birth, eunuchs who have been made eunuchs by men, and eunuchs who have made themselves eunuchs for the sake of the kingdom."[11] This saying of Jesus is so bizarre and impenetrable that it must certainly be authentic. Jesus must be using poetic hyperbole here, because no evidence exists that he in any way promoted the castration of males. Much later in church history this saying and the previous one, were taken as the primary scriptural injunction for celibacy, celibates being understood metaphorically as eunuchs for the kingdom. That makes two very slender reeds on which to erect the requirement of celibacy. A celibacy teaching would have been so countercultural in a Jewish environment, so extraordinarily controversial, that surely we would not be left solely with these two strange and oblique sayings to support it. Furthermore, none of Jesus' disciples appears to have been celibate, traveling with their wives as they did. If Jesus was promoting celibacy, it took most of his followers about one thousand years to finally comprehend the teaching, and only then by the use of hermeneutic contortions.

One scholar, William Countryman, has suggested that Jesus' saying on eunuchs, like the story of the woman with seven husbands, is simply a critique of patriarchal marriage.[12] The inability to procreate was a devastating impediment in a society that considered procreation to be the first divine command and the foundation of marriage. The eunuch is thus thrust into a socially degraded position. Jesus likely meant that we all should become eunuchs in the sense of abandoning male prerogatives and the privileges of patriarchy. Solidarity with the disenfranchised is a consistent theme with Jesus.

Any search for understanding on the question of what Jesus believed, practiced, and taught about sex, marriage, and women must take into consideration the provocative conclusions of Donald Capps, Professor of Pastoral

Theology at Princeton Theological Seminary.[13] He proposes that Jesus' personality and vocation were profoundly shaped by his own experience of illegitimacy. In proper Jewish practice of the day, Mary's pregnancy would have been the responsibility of the biological father. But if Mary were impregnated by a Roman soldier, as one tradition has it, she and her son would have been set adrift as social outcasts. Joseph, described as a noble man, took her under his wing and married her in spite of her illicit pregnancy. But Jesus was not Joseph's responsibility under Jewish law and custom. Thus Jesus would have been caught in a fault line between Jewish and Roman moral practices. He is likely to have experienced his condition as anomalous and disquieting, especially because no data suggests that Joseph adopted him. One text refers to him as "the son of Mary."[14] Capps argues that this disenfranchisement likely radicalized Jesus and was the source of his creativity and strength and of his willingness to challenge the boundaries of Jewish law and practice. In Capps' view, little wonder then that Jesus sharply critiqued marriage as an institution. But that critique does not lead to a conclusion that he was either a monogamist or a celibate. It is quite plausible that Jesus did not go beyond making a prophetic critique of exploitative marriage practices and that he actually had no new plan for organizing sexual relationships.

The source of the gross misunderstanding of Jesus in later Christendom is the relentless and scandalous obliteration of Jesus' identity as a Palestinian Jew. The Church has recast him in ever so subtle ways in the image of a sex-phobic Roman philosopher and/or as a quasidisembodied Roman god who tampers with the laws of nature. No authentic portrait of Jesus will be possible until he is finally understood as a thoroughgoing Jew and thoroughgoing human being who considered himself called to confront, serve, and teach his own Jewish people.

As an observant Jew, Jesus was likely married as a young man and fathered children. That the record makes no mention of a family is not anomalous. Jesus is clearly critical of marriage, which would mean, in his own context, polygamous patriarchal marriage. However, no credible data suggests that he proposed to replace polygamy with either monogamy or celibacy. Jesus' illegitimacy shaped his sense of self and his mission, making him a sharp critic of his culture and an innovative teacher who was at once both devout and radical. His life and teaching on sex and marriage were thus quite radical. For all his radicalism, however, he appears to support the Jewish law, the Torah, albeit in a radical and arguably humanizing interpretation. Thus he was likely tolerant of polygamy even while highlighting its abuses. The historical evidence has left us with a Jesus who affirmed the joy of sexual pleasure as a gift from God while at the same time being critical of the institutional forms—marriage, for example—by which culture seeks to control sexual behavior.

CHAPTER 2

JESUS: LEGITIMATE OR ILLEGITIMATE

The meager historical evidence available to us twenty centuries after the fact portrays a Jesus who was sexually tainted, both by the circumstances of his illegitimate birth and by the manner in which he lived his life. The sexual taint that marked him at birth, and which he exacerbated by his manner of living, undoubtedly provided fuel for the critical mass of public hostility required to put him to death as a common criminal.

Chronologically, the first signal of Jesus' sexual taint is disclosed in the genealogical list of his ancestors in the Gospel of Matthew,[1] where four women are inserted into the genealogical list: Tamar, Rahab, Ruth, and Bathsheba. A parallel genealogical list in the Gospel of Luke[2] contains no women. Such genealogical lists in Jewish tradition are of course invariably patriarchal, progressing from father to son, so the appearance of women at all is surprising and jarring.

The specific character of the four women inserted in Matthew's genealogical list is remarkable in that each woman is marked by a sexual taint.[3] Tamar disguised herself as a prostitute to trick her father-in-law into impregnating her, making herself twice a sinner; Rahab was a prostitute; Ruth attempted to seduce Boaz prior to clarification of her status under the marriage laws and before receiving the required permission of her brother-in-law; and Bathsheba committed adultery with King David while married to Uriah. Because Mary the mother of Jesus is marked by sexual taint as well—finding herself pregnant, but not by her fiancé—the point in the genealogy is obvious: Mary may be tainted, but there is a strong historical precedent.

The explanation that Mary's pregnancy was the responsibility of the Holy Ghost is a pious and belated cover-up and negates the rationale for appealing to the examples of the revered but tainted women in Matthew's genealogical list. A pregnancy brought on by the Holy Ghost, provided anyone would believe such a story, would hardly have been a cause for shame. While some among the early Christians adopted the Holy Ghost explanation of Mary's pregnancy, it certainly would not have been possible for Mary herself to have employed such an explanation of her condition. Even if such a fanciful tale were true, who would believe her? She was, after all, a real person. Thus we see in Matthew's peculiar genealogical list a residue of anxiety over Jesus' uncertain paternity.

The so-called virgin birth of Jesus is actually a fanciful revision of the birth narratives that disclosed Jesus to be, in imperial Roman terms, a bastard. The idea of a virgin birth almost certainly was invented some time after Jesus' death as a way to cover Mary's sexual taint. A retrospective interpretation, so to speak. Moreover, the Jerusalem Church, run by Jesus' brother, did not hold to a virgin birth. Paul, the earliest of the New Testament authors, who wrote some 25 years after Jesus' execution, seemed to know nothing of a virgin birth. The Gospels of Matthew and Luke, written probably 50 or more years after Jesus death, are the first promoters of a conception performed by the Holy Ghost. Neither Mark's gospel nor that of John's mention a virgin birth.

The virgin birth idea became a perpetual insidious assault on any positive posture toward sexual pleasure in the subsequent development of the church. The virgin birth did serve the purpose of attracting Roman religionists, who were fascinated with virginity and held it in high esteem. Stoic and Neoplatonist philosophers would surely have been sympathetic, too, as it would have supported their distaste for sexual pleasure. For the Jews, on the other hand, virginity was something to be blessedly lost as soon after the onset of puberty as dignity permitted.

Having been conceived in a sexually tainted context, Jesus then lived his entire life exacerbating his reputation as a sexual outlier. The number of women surrounding Jesus, as well as the nature of his interactions with them, is nothing short of astonishing, furthering the sexual taint.

The data show Jesus to have been what we today might call wonderfully boorish in his close relationships with women. The Jewish tradition at that time was quite gender-specific, reserving religious leadership to men. Custom and religious practice forbade men and women from socializing casually in that world. Roman imperial tradition was somewhat different, but it too prescribed gender roles, and male prerogatives prevailed in Rome as well. The political power of Cleopatra, with her sway over Anthony, was a turn of events roughly contemporaneous with Jesus and sent shock waves throughout the patriarchal empire. Her rise to power, thought to have been a brief flowering of feminism, was crushed before it got out of hand. Jesus may have been as favorable toward women as Anthony was, though the two men held quite different values and commitments, especially in their approaches to power.

The biblical texts show Jesus to have taught female disciples and to have traveled with them as well. In the conflict between Mary and Martha, the former sitting at Jesus' feet as a disciple, the latter waiting tables for them, Mary is said by Jesus to have "the better part."[4] For a rabbi to have female disciples would have rung alarm bells in first-century Palestinian Judaism. The texts also portray Jesus as allowing women to take sexual liberties with him. Mary of Bethany took a pound of costly ointment and anoints Jesus' feet at supper, wiping his feet with her hair.[5] Another woman, identified only as a sinner, made a similar gesture, this time using her tears to wash Jesus' feet.[6] This time the male host of the supper questioned the appropriateness of Jesus' permitting a sinner to touch him. Jesus assured his host that it was quite appropriate. At the house of Simon the leper, another unnamed woman entered during supper and poured costly ointment on Jesus' head.[7] Apparently, Jesus was not averse to having his body cared for in quite intimate ways at various times by various women. Those who fail to see the sexual content in such interactions, especially the massaging of the feet with oil and tears, are simply failing to see through the euphemistic language of the narrative. Jesus' own male disciples are described as reacting uncomfortably to Jesus' boorish behavior toward women. "Doesn't he know what manner of woman he is speaking with?" they asked.[8]

In a noncanonical text, which was rejected by church authorities centuries later, we have even more explicit data on Jesus' sexuality. He is portrayed by *The Gospel of Philip* as kissing Mary Magdalene on the mouth, to the consternation or jealousy of some of the male disciples.[9] When one considers Jesus' relationship with the Magdalene, as described even in the canonical texts, this report of kissing would appear to be neither incongruent nor surprising. He seems to have been on more intimate terms with her than he was with Peter, who is supposed to have been the principal disciple, according to the canonical texts.

The fact that Jesus had female disciples, and that they traveled with him from city to city, further enhanced his reputation among the pious as a sexually shady character. The texts relate the names of about eight women who seemed to be disciples of Jesus. They and unnamed other women traveled with Jesus, an example of daring behavior not calculated to win moral approbation from the guardians of public morality in that cultural context. Some of these women, unlike the male disciples, remained near Jesus during his execution, and women were the first witnesses to the resurrection, whatever that experience may have been.

The biblical texts themselves reveal that the authors of the texts are not altogether comfortable with Jesus' relationships with women. As the accounts unfold, the women recede into the background, and yet they often reappear where one would least expect marginal persons to appear, the crucifixion scene being the most glaring example. Mary Magdalene is certainly a disciple, likely even the chief disciple, but she does not make it to any list of the twelve.

There are good reasons to suspect that the construct "the twelve disciples"—all men—was a retrospective invention for the benefit of a profoundly patriarchal and gynophobic society. For one thing, it is a little bit too cute for Jesus to have appointed a disciple for each of the twelve tribes of Israel. That does not sound like him. Secondly, and more significantly, if "the twelve" were such an important institution, one would expect that the records would present a distinct list. The various lists are so garbled that no one can tell exactly who the twelve men were. There is agreement on only seven of the names. Roughly half the names that are alleged to make up any version of the twelve are no more than names. We are told nothing more about them. Furthermore, Nathaniel of Cana and Joseph of Aramathea are specifically referred to as disciples, but neither appears on any of the specific lists of the twelve. If indeed Jesus did appoint twelve male disciples, the early church lost interest in precisely who was on that list, an unlikely turn of events.

However, the epithet "the twelve" men does serve a later purpose. It conveniently trumps the women. Gender strife may well have been the matrix out of which the notion of "the twelve" was invented. The early church was struggling to survive *vis-à-vis* both Rome and the Jewish establishment, neither of which had much use for women in public leadership positions. Because several decades lapsed between Jesus' death and the first written texts that make up the New Testament, there was time enough for revisionists to make considerable mischief.

In the decades after Jesus' death, one would expect efforts to be made to round off the rough edges of Jesus' story. One of those rough edges likely was his relationship with women, a fact to which even the canonical gospels testify. The apostle Paul, only a couple of decades after Jesus' death, obviously made (or is victim of) such a revision. In stunning contradiction to all four gospel accounts, he wrote of the resurrection appearances, that they were all experienced by men, precisely the obverse of the record in the gospels.

> I delivered to you first of all that which I also received, that he rose again the third day according to the Scriptures, and that he was seen by Cephas, then by the twelve. After that he was seen by above five hundred brethren at once, of whom the greater part remain unto the present, but some are fallen asleep. After that, he was seen by James, then by all the apostles, and last of all he was seen by me also.[10]

Thus the women, who by several accounts were the first to experience the resurrection, summarily vanish from the record. We should note, however, that women appear in quite high profile in much of the extrabiblical, or noncanonical literature of the first and second centuries. There, women were specifically listed as "disciples."

The well-established association of Jesus with fish is a provocative one and not a little mysterious. No surviving early document comments on the origin or meaning of the association. Augustine, 400 years later, offered two explanations, neither of which is persuasive. He pointed out that the first letter in the five Greek words "Jesus, Christ, God, son, savior" combine to make up an acrostic for the Greek word "fish." However, no one ever seems to have used those five words in that sequence. Thus the acrostic explanation seems contrived; and this is a subject on which Augustine could be expected to have invented just such a gimmick.[11] Augustine also explained the fish symbol as an allegory for remaining alive without sin in the abyss of our mortal condition, in the depths of the sea, as it were.[12] That explanation hardly needs rebuttal.

Whatever the origins of the particular association, fish is a symbol of sex and the unconscious in cultures the world over. Anthropologists explain the association as derived from the phallic shape of fish and the manner in which they slip through the water, conjuring up thoughts of the penis in the vagina, along with the salty and fishy taste and smell of sex. Dwelling in invisible or dimly visible depths suggests the symbolic association of fish with the unconscious.

Fish as a symbol would not have been obscure to first-century Romans. Friday was the day to eat fish in the empire, a custom that well predated Christianity. The Romans ate fish as a tribute to Venus, the goddess of love and sex. In the empire fish was indisputably the food of love and sex. The much later Christian Church, when it was finally adopted as the state religion of the empire, continued Friday fish eating, merely changing the rationale for it. The Christian revisionist explanation for Friday fish eating was that Jesus was executed on Friday, and fish is the substitute for animal flesh. So latterday Christians continued the practice of eating the food of the goddess of love and sex, all the while claiming that it commemorated Jesus' crucifixion. In a very profound sense, they may have been correct. Jesus and the goddess of love and sex may not have been so far apart. The earliest association of Jesus with fish would ineluctably have conjured up thoughts of sexuality, especially in the imperial Roman culture.

Jesus' association with fish was plausibly related to the nature of his healing power and his grasp of unconscious processes. All of Jesus' healing acts were clearly of a psychological nature. He performed no magic. In modern times, Sigmund Freud was a healer who similarly effected psychological cures, and Freud himself is strongly identified with both sex and the unconscious. (As an authority on sex and the unconscious, it might have been appropriate for Freud, also, to be symbolically associated with fish.) If Jesus healed suffering persons of psychosomatic ailments, and liberated them from their sexual repression, fish would have been a very appropriate symbol of his life and work. Jesus' association with fish and all that fish symbolize would have further exacerbated his public relations problem, not least of which would have been the suggestion that he promoted sexual liberation, especially of women.

Archeologists at Megiddo, in 2005, found what they identify as "certainly the earliest church in Israel that we know of."[13] They assigned the supposed date of the church as early as the third century. The floor's mosaic shows motifs of fish and geometric patterns. The symbol of the cross was not found in that particular site. The discovery certainly adds more weight to the argument that the fish was a very important symbol in early Christianity, the meaning of which was forgotten in time.

The later Christian Church developed amnesia regarding the moral taint associated with Jesus, just as it forgot about the fish symbol. The pious cover-up began with the revision of his tainted origins in the tale of the virginal conception. As history obliterated the original taint in Jesus' life, it also removed the source of his power and authority. His illegitimacy was the likely touchstone of his personal power and the key to the riddle of his liberating power with others. The fish symbol, the meaning of which was also forgotten by the church, is an apt symbol for a man who was instrumental in liberating persons from unconscious conflicts and from tyrannical sexual repression.

The biblical charge that Jesus perverted the people should be taken at face value. It is no stretch, given the fragmentary evidence, to suppose that this accusation against Jesus was at least partly drawn from the perception that he was monkeying around with respected sexual norms. The rage against him was broad and deep enough to earn him a gruesome public execution, with no one coming to his rescue. It must be surmised that he touched many persons deeply, for better and for worse. This would account for the depth of rage against him.

Picking his lunch from a field on the Sabbath, and thus flouting strict religious practice, might have created animosity among the pious. Similarly, his disturbance of the temple in Jerusalem would have been seen as obnoxious and deserving of punishment. However, nothing so inflames anxious people as tampering with strongly held views on the boundaries of sexual behavior. On this subject, even Jesus' own disciples were troubled. The sexually tainted rabbi was in turn tainting the faithful and thus had to be crushed.

The portrait of Jesus as a liberator of women, and a liberator of sexual pleasure itself, has plenty of textual support. This hardly makes Jesus a cavalier antinomian. Far from it. But it does portray him as loosening the bonds of sexual convention, and especially the bonds imposed on the behavior of women. When women are liberated in any culture, sexual pleasure is, by definition, liberated with them.

Jesus' life and work were marked by permissiveness and acceptance, as opposed to restrictiveness and punitiveness. His posture of toleration and graciousness, along with his audacity, was taken by the guardians of the moral code as a lack of seriousness about moral standards. But for all his conflict with Jewish religious authorities, nowhere did he denigrate the Jewish law; rather he attempted to humanize the implementation of its requirements. A graciously contrarian posture on sex values is probably the surest route to ill-treatment at the hands of the guardians of morality in any culture.

Anyone who attempts to portray Jesus either as a monogamist, polygamist, or celibate will be left at the altar by the canonical texts. On the basis of the texts, it is far easier to make a case for Jesus as a libertine. But it would have to be a case of a qualified libertine, who was at the same time very respectful of the Torah, and in no respects frivolous in his approach to human behavior. Jesus seems clearly to have been a situational ethicist, but as J. Harold Ellens[14] declares, a situational ethicist with a bias. His bias was that any human behavior was permitted if it did not harm anyone and contributed to human well being in body, mind, and soul. Behavior must proceed from love for others.

Twenty centuries of Christians have been cognizant of Jesus' rejection as a social outcast and his disgraceful execution as a common criminal. But the effects of the bastardy of his birth has been glossed over, veiled by the fiction of the virgin birth. His subsequent biography has been similarly cleansed of its socially offensive features, particularly around issues of women and sex. The fact remains that the taint of his illegitimacy started him out on a lifelong course of social and religious marginality that became the very source of his personal power.

CHAPTER 3

THE TWO WIVES OF
PAUL THE APOSTLE

While Jesus is the central figure in Christianity, later Christendom's sexual ethic was for the most part based on readings, or misreadings, of the letters of the apostle Paul. Paul nowhere in the surviving texts expounds a clear sexual ethic; this was not on his agenda. But theologians have cobbled together an ethic using bits and pieces of Paul's writings drawn from here and there. The cornerstone of this confabulated ethic consists of the mass of Paul's denunciation of fornication. Fornication, however, is actually a mistranslation of the Greek word Paul used, *porneia*, which means "promiscuous sexual conduct."[1] The parameters of what was illicit in the first century Palestinian Jewish context are at some variance with what is considered illicit today in the modern West. Obviously the definitions and parameters of proper sexual conduct can and do vary considerably from culture to culture.

Adultery, for example, was considered illicit in first century Palestine, as it is today, but a man who took an additional wife or two would not have been charged with either adultery or illicit sexual conduct in first century Palestinian Judaism. The word "fornication" in today's English means any sexual contact except that between a man and a woman married to each other. Thus "fornication" should be deleted from English translations of the Bible and replaced with "promiscuous sexual conduct," which is to say, such conduct as construed to be immoral in Palestinian Judaism.

The presumed Rosetta stone of Pauline sexual ethics has long been considered I Corinthians 7. Virtually everyone who expounds upon Paul's sexual ethic turns first to that chapter. The chapter is ambiguously translated and almost universally misinterpreted. The first sentence in the King James translation reads: "Now concerning the things whereof ye wrote unto me: It is good for a man not to touch a woman." Some of the recent translations are in rather more current English parlance, but none of the modern translations correct the gross mistranslation. An accurate translation would read something like this: "You have written me to say that it is good for a man not to touch a woman, and this is my rebuttal to you." Thus the actual meaning of the text is just the opposite of the one commonly accepted ever since the Bible was put into English five hundred years ago.

In this same chapter Paul goes on to say that the married should stay married, and the single should stay single. He makes the case for leaving one's marital state as it is, and he takes this posture because he feels that the urgency of the times renders marriage irrelevant. He feels that the time is short. (This is the so-called eschatological challenge that may not necessarily be linear.)[2] It is noteworthy that he makes a similar argument regarding circumcision. Those who are circumcised are well as they are. Those who are not should not bother to be circumcised. In this time period it seems that many converts to Christianity were having themselves circumcised first, because virtually all early Christians were already Jews, and Christians had not yet separated themselves from Judaism. Paul makes a similar argument regarding slavery. He tells slaves who are able to acquire their freedom to do so, but those who cannot to continue in their slavery. They are after all slaves of Christ, as he puts it. Paul calls for the Corinthians to remain as they are, whether married, unmarried, slave, free, circumcised, uncircumcised. Marriage and other social conditions are thus irrelevant in the context of the urgency of their vocation as Christians, according to Paul, because Christians believed themselves to be at the "end" of history, in a manner of speaking. The later church misconstrued this pronouncement of the irrelevancy of marriage as the textual foundation for its call for celibacy and sexual abstinence. It is nothing of the sort.

Though Paul considers marriage irrelevant in the context in which he works, it is not at all clear that he himself is unmarried. In I Corinthians 8, the King James translation reads: "To the unmarried and the widows I say that it is well for them to remain single as I do." The word "single" does not appear in the original Greek text, and Paul may not have intended to communicate in this context that he himself was single. An alternate way of understanding the sentence is that Paul's wife may have been in another city, or he may have been living as if marriage is not a priority in his life. Paul is living as though marriage is unimportant relative to the tasks at hand, and he invites others to join him in such a vocation, to live "as he lives."

In summary, Paul in I Corinthians 7 is actually making an argument counter to those who are promoting sexual abstinence in the manner of the Stoics and Neoplatonists of the day.[3] Sexual abstinence as a sign of moral achievement, as in the teachings of the Stoics, is apparently of no interest to Paul. For centuries now Paul's argument has been turned on its head by theologians and has been understood to mean the opposite of what the texts actually have been thought to say.

In point of fact, Paul was almost certainly married twice. He was an observant Jew, and the Torah's commandment to marry and procreate was considered binding on observant Jews. As Paul nowhere takes issue with this religious requirement and had been very serious about the Torah in his preconversion days, we must presume that he attempted to be fully observant in his earlier years. He may, of course, have been widowed or divorced by the time he was writing his letters. However, the absence of any mention of his wife is not significant either way. The names of wives of famous rabbis are not typically disclosed in religious literature of the time, nor were the wives of Peter and the other married disciples.

Paul would almost certainly have married at about age 19 or 20 to a girl in her early teens. We do not have any data on such a presumptive wife. But more crucially, we do not have any data to suggest that Paul elected to live a celibate life, that most un-Jewish of practices. Thus we must presume that Paul had taken a wife in his youth. The wife of his youth was not likely the wife that Paul addressed in Philippians 4:3.

> And I ask you, faithful spouse, help these women, for they have labored side by side with me in the gospel together with Clement and the rest of my fellow workers, whose names are in the book of life.

This wife must have been Paul's second wife, and if his first wife were still living, Paul would have been a polygamist. For that matter the spouse addressed here could have been Paul's third or fourth wife.

The spouse Paul addressed in the letter to the Philippians is plausibly Lydia, a wealthy tradeswoman dealing in fabric in Philippi. When Paul was released from prison there, Lydia had invited him to come live with her, which he did, remaining with her for some length of time.[4] It is a reasonable presumption that a woman he is living with might have become his wife, especially if she were herself unattached. When a woman invites a man to live with her, assumptions of sexual intimacy are implied in most any culture. While such a version of events would come as a shock to adherents of later Christianity, there would be nothing shocking about it to religiously observant Palestinian Jews, even if Paul's wife of his youth were still living. Polygamy was neither immoral nor illegal in Paul's religious culture. No Torah-abiding Jewish moralist would have batted an eye at this.

The translation above, of Philippians 4:3, cannot be found in any published Bible, but it is a more correct translation of the Greek in which Paul wrote and far more accurate than any current English translation. Once again, the translators have done, and continue to do, their work on the text. The word "spouse," in Greek *syzyge*, is a word that has not changed in twenty-five hundred years or more. It means the same thing today on the streets of Athens that it meant in the time of Plato and Aristotle. But the Greek "spouse," preceded by the adjective "faithful," is translated in English as anything but. The King James translation reads "loyal yokefellow," whatever in the world that might mean. Other modern translators are equally inventive. Some suggest "comrade" is the meaning, a not entirely implausible translation, except for the fact that the word does mean "spouse." Others have conjectured that *syzyge* is a proper name.[5] Greek writing did not capitalize proper names. However, no one else in all history seems to have been given such a name. The problem is that Christian theologians simply have not been able to imagine Paul with a spouse, so they were driven to make contorted translations of what, on the face of it, should have been a simple and straightforward translation. The revisions and mistranslations of the texts by most of the theologians of Christendom have made it simply impossible for latter day Christians to conceive of Paul addressing his spouse in writing.

The characterization of Paul as a celibate was not established in the church until the medieval period. Paul's alleged celibacy was one of the errors of medieval Catholicism that the Reformation failed to correct, a surprising turn of events given the fact that almost all the Reformation leaders were themselves formerly celibate priests who then married.

The later sixteenth century Protestant translators of the biblical texts, the first to put the Bible in modern languages, relied on the original Hebrew, Greek, and Latin texts. However, the existing versions of the texts were not all exactly the same. A pure text does not exist. Because the texts were all hand-copied, a maddening number of scribal errors and editorial comments show up in the various copies. Thus the Reformation translators consulted and weighed all available Greek, Hebrew, and Latin versions to help them make a decision on the most likely correct text. They naturally consulted Jerome's own famous translation of the Hebrew and Greek into Latin, known as "The Vulgate."

The sex-phobic Jerome attacked the view that Paul was married, so it is interesting to see what he did with the word "spouse" in Philippians. He elected to create a new Latin word, *conpar*, which should mean something like "yoked together," a literal etymological rendering of the Greek word for "spouse." But because the word *conpar* was never seen before or after in the Latin language, no one has been able to decipher precisely its meaning. Latin has a perfectly good word for spouse, but Jerome declined to use it. He was clearly obfuscating. He intended to make it difficult to imagine a married Paul. The Reformation translators were to some extent influenced by Jerome. Indeed, "yokefellow" looks very much like *conpar.* The Reformation translators likely thought that Jerome was privy to something they did not know, and he was, of course, one of the esteemed church fathers. Thus it was that Reformation translators, who might have been comfortable, even delighted with the notion of a married Paul, declined to translate Philippians 4:3 as they should have.

The single most persuasive piece of data in support of a married Paul comes from the pen of Bishop Clement of Alexandria, writing in the late second and early third centuries. He is noteworthy for having left us the earliest surviving commentaries on the Pauline letters. Clement was a conservative, mainstream church leader of good repute. Because his native language was the same Greek as Paul's, Clement had no need to translate Paul's letters; he needed only to interpret them. He stated explicitly in his commentary on Philippians that Paul was addressing his wife in 4:3.[6]

Clement did not have trouble thinking of Paul as married because he lived prior to later Christianity's sex-phobic revision of the biblical texts. Origen, the prominent third-century theologian and other church fathers also agreed with Clement's view of Paul's marital state as disclosed in Philippians. So too did several Protestant leaders and scholars in later centuries. But one hears no word of this in today's seminaries, whether Protestant or Catholic. Any rational person without a sex-phobic axe to grind will concede that Paul, the Apostle, can be assumed to have had at least two wives, either concurrently or in succession. One of his wives was likely to have been the rich merchant woman he lived with for a time, Lydia of Philippi.

CHAPTER 4

SEXUAL PLEASURE IN JUDAISM

At the time of Jesus, the Jewish religion promoted standards of sexual behavior vastly different from those that emerged in later Christendom. Jewish religious leaders were utterly serious about matters of proper sexual behavior, yet were *not* serious about the same matters that concern modern Christian leaders in the West.[1]

The Pharisees, who made up the dominant religious party in first-century Palestine, attended to every detail (every "jot and tittle") of the law, and this included all sorts of rules regarding sexual behavior. Jesus himself is thought to have belonged to the Pharisee group, even though he quarreled with some of its points of view. Subsequent Christians quarreled with the Pharisees even more. In fact, the adjective, "pharisaical," meaning hypocritical and censorious self-righteousness, is an unjust slur against the Pharisees.

The French philosopher Paul Ricoeur (1913–2005) said that we observers today, like New Testament writers in their time, are too hard on the Pharisees.[2] He contended that they should be held in high esteem for their devotion to the commandments. Certainly, they did micromanage matters of conduct, and certainly they got caught attending to superficial details rather than concentrating on the deeper motivations of the human heart; but Jesus, like other Pharisees, shared a serious posture about the requirements of obedience to divine commands.

As New Testament writers unmistakably portrayed, Jesus held the law in high esteem; he was "obedient unto death." He obeyed the Torah, yet his parsing of its requirements was apparently more humanistic, more gracious than the interpretations of his fellow Pharisees. By its nature, all law must be interpreted. As Jesus implied, the law was made for man, not man for the law.

The Pharisees had worked out the details for proper sexual behavior, regulations they expected to be scrupulously observed. In the spirit of their later Talmudic successors, the Pharisees endlessly debated the requirements of the law. While that tradition is affirming of sexual pleasure, it is hardly cavalier. As one Talmudic Rabbi put it, concerning sexual desire, "let the left hand push away and the right hand bring close." The commentary goes on: "If he distances himself totally (from sexual desire), then he decreases the world; however, if he draws it very closely he will succumb to what is prohibited."[3] This is an apt representation of Jewish affirmation of sexual pleasure, balanced by scrupulous attention to the law, or Torah.

In first-century Palestinian Judaism, Pharisaic interpretation apparently held that a proper woman never conversed with a man in a public place; that is, never with a man who was not her husband or kinsman. Likewise, the Pharisees decreed that women should not travel from city to city accompanied by men who were not their husbands. Jesus made quite different interpretations of the law, flouting both of these interpretations. He spoke intimately with strange women in public places and, along with his disciples, traveled with women. But these Jewish regulations, as well as other similar sexual strictures of Pharisaic interpretation, were not based on negative attitudes toward sexual pleasure. Rather, they were based on an intense devotion to the commandments, in this case the commandment against adultery. Moreover, the laws reflected the Pharisees' intense desire to maintain faithfulness to such commandments. So it is hardly surprising that Jesus' own interpretation of such a law, rather free-wheeling as to what was permissible sexual behavior, did not sit well with the Pharisees.

In ancient Judaism the prohibition of "adultery" had a different interpretation from its modern English meaning. In Judaism, adultery was an offense that applied only to married women, or to a man who had sexual relations with a married woman. A married man who consorted with an unattached woman, a widow, a single woman, or a prostitute was not considered an adulterer, but a polygamist. Polygamy was permitted and at times even required. A man who consorted sexually with any woman was tacitly considered to be married to that woman, at least for a time, even if she was a prostitute.

The act of sexual intercourse amounted, according to Jewish law and practice, to a de facto marriage. This meant that the man had obligations to such a woman. On the face of it, such an expectation may seem absurd, but it was actually an attempt to create justice for the woman. If a pregnancy resulted from a chance encounter, the child had a father. There were no illegitimate children in Israel, except for children born of incest. Compared to Roman law and custom, where all children born out of monogamous marriages were classified as illegitimate, the Jewish practice was, in many respects, considerably more just and humane.

In the Midrash, an ancient Jewish commentary on Bible texts, we can see the idiosyncrasy of Jewish sexual ethics and the profound difference between such a Jewish approach to sexual pleasure and a typical attitude toward sex as expressed in modern Christianity: "Rabbi Jonah said in Samuel's name: 'If a harlot was standing in the street and two men had intercourse with her, the first is not culpable while the second is, on account of the verse: Behold, thou shalt die ... for she has been possessed by a man.'"[4]

The second patron of the prostitute observed that another man had had sexual relations with her. Because male sexual relations with a woman constituted de facto marriage, the first man was, at least by implication, married to the prostitute, whereas the second man was an adulterer. We see in this vignette a posture toward sexual pleasure that is radically different from the one taken by modern Christians, for whom the contamination of sexual experience itself is the prime concern, a taboo violated. The Jewish focus was on justice for all participants; in this instance, justice in the form of protection for the woman, and protection of the property of the man, that is, his de facto wife.

The so-called levirate law, the law requiring the brother-in-law to marry his brother's widow, dramatically illustrates the ancient Jewish approach to marriage and shows how different this attitude was from the monogamy required in later Christendom. This law specified that a widow must be taken in as an additional wife by her brother-in-law, and if she was still of childbearing years, must be impregnated as well. The crime of Onan was his resistance to impregnating his widowed sister-in-law, though he did not seem to object to the part of the law requiring him to have sex with her.[5]

In response to a question about the levirate law, Jesus responded that there will be no marriage in the kingdom.[6] Whether he meant the kingdom of heaven, or some version of a kingdom on earth, is not clear. It is noteworthy, however, that he did not critique polygamy in favor of monogamy, as he might have, but marriage itself. Nor did he say there will be no sex in the kingdom; but as always, we should add the caveat that no one saying of Jesus can be considered unquestionably authentic, from his mouth.

The Talmud promotes the view that sex will be found in heaven. So does Islam. Of the three Abrahamic faiths, only Christianity has no tradition of sex in heaven. Jesus' remark to the Sadducees, that there will be no marriage or giving in marriage, might mean that in the kingdom of God, holy promiscuity will prevail.

While polygamy, or more properly *polygyny* (i.e., the state of having more than one wife, as it was practiced in Judaism generally) gave protection to those who, in other cultures, would have been mistresses, concubines, and illegitimate persons, it did have its moral flaws. Polygamy, then as now, granted no sort of level playing field for women. And it was unfair to men who had minimal economic resources. Now as then, the more wealth a man possesses, the more wives he can afford. In addition, in every polygamous culture the rich men take the most attractive, most talented women for themselves. King Solomon was said to have been very wise and rich. He was also a bit greedy. Perhaps he was immensely active sexually. With his seven hundred wives and three hundred concubines, his life certainly must have been too complicated for his own good.

Christian monogamy, which supplanted Jewish polygamy, created a whole class of mistresses and illegitimate children. It only traded one set of problems for another. One of the obvious problems with polygamy, at least as practiced by Jews, was its patriarchal posture. Jewish sexual matters, in ethical terms, have always been hobbled by a patriarchal bias. However, Christianity did nothing to remedy that moral problem. It simply instituted a monogamous patriarchy, following the tradition of imperial Rome.

The relative toleration of prostitution in the biblical texts, and in the Jewish postbiblical literature, is also noteworthy as an indication of Jewish comfort with sexual pleasure. While prostitution was hardly a venerated profession, neither was it treated with the utter contempt later directed against it in the Christian West.

The prostitute, Rahab, is even venerated as a woman of faith, both in the Jewish tradition, and, astonishingly, considering subsequent Christian history, in the Christian New Testament. Rahab was a prostitute who lived in Jericho. Siding with the Israelis, she sheltered Jewish spies, misled the local police, and helped turn the city over to the invading general, Joshua.[7] In the Christian New Testament, Rahab is referred to as a woman both of faith in the Epistle to Hebrews[8] and of good works in the Letter of James.[9] She is also cited as one of Jesus' ancestors in the genealogical list in Matthew.[10] It is notable how nonchalant the texts are in reference to Rahab's line of work, both in the Old Testament and in the three Christian texts. Her way of earning a living would not have been highly esteemed in either the Jewish or early Christian communities, but her faith and works are nevertheless venerated.

Such a cavalier stance toward prostitution cannot be imagined in modern Christian times. Important as Rahab is in both the Jewish and Christian scriptures, one cannot envision a church built in her honor these days. Her sexual taint would, for modern Christians, overshadow all her faith and good works combined. Such is the nature of the divide that separates Christian from Jewish tradition, and for that matter, separates Christianity from its own roots.

The prophet Hosea married a prostitute, in response to a command from God. (Some Jewish interpreters think that his wife was not an actual prostitute, but a woman who became sexually promiscuous.) Yet Hosea remained committed to her, by direction from God, and their relationship became, for Hosea, a metaphor for the divine human relationship: one of repeated disobedience followed by continual unconditional forgiveness.

The issue of premarital sexual relations was not a significant issue in biblical writings, either in regard to Jewish or Christian girls. By modern standards, girls were betrothed and married at a very early age, between 13 and

15, which allowed little time for them to be tempted to engage in sexual activity prior to marriage. Marriage was essentially the transfer of a girl from the authority and property of her father to the authority and property of her husband. A man expected to find his young wife a virgin. Some girls undoubtedly had illicit sexual relations prior to marriage, either through their own daring or as victims of male aggression. Mary, the mother of Jesus, was found to be pregnant as a young girl and not by her fiancé; she is presumably a noteworthy example of just such a violation.

Unquestionably the most controversial, and arguably the most important, book of the Bible is the Song of Solomon, also called the Song of Songs. Yale professor Marvin H. Pope became its chief modern interpreter and defender; he was the author of the *Anchor Bible Commentary* on what he called the "Super Song."[11] This Super Song provides another lens, another angle by which we can infer Old Testament Jewish thinking about sexual pleasure.

The Song is unambiguously pornographic. Its theme, in the words of Roland E. Murphy, is "human sexual fulfillment, fervently sought and consummated in reciprocal love between a woman and a man."[12] Some English translations are less than candid, but a number of alternate translations exist. Here is a translation drawn from a variety of versions:

O kiss me with the kisses of your mouth.
　His left hand is under my head;
　His right hand clasps me. (Song of Songs 2:5)
Let my love enter his garden;
　Let him eat its delectable fruit. (4:16)
Under the apple tree I aroused you.
　There your mother conceived you. (8:5)
My love thrust his hand [a euphemism for penis] into the hole
　And my inwards seethed for him. (5:4)
Your curving thighs are like ornaments crafted by artist's hands;
　Your vulva a round crater. (7:2)
The scent of your vulva like apples,
　Open to me, my sister, my darling, my dove, my perfect one! (7:8)
I have removed my tunic.
　How shall I put it on? (5:2–3)
Your valley [a euphemism for the female pudendum], a rounded bowl
　That is not to lack mixed wine. (7:3)[13]
Eat, friends, drink.
　Be drunk with love! (5:1)
For love is strong as death;
　Passion as fierce as hell;
　Its darts are darts of fire.
　Mighty waters cannot quench love.
　No torrents can sweep it away. (8:6)

There is some violence in the Song that is impenetrable. The lovers are
    attacked by someone.
Then he fled and the guards struck and wounded her. (5:6)

The Song is thought to have its origins in Babylonian funeral rites, religious
rituals that proposed to assuage grief through themes of love and orgiastic
experiences, perhaps even sexual orgies. Such rites are known to have taken
place in Middle Eastern religions. They may well be related to Tantric Hinduism and Buddhism, in India and the East, where orgiastic sexual practices,
considered to be redemptive and therapeutic, are still practiced today.

The fact that the Song springs from Babylonian religion is not unique. Much
of the Bible consists of material borrowed from Babylonian and other Middle
Eastern religions, then recast with its own religious slant. The Book of Esther,
for example, is a recasting of the Babylonian cult of Ishtar, goddess of love.

One of the curious residual effects of the Ishtar cult are the Jewish cookies
hamantaschen (German word meaning, literally, "Haman's pocket.") Haman
was a figure in the Esther story, also featured in the Jewish feast of Purim;
but the cookie originates in Babylon and should more properly be called
Ishtar's (or Esther's) pubes. An examination of hamantaschen will show that
the cookie is constructed to represent a woman's pudendum.[14]

Religious scholars, both Jewish and Christian, have historically had trouble
with the Song of Songs. Some Jewish sages, like the seventeenth-century
Westminster Puritans, rebuked those who read the Song as a "hot carnal pam-
phlet."[15] They speculated that it was an allegory or metaphor of God's love for
humankind. To read the Song as a metaphor for God's love is not inappropriate. Nevertheless, it remains a vivid sexual metaphor. Still, if the literal meaning
is forgotten or erased, the power of the metaphor itself is also lost.

What is truly marvelous is that the Song was included in the Bible at all,
and that religious leaders were the ones who decided to include it in the list
of what were considered to be canonical or authorized books. The renowned
Rabbi Akiba ben Joseph of the first century was one of the strongest defend-
ers of the Song against those who objected to its inclusion in the Bible. It
is the holiest part of scripture, he declared. "The whole world," he wrote,
"is not worth the day on which the Song was given to Israel." He won the
argument.[16]

The Song is the strongest single work to counter the claims of the effete
Platonists and Stoics, who established themselves as the ultimate religious
authorities in the Roman imperial world and who, furthermore, pontifi-
cated that true religion separated itself from sexual pleasure. There is no
transcendence of sexual pleasure in the Song of Songs, nor is there in the
biblical world generally. The entire biblical world, Jewish and early Christian,
is comfortable with the blessings of sexual pleasure. It was only later in its
life that Christianity changed its point of view.

The prophet Ezekiel,[17] using a powerful sexual metaphor, writes of the relationship between God and his people. The Lord saw that Israel, like a daughter he had raised from birth, had come of age and was "ripe for love." So he spread his robe over her, covering her nakedness, and had intercourse with her. Afterward, he washed away the hymenal blood and, after anointing Israel with oil, married her. Then, as the prophet goes on to relate, Israel had proved unfaithful to him. These days, we shouldn't expect to hear any Christian sermons on *that* text.

In a similar metaphor, Ezekiel characterized the Lord as married to both Jerusalem and Samaria, each of which has become an adulterous wife. God himself is thus characterized, metaphorically, as polygamous. So we see how, in Judaism, sexual intimacy is a common metaphor for the love between God and his people.

For illustrating the gulf between the biblical world and the world of twenty-first century Christendom, the tale of Abishag the Shunammite is one of the Bible's most telling passages.[18] It is regrettable that, in modern times, so few Christian sermons have been heard on the life and work of this wonderful figure named Abishag.

King David was in his declining years. He had been so effective that subsequent generations would consider his rule to have been the golden age of Israel. Christians even gave the title "Son of David" to Jesus, hoping to suggest Jesus' preeminence by representing him as a personified Davidic return of power and wisdom.

In his last days, when David could not get warm, his attendants strove to keep him comfortable and strong. Then someone came up with a simple solution: David's caregivers sent out word to find a beautiful young woman to attend to David and "to lie in his bosom." If anything could restore his vitality, they concluded, this medicine would.

The texts do not say how long David lived intimately in the company of Abishag, but he did live long enough to put down an attempt at usurpation of his throne by one of his sons named Adonijah. David had already decided to make Solomon his successor to the throne, but during David's declining period, Adonijah moved to preempt Solomon. The biblical account describes how David's wife, Solomon's mother Bathsheba, came to appeal to David for action to thwart Adonijah's coup. The text reports that Bathsheba made her appeal while Abishag waited on David: a poignant description of intercourse between the old wife and the new one.

David put down the rebellion, as requested. Furthermore, he did not wait any longer to enthrone Solomon and made him king immediately, and Bathsheba, queen mother. In turn, Solomon pardoned his brother Adonijah and sent him home. Later David died. The biblical text states that David had not consummated the relationship with Abishag sexually, although some Rabbinic literature seems to be of the opinion that he had. (One can never be sure whether or how much any particular text has been edited by scribes and copyists through the ages.) In either case, Abishag had certainly been sexually available to David, whether he consummated the relationship or not.

In an interesting sequel, after David's death Adonijah appealed to Solomon, asking to have Abishag as his own wife. In so doing, Adonijah displayed what modern psychology calls a lack of self-awareness. His request was audacious, as he would be marrying one of his deceased father's *wives*, whether her relationship with David had been consummated or not. By marrying a widow of David, Adonijah, in psychological terms, would have achieved an "oedipal" victory. In response to the request, the wise Solomon ordered Adonijah immediately put to death. Adonijah had shown that he had not given up his rebellious ways, that his lust for power was still covertly operative.

The Jewish religious tradition has remained as affirming of sexual pleasure as the Bible itself, although Judaism did trim its sails to a certain extent in medieval, Catholic-dominated Europe. Ashkenazi Jews, the branch of Judaism that existed mainly in Western Europe, adopted monogamy as its marital norm in the eleventh century C.E.

The good conscience that Jews historically have had about sexual pleasure has had negative consequences for Jews during certain historical periods. The Stoics and Platonists of the imperial Roman period, who were convinced that sexual ecstasy inevitably led to a disordered mind, held the Jews in contempt, branding them a dirty race. This frequent allusion to filth is clearly related to sexuality. Later in Christendom, Jews were often pilloried, charged with such lurid crimes as lusting after pure Christian girls. Throughout history, sexually repressed, guilt-ridden Christians have echoed this charge, culminating with Adolph Hitler, the most successful anti-Semite ever. Hitler did not invent the slur of the dirty Jew, with its sexual innuendo, but he effectively repeated and elaborated the theme.[19]

It should strike us as no historical coincidence that Hitler personally promoted a public image of sexual abstinence. He countenanced no display of sexuality in his presence. Keeping his mistress, Eva Braun, in virtual hiding, he maintained an asexual public image; he and Eva didn't marry until just prior to their mutual suicide. Hitler's presumed sexual purity played well with anti-Semites, who portrayed the Jews as lustful, filthy, and perverse. But Hitler was not the creator of such anti-Semitism; it had a long history in Christendom. The Jews have paid dearly in Christendom for their affirmation of sexual pleasure.

Novelist Herman Wouk captures in a few words the distinctive character of Jewish sexual values and how they stand in contrast to our current, culturally dominant form of Christianity: "What in other cultures has been a deed of shame, or of comedy, or of orgy, or of physical necessity, or of high romance, has been in Judaism one of the main things God wants man to do. If it turns out to be the keenest pleasure in life, that is no surprise to a people eternally sure God is good."[20]

CHAPTER 5

SEXUAL CONDUCT IN THE EARLY CHRISTIAN CHURCH

During the first three centuries of Christianity, no voice emerged to define proper sexual conduct in a manner that indicated any degree of consensus. No central authority existed to define such a position even if there had been a proposal for one. Evidence shows that among the various and varied Christian communities, some promoted a tilt toward sexual asceticism; others, a tilt toward libertinism of one sort or another. An argument was taking place in the young Christian community, but neither the sexual libertines nor the sexual ascetics carried the day. During its first centuries, Christianity was quite polymorphous in creed and in sexual conduct.

We do know, however, that even as Christians were sporadically persecuted by Roman authorities, the various Christian groups also made efforts to ingratiate themselves with the better elements of Roman society. In this effort, Christians were often quick to dissociate themselves from Judaism. Certain imperial philosophers held a low view of Judaism; and this was hardly a minority opinion. Strabo, a Greek geographer and contemporary of Jesus, judged Jews to be degenerate.[1] The esteemed historian, Tacitus, who lived in the period shortly after Jesus, said this of the Jews:

> Among the Jews all things are profane that we hold sacred; on the other hand they regard as permissible what seems to us immoral ... though a most lascivious people, the Jews avoid sexual intercourse with women of alien race. Among themselves nothing is barred ... the very first lesson they [proselytes to Judaism] learn is to despise the gods, shed all feelings of patriotism ... Their kings are not so flattered, the Roman emperor not so honored ... the Jewish belief is paradoxical and degraded.[2]

Celsus, a third-century critic of Christianity, added that there is "not the shadow of an ass's difference between Christians and Jews."[3]

The early Christians found themselves in a double bind. They were subject to Roman anti-Semitism, as they were themselves initially a sect of Judaism; and as members of allegedly liberated Jewish communities, they were sometimes marked by their imperial detractors as sexually even more libertine than the Jews. In the course of time, Christianity radically separated itself both from Judaism and from sexual libertinism, in both instances going to the extreme.[4]

We also know that certain early Christian groups carried out practices that would have been viewed as scandalous both to Roman and Jewish authorities, yet it is impossible to sort out, from our historical vantage point, exactly who the actors were, what the extent of their influence was, or what their precise relationship may have been with the earliest Jesus traditions. Charges of sexual misconduct were hurled back and forth throughout the early Christian world. While some of the invective may be discounted as mere hyperbolic slander, we know that liberated sexual behavior, from one viewpoint or another, was increasingly on the minds of early Christians. As early as the letters of Paul, the earliest biblical documents of Christianity, both sexual libertinism and sexual asceticism were matters of some concern.

For reasons now lost to history, the kiss of peace was a novel and also widely established institution in early Christian communities, and one that must, physically, have suggested sexual liberation and intimacy.[5] In addition, its cross-gender physicality would have rendered it a very un-Jewish practice. Jesus must be given some, if not all, of the credit for the wide use and significance of the kiss. It seems unlikely that a practice of such significance would have arisen within a couple of decades of Jesus' demise with no obvious link to Jesus himself. Moreover, the scripture records Jesus exchanging kisses with others, for example, with Judas at the betrayal.

Two thousand years ago, a kiss must have meant roughly what it means today, aside from such periphera as kiss-proof lipstick. One can hardly kiss without some degree of sexual innuendo. The kiss, as practiced in early Christian communities, was no sex-phobic cheek-to-cheek brush, as practiced in certain churches today. It was mouth-to-mouth, as indicated by some of the Nag-Hammadi manuscripts.[6] The rationale seems to have been related to the association of the breath with spirit and soul. It was also referred to as "the kiss of love." Modern theologians, such as J. B. Phillips, who proposed that the handshake be taken as a modern equivalent to the early Christian kiss of peace or love, reveal their own anxiety about sex, not to mention a certain density of thought.[7]

The kiss eventually and predictably fell out of favor, and by the third century was not described as a feature of Christian gatherings. It went the way of the association of Jesus with fish, likely for much the same reason. In

200 C.E., church leaders were concerned that their "assemblies resound with nothing but kisses." Bishop Clement of Alexandria wrote: "We should realize that unrestrained use of the kiss has brought it under grave suspicion and slander. It should be thought of in a mystical sense ... Let us taste the kingdom with a mouth that is chaste and self-controlled."[8] Bishop Athenagoras announced that he would penalize "any man who takes a second kiss for the motive of pleasure."[9] By the third century, it appears, men and women were separated in church gatherings, a practice that continues today in some Orthodox churches of the East.

This nervousness of the bishops about the religious kiss was a harbinger of the ultimate obliteration of any sort of approval of sexual pleasure in official Christian ethics. This revision of the practices and teachings of the early church paralleled an increasing amnesia about the Jewish origins of Christianity, an amnesia that has also permitted almost two millennia of pervasive and brutal anti-Semitism.

As the young Christian churches moved from their birthplace in sex-positive Judaism into sex-negative Roman imperial philosophy and religion, they underwent a sea change and adhered increasingly to imperial Roman standards. But such a sea change, though it did come, was slow to take place. Almost none of the literature of the first three centuries speaks with the voice, say, of the modern popes on the subject of what constitutes proper sexual behavior. The early Christian literature was not universally marked by the kind of prudery that was exhibited in the writings of Stoic and Neoplatonist philosophers, the moralists of imperial Rome, whose writings, astonishingly, are exactly congruent with modern, official, Roman Catholic sex ethics; but this gets ahead of our story.

In the final analysis, the winner in the internecine conflict within Christianity was the group that came to identify itself as the Catholic party, and history is always written by its winners. Thus any group that appeared not to represent the principles of the victorious Catholic party was labeled heretic or gnostic or both. The label "heretic" was generously thrown around in the early centuries, and "gnostic" was a particularly common heretical label of the one-size-fits-all variety. Not until the fourth century, with the imperial adoption of Christianity, did the label heretic become a threat to one's health and welfare.

One of the ultimate literary losers in the heresy debates was the Gospel of Philip, with its intriguing sacrament of the bridal chamber. The gospel presented itself as a report on the earliest Jesus movement but was rejected, along with many other documents, by the victorious Catholic party. No record is left to indicate what actually took place in Philip's sacrament of the bridal chamber, but the innuendo is clear. The bridal chamber is a place of sexual encounter, however sublimated such an encounter might have been in actual practice. We can assume that this was an attempt to carry forward the sexual liberationist agenda of Jesus, however embroidered its account, historically speaking, may or may not have been.

The sacrament of the bridal chamber was not the only piece of evidence suggesting sexually liberated agendas in the early church. Surviving documents from the first three centuries disclose numerous charges alleging, from the imperial Roman perspective, sexual misbehavior among Christians. A tutor of the philosopher Marcus Aurelius, M. Cornelius Fronto, wrote this about Christians:

> Hardly have they met when they love each other ... a veritable religion of lusts. Indiscriminately they call each other brother and sister, thus turning ordinary fornication into incest by the intervention of these hallowed names ... It is also reported that they worship the genitals of their pontiff and priest ... a suspicion that befits their clandestine and nocturnal ceremonies ... On a special day they gather for a feast with all their children, sisters, mothers, all sexes and ages. There, flushed with the banquet after such feasting and drinking, they begin to burn with incestuous passions. They provoke a dog tied to the lamp-stand to leap and bound towards a scrap of food which they have tossed outside the reach of his chain. By this means the light is overturned and extinguished, and with it common knowledge of their actions; in the shameless dark, with unspeakable lust they copulate in random unions, all equally being guilty of incest, some by deed, but everyone by complicity.[10]

We do not have to credit this alleged historical account, and others like it, with veracity. Almost certainly it was hyperbolic slander. It has the ring of invention. At the same time, such accusations were plausibly based on anxiety about the sexual behavior of Christians; and they do reveal what some presumably intelligent Romans thought of early Christianity. Their disdain for the sexual practices of Christians was likely based on an element of truth, however exaggerated. The early Church was thus doubly tainted, both by identification with Judaism and by its own liberationist teachings. Early Christian sex ethics did not conform to Roman imperial notions of an antithetical relationship between religion and sexual pleasure. That was to come later in the church's development.

In 330 C.E. Constantine abandoned Rome to set up his new imperial capital, Constantinople, in Byzantium, the city now know as Istanbul. Thus he set in motion a series of events that eventually divided Christianity into East and West, Orthodox and Catholic, a division that continues to this day. In effect, he moved the center of the world eastward one thousand miles, leaving Rome a city of lesser consequence. However, the aura of Rome as the center of things did not entirely depart; and curiously, in an ancient illustration of synecdoche, the empire continued to refer to itself as the Roman Empire, even after Rome itself was overrun by the encroaching "barbarians."

Modern historians now call it the Eastern or Byzantine Empire. Rome was finally severed from the Roman Empire in the seventh century, but the empire lasted until the fifteenth.

Succeeding bishops of Rome, moving into the vacuum left by the departing emperor and his civil servants, attempted to assert themselves as the authority over the entire Christian Church; but the bishop of Constantinople, eventually entitled "the Patriarch," possessed authority of his own in the now-Christianized empire. His office was situated in the new imperial capitol of this theocratic Byzantine state. Meanwhile, back in Rome, the bishops there argued from tradition, contending that the original apostles, more particularly Peter, had set up shop in Rome. The bishops of Rome almost won the argument. For several centuries letters and embassies went back and forth between Rome and Constantinople, leading to tentative agreements from time to time, all directed toward settling the question of who would serve as ultimate religious authority in the Christian world. The matter was never resolved, and gradually the two centers, Rome and Constantinople, settled into a perpetual rivalry, each developing its own particular and separate traditions.

The rivalry between Constantinople and Rome was not always as polite as it is today. After Pope John XIII sleighted Emperor Nicephorus III in the tenth century, the Byzantine legate sent the following message to Rome: "That fatuous blockhead of a pope does not know that the sacred Constantine transferred to this city the imperial sceptre, Senate, knighthoods, leaving in Rome nothing but vile slaves, fishermen, confectioners, poulterers, bastards, plebians, and underlings."[11]

The Church in the East under the patriarchs, like that in the West under the popes, was infected by Stoic and Neoplatonic anxiety about sexual pleasure. Both centers increasingly exhibited extreme amnesia about the sex-affirming Semitic roots of Christianity. While Rome slogged on, institutionalizing a severe strain of negativity toward sexual pleasure, and finally establishing celibacy as the rule for everyone in leadership in the church, the East developed a different set of rules, also negative toward sex but considerably less stringent. The Eastern Church actually required parish clergy to be married, and married prior to ordination, but at the same time, it cultivated monasticism as a parallel system. More ominously, it decreed that bishops were to be selected only from among the monastics. Thus the highest level of leadership, the bishops, consisted exclusively of persons who, it was claimed, were bereft of sexual pleasure in their lives, whereas the frontline clergy, the priests who served congregations, had wives. These distinctions between the Catholic West and the Orthodox East remain in place today.

As true as the dichotomy may be, to portray the Greco-Roman world as sex-negative, and the Jewish world as sex-positive, runs a risk of oversimplification. More precisely, we should say that the bearers of values in the respective cultures took radically opposite positions on the value of sexuality in the, so-called, good life. In the Roman imperial world, it was the Stoics and Neoplatonic philosophers, along with priests of the imperial cult, who were the public bearers of the highest values. They believed sexual pleasure and religion were antithetical, a conviction quite alien to biblical literature and to Jewish tradition generally.

But the Roman imperial cult was polychrome as well as polytheistic. On the one hand there were vestal virgins, and on the other, orgiastic Bachannalia. On the one hand there was Venus, goddess of sex and love ... on the other hand, sexual abstinence was a stated requirement as preparation to worship in various temples.

Christianity remodeled many of the existing Roman gods, making them appear to be sexually abstemious ones. Venus was remodeled as a virgin, and Dionysus, the Greek precursor of Bacchus, was somewhat cleaned up as Jesus. The feast of the unconquerable sun, the Sol Invictus, on December 25, was turned into a festival to celebrate the birth of Jesus. The virgins of Vesta needed little retooling; only some name changes were required to Christianize the characters.

The Roman Bacchanalia was not the sole cultic event with orgiastic associations. The union of sexual activity and religious rituals has a long and multicultural tradition. The religion of the Palestinians, whom the Israelites encountered while conquering the promised land, included what are euphemistically called fertility rites. These orgiastic rituals had more to do with pleasure than fertility.

The biblical Song of Solomon (or Song of Songs) is a vestigial remnant of such an orgiastic funeral rite. (See chapter 4 of this volume, "Sexual Pleasure in Judaism.") "Kiss me with the kisses of your mouth," it proclaims, for "love is stronger than death" (8:6). Grief is assuaged and life is affirmed through sexual pleasure. Paul Tillich must have had this in mind when he claimed that the only "argument against death" was the forgiveness of sins.[12]

We do not know all the practices that characterized this type of religion. They are lost to history but continue today, at least in part, as expressed in Tantric Hinduism, where orgiastic practices and sexual pleasure are considered to be both therapeutic and sacred. Early Christians were influenced by such religious practices, and their response seems to have been revulsion, as felt by some, but acceptance, as felt by others. Antipathy toward sex ultimately won the debate; and for the most part, the winners were the ones who preserved the documents, passing down to us mainly the documents that they chose to preserve.

Thus we have inherited in the West a rather severe prohibition against any suggestion of sexuality in the context of any religious practice. Modern dance, for example, with its explicit sensuality, has not been well received in the context of religious liturgies. Tantric Hinduism has never gained much respectability in the West.

Roman culture was an eclectic, polyglot culture, as is our own. The John Ashcrofts and Billy Grahams of Rome lived side by side with its Hugh Hefners and Larry Flints. We have our lurid, eroticized advertisements; the Greeks had their Dionysian cult, in which large plaster effigies of the phallus were paraded through the streets of Athens. Even today, on the Greek isle of Delos, one can see stone phallic pillars that are none too subtle remnants of the cult of Dionysus. Heraclitus the philosopher is recorded saying, "If it were not Dionysus for whom they march in procession and chant the hymns to the phallus, their action would be most shameless."[13] Likewise, *we* should admit that many ads in *Vanity Fair* and other magazines would be thought of as obscene were they not considered essential to business. As polychromatic as Roman imperial culture and religion may have been, the sex-negativity of the Stoics and Neoplatonist philosophers finally carried the day. Unfortunately for us all, Christianity has brought us down the same philosophical path.

CHAPTER 6

CONSTANTINE'S IMPERIAL COOPTATION OF CHRISTIANITY

When the Emperor Constantine adopted Christianity as the state religion in the early fourth century, a new uniformity was imposed on the religion. Since its beginnings, Christianity had been very diverse and polymorphous. After Constantine, dissenters became enemies both of the state and the church. This new uniformity was increasingly congruent with Stoic and Neoplatonic values, with dramatic implications for sexual values. The values and theology inherited from biblical literature were gradually eclipsed and done away. The church left its Semitic origins far behind.

According to popular tradition, Emperor Constantine himself converted to Christianity as a result of a vision of a cross in the sky prior to the battle of the Milvian Bridge in 313. This apparition led him to establish Christianity as the official religion of the empire. The message Constantine claimed to have received from the heavens was, "By this sign you will conquer." The truth is likely more subtle; Constantine did not convert to anything. He was, after all, not baptized in 313 but just before his death in 337. While his actual motives are undiscoverable, he undoubtedly saw an opportunity to bring new cohesion to a disintegrating empire that was increasingly threatened from both east and west. In a couple of centuries, the city of Rome would fall to the barbarians. Joseph Brodsky was probably correct in his judgment that Constantine was attracted to Christianity's extensive, empirewide network that was something of a combination of a food stamp program and the Red Cross.[1]

Constantine was, and remained throughout the rest of his life, a powerful and unsavory leader whose personal life reveals no evidence of religious or moral transformation, nor of any real appreciation for the biblical tradition. He had his wife Fausta murdered, as well as his sons Crispus and Licinianus, all years after his alleged conversion. He waited for baptism until his death-bed because baptism, supposedly a symbol of resolve to live a new life, was for him a magical erasure of all accumulated sins to date. Many others after Constantine attempted the same feat, a risky gamble to be sure. Not everyone successfully plots the hour or day of dying.

Constantine continued to cling to the title that he and previous emper-ors inherited, that of *Pontifex Maximus*, the high priest of the imperial cult, the title later assumed by the bishop of Rome in his ascent to increasing power. Moreover, Constantine continued to have temples built and dedicated to himself, temples that coexisted with Christianity. The preponderance of evidence supports a view of an emperor who was successful in converting Christianity to his own purposes rather than one converted to the values and commitments of Christianity.

Constantine dramatized the imposition of his will on the church by con-vening and presiding over the opening session of the first and most sig-nificant ecumenical council of the church, the Council of Nicaea, in 325. At Nicaea Constantine deputized the Catholic party as the one true Christian faith. The Arian party was the principal loser in this particular political skir-mish. With the power of the state behind them Christians for the first time in history were authorized by the state to impose sanctions against fellow Christians who held opinions different from the position approved by church and state. Not too many years later, Christians would sentence each other to death for holding unacceptable theological views. The Manichaean Chris-tians were said to be the first in a long list of heretical groups to suffer that insult and near extermination.

If Constantine posed as God's anointed representative on earth, his successors made the claim more explicit. Emperors who followed adopted the epithet, "Equal to the Apostles," thereby elevating themselves a step higher than the bishop of Constantinople, the patriarch, and assuredly higher that the bishop of Rome. After 325, the Roman Empire continued to be the theocracy it had always been. Only the name of the god had changed.

Prior to the Council of Nicaea, Christians had, for three centuries, fiercely debated the philosophical question of Jesus' own relationship to God. This debate started even during Jesus' lifetime. No rational person can doubt that Jesus was a real person, living in history; but he was also seen by some as a very special religious authority. At some point, probably only after his death, he was given the title of Messiah. The notion of Messiah came out of late Judaism and was understood as the one anointed to usher in the new reign of God at the end of history.

The New Testament documents, all written after Jesus death, are quite coy on the subject of Jesus' relation to God. While they proclaim him the Messiah, they add that Jesus himself kept the fact of his messianic role a secret. Obviously, he may have kept it a secret simply because he did not see himself in that role. In any case, some in the early church understood Jesus to be the Messiah, but harboring a "messianic secret."

As the decades and centuries passed, the theories about Jesus' relationship to God became more convoluted and fanciful. His role as Messiah was gradually eclipsed by notions of Jesus as the Son of God. This shift was due partly to the expansion of Christianity into the empire where the Jewish concept of Messiah was an unfamiliar concept and where Judaism itself was a relatively obscure, even distasteful, religion. Jesus as the Son of God, on the other hand, was language compatible with the empire. In the religion of imperial Rome, the gods "appeared" often disguised as humans, who sired children and tampered with the laws of nature in a variety of ways. In that sense the Romans were very religious. Thus the imperial Romans were much quicker to believe that Jesus was the Son of God than to believe that he was the Messiah, whatever that may have meant to them.

Once it was agreed that Jesus was the Son of God, it became necessary to clarify who the father might be, and what kind of relationship existed between the two. The Holy Spirit (or *Ghost*, archaic) was then put in place to represent the continuing historical relationship between God and the world. Finding itself with Father, Son, and Holy Spirit, the church had a trinity. The idea of a trinity does not appear in any biblical texts. It evolved later and was officially legislated at the Council of Nicaea. No one was bothered by the absence of any mention of a trinity in the Bible.

At the Council of Nicaea, the question of Jesus' status in the now-state-approved trinitarian godhead was the major subject of contention. The Arian party argued that the Son was subservient to the Father, as common sense and family relationships would dictate. The Catholic party argued that all three persons of the godhead were fully equal to one another. As Constantine backed the Catholic party, the question was resolved by decree, and the Arians were officially classified as heretics.

In the three hundred years from Jesus to Nicaea, the church had finally lost interest in Jesus' role as messiah. As a substitute, Nicaea proclaimed a tautology: Jesus as both fully God and fully human. Common sense would dictate that one negates the other, by definition. Nevertheless, the tautology carried the day. It was called a divine mystery and has remained so ever since. Particular schools of thought within Christianity have taken up a variety of positions along the spectrum of the "God and man" debate. At its best, the debate promoted a view of Jesus as fully human but with a special divinely appointed commission. At its worst, the debate has promoted the view of Jesus as a God traipsing around Palestine in mufti, pretending to be a human being.

Thus it was that in the course of 300 years, the Palestinian rabbi was gradually elevated to a status in which he was equated with God himself. This inflation alarmed many Christians, and not only the Arians, but also those famously known as Christian humanists, most of whom in the fourth century seem to have been linked to the church in Syria, particularly the archbishopric of Antioch. This was the section of the church most closely linked with Jesus own family and the Jerusalem Church, led originally by Jesus' brother James. Even as late as 250, Theophilus, Archbishop of Antioch, contended that Jesus was a human being whose redemptive value for us was that he followed the law of Moses perfectly and set us the supreme example.

The imperial dominance of the church by Constantine was a colossal defeat for the Jewish biblical affirmation of sexual pleasure, just as it was a defeat for the view of Jesus as a human being. The curious fact is that the two go together. Furthermore, those who understood Jesus as a human being were generally more positive in their appreciation of sexual pleasure, and those who understood Jesus as divine were more negative and abstemious regarding sexual pleasure.

We know the names of several defeated Christian leaders who were declared heretics and disgraced during that time: Jovinian, Helvidius, Vigilantius, Julian of Eclanum, and Theodore of Mopsuestia. They all held in common a more Jewish approach to sexual pleasure and its corollary, the view of Jesus as a human being. Theodore is the best known, and the only one whose own writings survive. They were preserved in secret in a monastery after he was declared a heretic, disguised ironically by a cover designating the work as that of a certain Ambrose. The others are remembered only by way of the polemics written against them.

Theodore of Mopsuestia has lately received some renewed attention. Two theologians in this generation have written excellent studies of his life and work, R. A. Norris, Jr., and Rowan A. Greer.[2] They have contributed much toward restoring his undeservedly besmirched reputation. Theodore was what we now would call a Christian humanist. He was informed more by biblical literature than by Stoic and Neoplatonic philosophy. While he was a monastic, he was not typically phobic about sex. He had fallen in love as a young man and only with difficulty decided on the monastic life. He declined to promote the celibate life as superior to marriage. Theodore also opposed the drift toward a view of Jesus as a god in disguise, such as was promoted by Nicaea.

So the heresy of Theodore and his fellow Christian humanists was their view that Jesus was a fully human being. There was no longer any room for them in Christianity. From the fourth century onward, Christianity was a Roman imperial religion, not a Semitic one, and Jesus was understood as a divine manifestation in human form, a god disguised as a human, with sexual purity as his defining moral trait. From this point on in the history of the church, those who have held the view that Jesus was a human being have either dwelt on the outer fringes of Christianity or been branded heretics and expelled.

Thus the fourth century brought an end to all but a few meager vestiges of the original Jesus movement. Jesus was now emblazoned on the shields and banners of the conquering Roman legions; in his name they conquered. Jesus was no longer in any sense a Palestinian rabbi who explicated the meaning of the Torah. Now he was an incarnated imperial god who had once paraded around Palestine disguised as, and pretending to be, a human being. Now he trumped all the countless other imperial gods. The fourth century witnessed the final defeat of those who held Jesus to be an actual human being.

The political transformation of Christianity had a powerful, and devastating, impact on the church's ethics and sexual morality. For the first three centuries of the Jesus movement, idolatry had been the preeminent distinguishing ethical mark that separated Christians from non-Christians. Christians were actually viewed as atheists and were identified as such in the context of imperial religion. Those Christians who were sporadically persecuted by the state were sometimes invited to denounce Christ and offer sacrifices to the imperial gods or face summary execution.[3] Among the gods in this polytheistic culture was the emperor himself. Among the devotees of the imperial cult, idolatry was not a moral or ethical problem, as it was in Christianity. There were always many gods to consider. Sexual purity was the principal moral feature of the imperial religion, and this ethical cornerstone was given major attention by the Stoics and Neoplatonist philosophers who were considered the bearers of values in that culture, as we have noted above.

During the time of Constantine, sexual innocence or purity was increasingly promoted as the central distinguishing feature, the preeminent ethical mark, of a Christian. Christianity simply made a radical exchange of moral focus, jettisoning idolatry, which then was supplanted by sexual abstinence as the hallmark of Christianity. The temple of the virgins (Parthenon means "of the virgins" in Greek) had dominated Athens, just as the Vestal Virgins held places of highest esteem in Rome. Virginity was no blessing in Israel, except for a nubile young girl prior to marriage. In mature women, it was a curse. The virgins of Vesta continued in power in their new Christian array, and they trumped the biblical affirmation of sexual pleasure.[4]

The impact of Constantine's cooptation of the church was felt in several significant ways. Jesus was elevated to the fullness of the godhead, with the full warranty of the state, jeopardizing his standing as an actual human being. This transformation of the personal identity of Jesus radically separated him and the church from its Jewish origins. Abstinence from sexual pleasure became the new mark of the ethical life in the church, and this standard had a damaging longterm effect on Western culture in the years since. Finally and more ominously, the uniformity imposed on what all along had be a diverse and polymorphous Christianity, meant, in the perceptive words of Charles Freeman, "the closing of the western mind."[5]

CHAPTER 7

ECCE UNDE —THAT'S THE PLACE

In the century after Constantine's adoption of Christianity, three individual figures emerged as preeminent among the Christian leadership: Jerome, Ambrose, and Augustine. In subsequent history, the latter stands head and shoulders above the others. His writings remain still today one of the major achievements of the Christian religion and culture.

Among all the great personages of early Christendom few exerted as much influence and none is more fascinatingly kinky than Jerome. If he could return to life today he would be a psychologist's dream case. Jerome was a leading figure in the Catholic party that ultimately declared all the Christian humanists heretics. He was fascinated with and repelled by sexuality. Sex was his obsession. Jerome carried the Stoic and Neoplatonic revulsion over sex to new heights. That Jerome and his party, thanks to a boost from the emperor, were ultimate victors in the early Christian culture wars was a blow from which we still suffer today.

Jerome taught that all sex is impure in whatever form. The only good that comes out of marriage, he argued, is the production of more virgins.[1] For him virginity and sexual abstinence were the highest marks of the Christian life. He attacked those who, like Bishop Clement of Alexandria, held the view that Paul had been married. He promoted the innovative notion that the mother of Jesus was a perpetual virgin, and he attacked those Christians who believed that Jesus' brothers were actually born of Mary. Such views foul the sanctuary of the Holy Spirit, he said.[2]

One of Jerome's religious fascinations was the practice of bathing, specifically, bathing by virgins. He held the not-so-unreasonable view that attention to personal hygiene might lead to an interest in sexual pleasure.

Speaking personally, I altogether disapprove of baths for a full grown virgin. She ought to blush at herself and be unable to behold her own nakedness. If she mortifies and enslaves her body by vigils and fasts, if she desires to quench the flames of lust and check the hot passions of youth by cold chastity, if she hastens to spoil her natural beauty by deliberate squalor, why should she rouse a slumbering fire by the inventive of baths?[3]

The great Christian humanist contemporary, Julian of Eclanum, who was eventually labeled a heretic, said of Jerome that he was so puerile that one could scarcely refrain from laughing on reading him.[4] Now a millennium and a half later we see that Jerome actually had the last laugh, to the great misfortune of us all in the West.

Jerome spent the last 33 years of his life in a monastery in Bethlehem with, as he put it, beans in his belly while Romans ate sturgeon. To his credit we must acknowledge that his move to Palestine was an admirable protest against the new-found prosperity and luxury of the church and its attendant corruption. In his self-imposed exile Jerome was accompanied to Palestine by Paula, a 35-year-old woman of social standing and wealth who had raised five children and was now widowed. It was certainly one of the more idiosyncratic love affairs in the annals of human relationships. Fascinated with Jerome as she was, Paula also concurred with Jerome's view of the devilishness of sex. She had ceased to have sexual relations with her late husband after their fifth child. In Palestine she declined to bathe, presumably making it easier for the two of them to control their sexual desires. She finally died there in Jerome's company at age 56.[5]

Jerome wrote that sex was his one crime and that specifically only in relation to Paula. No one knows whether he meant the sin of sexual fantasies, or whether he and Paula, despite their lack of personal hygiene, were propelled, to their chagrin, into consummating their relationship. If so, it would not likely have been a pretty sight. Jerome was, in more current lingo, a piece of work, and his dark, sex-phobic shadow casts itself across the church right into the present generation.

The second of the fourth century triumvirate was Ambrose, bishop of Milan. He was originally a Neoplatonist philosopher of some stature. He was thrust by popular will into ecclesiastical leadership in a manner that tells much about those times. He was baptized, ordained a priest, and elevated to the episcopate over a three-day period, an instant bishop, as we might say today.

Ambrose was a world removed from Christians who only a few decades earlier lived in danger of being made public examples as enemies of the state. Ambrose's career path was an apt illustration of the monumental impact on the church that came as a result of its merger with the empire. An unknown number of pagan priests immediately transferred their credentials and loyalty from the former imperial gods to the Christian gods. The state religion changed in form, if not in substance, with the human personnel often the same. This sea change was cynically commented on by the pagan priest, Praetextatus, who is said to have offered to convert to Christianity if he could be made a bishop.

Augustine, like Jerome and unlike Ambrose, made a stand against the newfound riches and respectability of the church and the attendant corruption stemming from its new and cozy relationship with the state. Augustine in dissent was to take himself to North Africa, to Hippo near Carthage, a sort of self-imposed exile. But he was fleeing more than simple corruption and insidious imperial respectability. He was also going home to Africa.

Augustine's mother, Monica, was a hovering and domineering personality. It is significant that history preserves her name but not the name of Augustine's presumably Christian common law wife. Augustine's relationship with his mother has the key features of what psychoanalytic theory calls an oedipal victory, Oedipus having killed his father and married his mother.

Monica earlier had followed her son to Italy and became a protégée of Ambrose. Her design for her son was an inflated one and included plans for him to be married to a young woman of high social standing. She asked him to abandon his mistress of 14 years, whom he deeply loved and with whom he had a child, Adeodatus, meaning "gift of God." Augustine followed a course of submission to his mother's will. He sounds like a victim not in control of his own life: "She with whom I had lived so long was torn from my side as a hindrance to my forthcoming marriage. My heart which had held her ever dear was broken and wounded and bleeding."[6]

The callousness of this social strategy does not seem to have been a concern to anyone involved, except perhaps the mistress, whose voice is nowhere to be heard. Augustine did abandon his mistress, in accordance with his mother's wishes, but he soon backed out of the engagement that she had devised. He abandoned the society religion of Rome and retreated to North Africa, there to promote celibacy as the bishop of Hippo. Augustine's more important psychological victory was likely his ultimate rejection of his mother's manipulative social climbing plans for him. What he learned in his struggle with his mother was a major resource for his profound theological and psychological insights.[7]

Augustine's ultimate greatness stemmed from two principal insights: his vision of a universal caring community, the "City of God," and his capacity to see into the dark recesses of the human heart, as expressed in his celebrated book, *Confessions*. Unlike Jerome and Ambrose, and most everyone else for that matter, Augustine's mind and soul greatly enriched subsequent religion and culture in the West. His ruminations have haunted reflective people ever since.

Augustine did not get everything right, to be sure. In some ways he was a pedestrian and narcissistic man of his time, but he did see through the thin veneer of this new shallow Christian culture and its cozy relationship with the state. He recognized the material luxury and shallow optimism of the new church for what it was, a form of pretentiousness and corruption. He eventually saw the flaw in his mother's social pretensions, as well as the pretensions of the new generation of Christian leaders and their incestuous relationship with the state.

In his *City of God*, Augustine envisioned the church as a new universal human community, a partnership of warm and lasting friendships based on service to others. Augustine harbored tyrannical and sadistic impulses toward those who opposed him and those who refused him; but perhaps he can be forgiven for striving, at least, to compensate for his own dark impulses. Augustine's vision of a new city of God was not a replica of pretentious Rome or Athens. He rejected the Rome where bishops walk the red carpets with emperors and kings and believed themselves worthy. Except for those written off as heretics, Augustine was the only significant and effective voice to challenge the grandiosity of this new, proud, confident, and politically empowered church. But Augustine's imagined godly city was in one respect a replica of Athens and Rome. Both Theseus and Aeneus, like Augustine, abandoned their lovers to create a city.[8] David and Solomon abandoned no lovers to create Jerusalem; rather they added a few.

Having witnessed the cooptation of the church by pretentious imperial power and glitter, and the complicity of the religious leadership in that usurpation, Augustine strove to explain the human propensity for corruption. Thus he invented his famous doctrine of original sin. He speculated that there must be some inherited flaw in the human heart that derailed the best of intentions and the noblest of wills. He thought this explained his impulsive and compulsive life before his middle-years conversion to the Catholic party (he was already a Christian), during which early life he lived in extreme sexual licentiousness and experimentation until he fell in love with his mistress, the mother of Adeodatus. It is noteworthy that when he converted to the Catholic party, he became as obsessive and compulsive about his celibacy as he had been about his former sexual freedom. With his notion of original sin, Augustine attempted to warn of the perpetual warfare in the human heart and its propensity for self-deception. "Build up yourself and you build a ruin," he proclaimed.[9]

Augustine became the precursor of all those who observed the crack in the foundation of the self-aggrandizing world views that infected the fourth century church. He became the precursor of Luther's challenge to the self-confident and politically empowered medieval church. He foreshadowed Kierkegaard's *Attack on Christendom*. He was the precursor of Marx, who exposed the dark underside of the nineteenth-century economic prosperity. He was a precursor of Nietzsche's expose' of the thin veneer of late nineteenth-century religion and ethics. Freud's invention of the unconscious and the disjunctive nature of human personality are direct inheritances of Augustine's notion of the irreparably divided will from which humans universally suffer.

There was a troublesome aspect to Augustine's genius. He sought too vigorously to discover the principal source of original sin. Even worse, he thought finally that he had found it. It was sex! This discovery was in part shaped by Augustine's admiration of Greek and Roman philosophy and mythology, to the neglect of the Semitic Bible. Thus his *City of God* was in this respect an imperial city, sexually abstemious, more than a Semitic or biblical one, celebrating sex as a gift of God.

This notion was also shaped, undoubtedly, by Augustine's personal journey, his abandonment of his common law wife, and his rejection of the society marriage that was to be arranged for him. His choice of celibacy instead, and his return home to the North African provinces, reflected his negative view of sexual pleasure.

Even more decisive in shaping Augustine's negative view of sexual pleasure was his discomfort with the weakness of the will in the face of erotic impulses. Following the Platonists and their emphasis upon the power of the mind and will, he was troubled by the inability of the will to command sexual response. He was dismayed that the penis does not respond to command. He proposed the view that in the Garden of Eden, before the fall, sexual intercourse was engaged in by way of a deliberate decision and act of the will rather than a deed driven by forces that the will seemed powerless to control. Augustine concluded that the involuntary character of the libido demonstrated it to be a tool of the devil. He concluded that we are all driven by an evil force greater than the power of the human will. He thought he had found in sex the key to mankind's propensity to sin. "*Ecce unde,*" he wrote, in Latin. "That's the place."[10] Sex was to be understood as the original human flaw, the true source of human sin, from this time forward. Tangentially and regrettably Augustine threw the weight of his genius against sexual pleasure, tarnishing it forever in the West. That was the price the West paid and continues to pay for his genius.

In his assault on sexual pleasure, Augustine could become petty and hysterical. In reply to the "humanist" Christian heretic, Julian of Eclanum, Augustine wrote:

> You would not have married couples restrain that evil …? You would have them jump into bed whenever they like, whenever they feel tickled by desire. Far be it from them to postpone this itch till bedtime; let's have your "legitimate union of bodies" whenever your "natural good" is excited. If this is the sort of married life you led, don't drag up your experience in debate.[11]

The great Christian humanists of the fourth century were routed by Jerome, Ambrose, and Augustine in concert with the powers of the state.

They drove the last nail into the coffin of the heretics who had attempted to preserve the Jewish character of the Jesus movement, the notion that Jesus was a human being, and a positive valuation of sexual pleasure that was promoted in the biblical texts. The destruction of the Christian humanists and the spoiliation of sexual pleasure tragically undercut the power of Augustine's profound and idiosyncratic vision.

Augustine, in conjunction with Jerome and the victorious Catholic party, laid the philosophical foundation for subsequent Christendom. The vision was one of a compassionate and just society where no one was discarded or abused, but it was also to be a society bereft of natural and normal sexuality and in time the latter trumped the former. Because of Augustine, as Peter Brown so eloquently and sorrowfully put it, "the loving cleaving of Israel to God would never be reenacted in the marriage beds of Western Christendom, only the sad shadow of Adam's estrangement from the will of God."[12]

CHAPTER 8

The Victory of Monasticism
in the West

Rome was sacked by Aleric and his Goths in the year 410. This event is remembered as the collapse of the empire, but in fact it affected only Rome, and part of the western half of the empire. Moreover, it was hardly a collapse. The Goths and the Huns after them were converted to Christianity and continued the institutions of the Roman Empire in the West until the Muslim conquest in the seventh century, indeed, for a century thereafter. The imperial capital remained Constantinople, where Constantine himself had moved it, and that empire survived for another thousand years, until it was overrun by the Saracens, in 1453. In terms of political power alignments, the fall of Rome was more symbolic than substantial: Rome, by that time, was not the capital of anything; and the sacking of Rome was not really such a bad day for the church. Aleric himself was a Christian; he ordered that rules of asylum be observed and that no churches be touched by his rampaging, pillaging troops.

The fall of Rome was simply the separation of north-central Italy, and much of western Europe, from the Byzantine Empire, still calling itself the Roman Empire. Europe would remain, from this time onward, politically fragmented, governed by countless smaller states, the borders of which were sometimes unstable. Some parts of Italy, Spain, North Africa, and the Balkans stayed under the control of the emperor in Constantinople for centuries to come.

The popes seated in Rome, one after the other, were in subsequent centuries simply bishops of Rome, each harboring dreams of becoming bishop of everybody but lacking the power to bring their dreams to fruition. When the Goths drove the imperial forces of Constantinople out of Rome, the way was left open for the popes to create for themselves a secular papal state, a constricted vestige of which the popes still possess today. But the pope also gathered to himself political power extending beyond his own territory and throughout the West. Typically, successive popes sought to act as kingmakers among European states, large and small. And eventually, by Christmas Day 800, when Pope Leo III placed a crown on the head of Charlemagne, instituting the new "Holy Roman Empire,"—famously said to be neither holy nor Roman nor an empire—an alternate Roman Empire was created. The rulers in Constantinople, who still considered themselves Romans and who still ruled the Roman Empire, were perplexed and chagrined, in spite of the fact that they had changed the *lingua franca* from Latin to Greek (in 641) and had long since changed *Imperator* to *Basileus*, the Greek word for king.

By his crowning of Charlemagne, Pope Leo fired a shot across the bow of Constantinople. Now, for the first time in history, there were two coexisting Roman Empires; but as history has made clear, Charlemagne's empire was a minor, backwoods kingdom compared to the rival, ruled from Constantinople. Never again would Europe be as politically united as it had been under the old empire. Although the day would come when the East was surpassed by European prosperity and power, and the pope would ride the crest of that wave, eclipsing the power of the Eastern Church, such a development was still six centuries in the future.

The monastic movement emerged late in the third century, with Anthony of Egypt as its central figure. In those days, many Christians were retreating to remote places to lead lives of communal piety, uncontaminated by the dominant society beyond. As such, early monasticism was both a protest against the world at large and a refuge for the most pious, and probably a protected society for homosexual persons who experienced a spiritual vocation. In the middle of the fourth century, this vision of a communal, separatist life was touted in Rome by both Athanasius and Jerome, key leaders of the victorious Catholic party.

As the centuries passed, the monastic movement gathered more and more power and influence, especially in the West among the various secular states, but also in the East. Politically, the monastic orders created an international network that in the East was less necessary, because social cohesion was provided by the imperial bureaucracy. As the centuries passed, the pope increasingly used the monastic system to enforce his will and to tighten his grip on both the church and on various European states.

When Constantinople fell, in 1453, the eastern churches evolved quite naturally into various autonomous national churches and in most places were treated with toleration and respect by the new Muslim rulers. The patriarch was accustomed to being mostly a symbolic leader, and he was able to maintain such a status even after the Turks took control in Constantinople of the last remains of the Roman Empire, or what we now, in retrospect, call the Byzantine Empire.

By this time, in the West the pope was a virtual autocrat, presiding over the entire western church. Except for Protestant defections, he remains so today. The pope was thus able to force on the western church an austere discipline regarding sexual behavior that made the East seem comparatively permissive. Unlike the East, the entire membership of the clergy was monasticized in the West, in the sense that all were required to take the vow of celibacy and chastity, a process not completed until the eleventh century.

Benedict of Nursia, who died in 547, first gained fame as a hermit, then founded a number of monasteries at Monte Cassino and its environs. He was the man who provided the written bylaws for monks, setting the behavioral standards for monastic living. The *Rules of Benedict* gave him a place in history.[1]

These rules made it clear that sexual behavior, and more specifically homosexual behavior, was a large problem in monastic life. Benedict addressed the problem head-on. A separate bed was mandated for each monk. Further, all monks were required to sleep together in one room, fully clothed and girdled, without weapons; and a light must be kept burning all night. The beds of the older members must be interspersed with those of the younger. For those monks who did experience homosexual urges, such rules must have felt something like Chinese water torture.

Gregory the Great, one of Benedict's protégés, became Pope in 590 and reigned until 604. If Augustine was negative regarding sexual pleasure, Gregory carried the negativity significantly further. Unlike Augustine, he denigrated even marital sex, even marital sex performed with the intention to procreate if any pleasure was experienced. When a couple, as he put it, "transfers the occasion of procreation into the services of pleasure ... though they do not then pass beyond the bounds of wedlock, yet in wedlock they exceed its rights."[2]

For Gregory, any sort of sexual pleasure was culpable, and the penalty for sex outside wedlock was eternal damnation. By anyone's measure, he drove a hard bargain. Gregory also promoted clerical celibacy, making *de facto* monks of all the clergy, but he lacked the power to impose such a rule on the whole church. His namesakes four hundred years later, the so-called Gregorian popes, implemented his vision.

The influential Venerable Bede in England, a century later, in the midst of the so-called Dark Ages, echoed Gregory. Even lawful intercourse, he argued, is not blameless when accompanied by pleasure.[3] He set his own rules regarding sexual activity and the church. He said that no one should ever enter a church after sex without washing and only then after a decent interval of time.[4] The washing part seemed not a bad idea even for non-Christians, but Bede was not thinking of hygiene. He had in mind the sinful taint of sexual pleasure. He had come a long way from the Jewish belief that sex on the Sabbath was a special mitzvah.

In the several centuries following Gregory, documents called "Penitentials" became popular in European churches. These devotional guides for pious behavior evolved into an art form, as they were filled with detailed descriptions of various sorts of prohibited sexual behavior. As might be expected, they inveighed against any sexual activity performed for purposes other than reproduction. Not stopping there, they described various prohibited sexual positions, such as retroposition, meaning the male behind the woman, and dorsal position, meaning the woman on top. The popularity of the Penitentials was undoubtedly due, at least in part, to their explicit sexual imagery.[5] No normal person can consider such fine details of prohibited sex without experiencing some degree of arousal. One can only imagine cloistered monks obsessing over the fine details of prohibited sexual activities and the consequences for their own libidinal impulses. Thus the Penitentials may be considered a sort of Dark Ages equivalent to *Penthouse* or *Playboy*. This is all the more interesting when we remember that the readers of this erotic literature were almost exclusively monks or parish clergy as, in those days, nearly everyone else was illiterate.

In spite of this ecclesiastical juggernaut directed against sexual pleasure, some and perhaps most of the clergy continued to marry. There seems to be no data on the question of how many did or did not marry. Records show that some bishops, and even one pope, took wives in these centuries of the Dark Ages; but given the widespread obsession over sex among so many church leaders, it was only a matter of time before clergymen found it impossible to take wives legally.

The western church, in the mid-eleventh century, underwent a transformation known as the Gregorian Reform. This was both a realignment of power and the creation of new sex regulations. For the first time in history, the pope seized total administrative control over the whole church in the West, ending local autonomy and making every cleric accountable directly to him, in theory and often in practice. This power grab was made in tandem with the abolition of clerical marriage, which had previously coexisted with monasticism. The married clergy typically had money, property, and the independence that goes with them. Often their priestly offices were handed down from one generation to another, much like family heirlooms.

Some have contended that the abolition of clerical marriage was motivated by a papal desire for additional wealth, but this is too simple an explanation. More likely, powerlust, or the lust for control, was the dominant motive, especially because the money involved was probably not that significant. With the seizure of absolute power, one does not need money. When power becomes absolute, money follows.

The popes essentially monasticized all clergy in the West. The parish rectory became a little monastery where clergy were expected to monitor each other's behavior. This change made the entire clerical order dependent on the pope, both materially and spiritually. The former insured the latter. In the abolition of clerical marriage, the popes now had absolute power over all the personnel in the church and had universal celibacy as well. This new and stringent sexual code in the West also established another significant point of contention between Rome and Constantinople.

The abolition of clerical marriage did not come without a price.[6] There were riots and public disorder in various places in Europe. There were killings; there were suicides; wives and children of priests were given no grace period for a continuation of family life. A number of bishops revolted. A rival pope, Honarius II, was installed in rebellion against Rome; but Rome had its way. It was an authoritarian religious coup, a radical centralization of power in Rome, and a total elimination of sexual gratification, at least in theory, for all the clergy, which is to say, the entire literate class in the West.

The eleventh-century monastization of the clergy remains in effect even today. Virtually no working priests are permitted to live in private apartments. With rare exceptions, they are required to live in closed communities where they can be under surveillance. Even today, the pope can reach down to any cleric in the church and summon him for an accounting. This makes for an extensive, single-gender, autocratic, international system that has no parallel in history. All ordinations were, from the Gregorian Reform onward, monitored and approved by Rome. In this autocracy no sexual pleasure was permitted any priest, whatever his position. Any who venture into an exploration of sexual gratification of any sort risked disciplinary action. Needless to say, plenty of evidence demonstrates that Catholic leadership is willing to look the other way in many instances of misbehavior. But the strictures remain and carry weight, even if enforcement is capricious.

We should not assume that the laws of monasticism were followed to the letter. In any culture, dissenters have a way of materializing from nowhere. The marvelous and explicitly erotic poem, *Carmina Burana*, was, in modern times, discovered safely and blessedly protected in a Benedictine monastery. Scholar John Boswell contends that the century of the Gregorian Reform coincided with what he calls the triumph of Ganymede. Ganymede was a youth in Greek mythology who was taken to heaven to be cupbearer or, implicitly, the homosexual consort for the gods. Those hundred years, says Boswell, marked a great flowering of homosexual literature among the clergy.[7]

The organizational structure of the single-gender monastery and rectory placed *all* the clergy in a double bind. Having created a strictly monosexual community, the church inadvertently fostered homosexuality, while, at the same time, forbade physical gratification. Just as homosexuality has a tendency to blossom in modern American prisons, and aboard naval ships, and at the YMCA, it should come as a surprise to no one that it has similarly flowered in the monastery and rectory. In general, nature has its way. Nothing is more natural than striving for sexual gratification, in whatever form may be available.

Thus by about 1100, the entire leadership in western Christianity was committed, on paper at least, to a life bereft of sexual gratification. The monasteries were the dynamos of medieval culture. They were planted all over Western Europe, and they were the centers of learning for both church and society. They were the repositories of culture and writing. The word *clerk*, someone who can read and write, derives from the word *cleric*.

The Arab world during the Dark Age and early Middle Ages was further advanced academically than the West. The works of Plato and Aristotle and other Greek literature were studied, copied, and preserved by Muslim scholars, producing manuscripts that would later be inherited by western scholars. These Muslim scholars were also sexually liberated compared to their European counterparts. The tide would turn, and the West would eventually surpass the East culturally as well as economically, but the reversal would take another four hundred years.[8]

From Jerome, in the fourth century, through the Gregorian Reform in the eleventh, Christianity in the West metamorphosed into the world's most sex-negative religion. The rejection of sexual gratification became the central ethical principle of Christianity in the West. The eastern church, centered in Constantinople, was hardly a promoter of the goodness of sexual pleasure, but at least its parish clergy married. Moreover, compared to the West, the Orthodox East was sexually liberated. Later Protestantism challenged Rome's disdain for sexual pleasure, but its challenge was not eminently successful in the long term. The central moral and religious claim that was firmly established in the eleventh century in the Christian West, the claim that the best people have the least amount of sexual pleasure, was fixed and remained dominant even into modern times, in both Catholic and Protestant cultures.

CHAPTER 9

BERNARD, ABELARD, AND HELOISE

Bernard of Clairvaux, who died in 1153, and Peter Abelard, who died in 1144, were the principal protagonists—and antagonists—of the Middle Ages. They were adversaries while they lived; in death their conflict continued. The former was a confidant of bishops and popes and a strong proponent of medieval values; the latter was a challenger, skeptic, and harbinger of the future. Bernard was victorious and Abelard was crushed, at least in the short term; Bernard was made a saint and Abelard condemned in his own lifetime as a heretic. In a real sense, their issues continue even more heatedly today; the end of their struggle has not been told.

Bernard was a mystic—pious and ascetic—who represented, at least publicly, all the established values of the western church subsequent to the Gregorian Reform. He was an organization man who preached absolute obedience to the hierarchy of the church. Performing well for the Roman bureaucracy, he was the most influential cleric of his generation. At the urging of Rome, in 1147, he energetically whipped up enthusiasm for the Second Crusade, that most destructive of social movements, which wreaked a trail of mayhem on the Mediterranean world, especially the Balkans, Greece, Turkey, and Palestine.

John Julius Norwich, in his wonderful trilogy on Byzantium, describes Bernard in inimitable fashion: "Tall and haggard, his features clouded by the constant pain that resulted from a lifetime of exaggerated physical austerities, he was consumed by a blazing religious zeal that left no room for tolerance or moderation."[1] Bernard was a genuine ascetic who saw the world through the eyes of a fanatic; in public he was a mesmerizing speaker.

When Bernard was working up a general frenzy for the Second Crusade, he had to know that half a century earlier, on July 15, 1099, the forces of the First

Crusade had taken Jerusalem, and on entering that city had slaughtered all the city's Muslims and had burned all its Jews to death in their central synagogue. This was a city where Muslims, Jews, and Christians had lived together in relative harmony for almost five centuries. The Crusades unleashed a kind of violence and social disruption comparable to the Nazi movement in the twentieth century.

It cannot be determined whether the crusaders were simply the dregs of European society, or whether Europeans generally were simply less civilized than their neighbors. Perhaps it was some of each. But it was never good news for a city or village, regardless of its religious affiliation, to hear that crusaders were headed their way. The crusaders had their eyes on Palestine, the holy land, with the goal of expelling Muslims and Jews, but they had a long way to go before they reached Palestine, and they were hungry and aggressive. Virtually all the crusaders followed the land route from Europe through Constantinople to the Middle East. The first crusaders dealt gingerly with Constantinople as they passed through, and in exchange for food, they treated the city with respect. But later crusaders sacked Constantinople, in 1205, they occupied the city for 60 years—which resulted, according to Norris, in a more devastating loss to culture than either the sacking of Rome or the infamous burning of the library in Alexandria.

Christians of the eastern church preferred occupation by Muslims to that of their fellow Christian crusaders from the West. "Better the Sultan's turban than the Cardinal's hat," they famously said. When the Sultan, Saladin, retook Jerusalem from the crusaders in 1187, he ordered no looting, no murder, and no reprisals, even though he certainly had not forgotten the events of 1099. His magnanimity and restraint contributed to his reputation as the greatest Muslim hero in history. He was the kind of man who inspired some of the more thoughtful crusaders even to adopt his name, which still pops up among a few Europeans and American Christians even today.

Bernard was particularly offended by Abelard and his works. He argued that Abelard explored even the deepest matters without "reverence." He also charged that Abelard "argues with boys and associates with women."[2] Bernard was instrumental in persuading the pope to make Abelard a heretic and to order his books burned.

Abelard was the voice of a more humane spirit in the depths of the Middle Ages. In so many ways, he pointed to a more humanizing future, and he exposed many inherent flaws of the medieval establishment. As a dialectician who tried weighing all sides of an argument, he is remembered as the theologian of "yes and no." Wisdom, he argued, is to see the contradictions that can be elucidated through dialogue. Medieval theologians were famous for their airtight, all-encompassing systems stripped of ambiguity. Their theological constructs proposed answers for everything. They provided a place for everyone: heaven, hell, purgatory, limbo. Abelard was never so certain of well-crafted explanations. For him, questioning, not blind obedience, was the meaning of faithfulness. Abelard was heir to his fellow heretics, the

Christian humanists of Antioch. Like them, he rejected the notion that Jesus was a divine being, an appearance of the divine logos disguised as a human being. Abelard was a precursor to the Protestants, to Martin Luther, to Sören Kierkegaard especially, and in modern times, to Karl Barth and Paul Tillich.

Abelard was the leading advocate of the cathedral school, the forerunner of the modern university. In the twelfth century, cathedral schools were competing with monasteries for the dominant role in higher education. Cathedral schools were upstart urban competitors. They represented free thinking and questioning, and thus became centers of unorthodoxy. The monasteries represented piety, right thinking, obedience, and orthodox belief. Cathedral schools attracted students who wanted to question and think new thoughts. These schools eventually evolved into the modern university, where thinking could take place under a little—and sometimes a lot—less surveillance by ecclesiastical authorities. Posthumously, Abelard won the debate with Bernard on this matter, but the antagonists had been long dead before the western world saw the emergence of the university as the center of creative new thinking, relatively independent of control by church authorities.[3]

Abelard took delight in challenging the teachings of the church on sex. He recognized the silliness of the church's injunction to perform sex without pleasure. He recognized, as any person with common sense would, that without pleasure sexual intercourse would hardly be possible. In his Ethics he wrote:

> they say that marital intercourse should be performed wholly without pleasure. But assuredly, if this is so, they are allowed to be done in a way in which they cannot be done at all.
>
> If to lie with a wife or even to eat delicious food has been allowed us since the first day of our creation, which was lived in paradise without sin, who will accuse us of sin in this if we do not exceed the limit of the concession?[4]

Abelard defied the religious establishment in his sexual behavior, as well as his thinking and writing about sex. When he was in his mid-30s, he was assigned to tutor the 17-year-old, or perhaps 20-something-year-old, Heloïse, who was the niece of the cathedral dean, a man named Fulbert. (She is thought by historians to have been Fulbert's illegitimate daughter.) In the course of their tutoring sessions, Heloïse and Abelard fell into a sexual liaison, which turned out to be a lifelong love affair. The couple were caught *in flagrante delicto* by Fulbert himself, after which Heloïse, pregnant, was sent to her family in Brittany for her lying-in. There she gave birth to a healthy son they named Astralabe. After the couple secretly married, Heloïse entered a convent. Abelard visited her there, and, on at least one occasion, they had a tryst in the refectory.

As lovers, Heloïse and Abelard did not have good options since, in medieval society, the church offered the only chance of an intellectual life. In marrying, Abelard risked his professional status as a cleric. In addition, as if the couple did not have troubles enough, Fulbert commissioned bullies to attack Abelard in his bed at night and castrate him. (They likely cut off his penis as well.)

The relationship between Abelard and Heloïse continued through the remainder of their lives. Abelard later became abbot of a convent he himself founded, Le Paraclet; Heloïse served as the abbess. They published several books together, including a book of hymns. One fact known about Le Paraclet is that, unlike a typical monastery, there was no attempt to separate the genders for the liturgies. The couple's marriage was either kept secret or the authorities mercifully declined to use it against Abelard. Late in his life, Abelard was declared a heretic by the pope, who ordered his books banned and burned. This decree was lifted just before he died, but Abelard continued to be a problem for pious and orthodox medieval church leaders even from the grave. In fact, his death was unquiet in several ways; his body was interred seven times before reaching its final resting place. Eventually, more than six hundred years after his death, he was buried—with Heloïse—in the Père Lachaise cemetery in Paris, where they have shared a sepulchre since 1817.

Now the story becomes problematic. It seems likely that, as some historians contend, Abelard's later letters were tampered with and reworked. What has been passed down to us may well be doctored versions of his original letters. Heloïse's letters late in life communicated deep love and devotion to Abelard, but some of his late letters, on the contrary, sounded like a traditional medieval Catholic, repenting of the sexual sins of his youth.

Joseph Campbell gives Abelard bad marks on the basis of the letters in their current form. "Adequate was he to the deed when he did it, but the idea of it he could not bear when it was done," said Campbell, borrowing a line from Nietzsche.[5] If the letters are credibly authentic, one would have to conclude that Abelard underwent something of a philosophical and religious change late in life. Certainly, his numerous enemies, entrenched in the church as they were, had ample motivation and access to tamper with his texts posthumously.

The letters of Heloïse, on the other hand, reveal her steadfast love for Abelard, and, perhaps more importantly, show that she continued to celebrate their relationship in no uncertain terms, even though she expressed, at points, some feelings of having been neglected by Abelard. We can presume that her correspondent is in a real conversation with her, and that a drastic reversal by him would have been reflected in her letters. It is not.

We can feel the impact of Heloïse's personality and character in her letters, and we can also feel the profound love she continued to feel for Abelard:

the name of wife may seem more sacred or more binding, but sweeter for me will always be the word mistress, or, if you will permit me, that of concubine or whore.

God is my witness that if Augustus, Emperor of the whole world, thought fit to honor me with marriage, and conferred all the earth on me to possess forever, it would be dearer and more honorable to me to be called not his Empress but your whore.[6]

She wrote that she "preferred love to wedlock and freedom to chains," and made clear that even their secret marriage was entered into by her only because Abelard thought it best. Also, she made it unambiguously clear that she never repented of her relationship with Abelard.

> I expect no reward for this from God, for it is certain that I have done nothing as yet for love of him ... I would have had no hesitation, God knows, in following you or going ahead at your bidding to the flames of Hell.
>
> I should be groaning over the sins I have committed but I can only sigh for what I have lost. Everything we did and also the times and places are stamped on my heart along with your image, so that I live through it all again with you. Even in sleep I know no respite ... now particularly you should fear now when I no longer have in you an outlet for my incontinence.
>
> Wholly guilty though I am, I am also, as you know, wholly innocent. It is not the deed but the intention of the doer which makes the crime, and justice should weigh not what was done but the spirit in which it is done.[7]

Heloïse shows herself to be a dialectician, like Abelard, a theologian of "yes and no."

Late in his life Abelard wrote a poem for their son Astralabe. The poem adds weight, perhaps, to the view that the letters, which portray a pious, repentant Abelard, were likely redactions of the original texts.

> Yet there are those whose past sins still so allure them
>   That they can never feel truly penitent.
> Rather, the sweetness of that bliss remains so great that
>   No sense of atoning for it has force.
>   This is the burden of complaint of our Heloïse, whereby
>   She often says to me, as to herself,
>   "If I cannot be saved without repenting of what I used to
>   commit, there is no hope for me.
> The joys of what we did are still so sweet that, after delight
>   Beyond measure, even remembering brings relief."
>   For one who tells the truth there is no strain in telling—it is feigning
>   that's the effort, before one speaks.[8]

Peter the Venerable, who was the abbot of Cluny and a friend to Abelard, gave him shelter in his last difficult years as a condemned heretic. After Abelard's death, he wrote to Heloïse:

> My illustrious and dearest sister in God: this man to whom you cleaved, after the sexual oneness, with the stronger and finer bond of divine love, he with whom and under whom you have long served God—I tell you, God is now cherishing him in his lap, in place of you, or like a replica of you. And at the second coming, at the sound of the archangel and the trumpet

heralding God descending from the heavens, God will restore him to you through his grace, having preserved him for you.[9]

Whatever pieties Aberlard may or may not have expressed in his late years, or however much he may have neglected Heloïse, or however much he may have reverted to the official Catholic position on sexual pleasure, the bulk of the data shows Heloïse and Abelard significantly involved with each other in a lifelong, loving, and unabashedly sexual relationship.

The love between Abelard and Heloïse captured the imagination of countless people through the centuries. Their tale may well be the preeminent love story of western history.

At any rate, Abelard certainly rattled the Middle Ages and its airtight, authoritarian, sex-phobic Catholic ideology. Church authorities had no wish to see his ideas and behavior known, or his influence felt. No more fully human individual exists in Christian history than Abelard—a brilliant mind, a visionary, and a courageous yea-sayer to life in all its fullness.

The position in which Heloïse and Abelard found themselves was unique and extraordinarily difficult. They must have experienced self-doubt. They had their friends, but stood on ground no one else had trodden, at least in public. In retrospect it is difficult to imagine how they persevered in the religious and cultural context in which they lived. If there are any more compelling figures in Christian history, they did not survive in the written record.

The paucity of data makes any attempt at a full biography of either Abelard or Heloise a problematic undertaking, requiring some degree of speculation. The recent *Heloise and Abelard* by James Burge is a careful, judicious, and loving portrait.[10]

Any church today bearing the name of Bernard of Clairvaux should have sufficient wisdom, and enough sense of shame, to rename itself. A polarizing figure and consummate bureaucrat, Bernard was destructive of the highest human values. His pious deeds caused immeasurable suffering to countless people. The Second Crusade led to the most shameful humiliation of Christians in the entire Middle Ages, according to John Julius Norwich.[11] Bernard impeded the emergence of innovative thinking and ideas of individual freedom. He was leader in the movement that condemned Abelard and all his works. Bernard's words and deeds bear the marks of a pious sadomasochist.

One does not find churches today dedicated to the memory of Peter Abelard. He was a man too human and idiosyncratic to be appreciated by the religious establishment of his time or ours. Also, he was a man of too much personal audacity. The church did not kill him, as it might have, but it mutilated him, silenced him, and burned his books. Nor does one find churches named for Heloïse. Such a church would signal a rebellion against the pervasive fear and loathing of sexual pleasure in the Christian West.

CHAPTER 10

THE CATHARS

One of the most bizarre movements to emerge from the Middle Ages was Catharism. The appearance of the Cathars seems to demonstrate the fact that irrational social organizations tend to breed even further irrationality. And so the antilibidinal Middle Ages spun off a yet more peculiar variant of contempt for sexual pleasure in the form of the Cathars. Their name most likely comes from the Greek word for clean or pure, *katharo*. The Cathars took the dream of purity to its outer reaches, holding the world and everything in it—save the content of their own imaginations—to be unclean, always paying special attention to the presumed uncleanliness of sexuality.[1]

Yet in their peculiar way the Cathars could be said to have rediscovered a repressed libidinal energy of the Middle Ages, because in their structure of redemption an idealized, sexually stimulating woman led the way. They practiced heterosexual pair-bonding infused with ideals of cosmic pairing, but they also preached restraint from genital contact. Sadly, they entirely projected the libido's gratification safely into the next world, where it would be subject neither to physical messiness nor to scrutiny and criticism. Striving for detachment from the world, they practiced a severe asceticism, to the extreme degree of seeking "the death of the Perfect," meanwhile trying to focus their full attention on the "other world." In this respect Catharism was even more perverse than medieval Catholicism. Thus the Cathars referred derogatorily to the Catholic Church as *ecclesia carnalis*, "the church of flesh." They replaced baptism by water with a cerebral rite of their own, and for the bread and wine of the traditional Holy Communion, or Eucharist, they substituted their own Consolamentum, in which their protegés had their souls restored to them. Life was to be lived, according the Cathars, for the next world. They judged that even marriage was more for the world to come than for this one.

A Cathar heterosexual couple was not expected to be involved in such earthly and contaminating undertakings as sexual intercourse. As a result, they typically, if not invariably, had no children. They tended to cluster in particular areas of the world, such as the south of France, or Verona, or Bulgaria, to name a few. The slang word, "bugger," referring to anal intercourse, derives from "Bulgar." It seems that popular opinion, considering that many Bulgarian Cathar couples had no children, concluded that they engaged in buggery.

The Cathars evolved into a kind of church within the church, a quasisecret community. They—and all their variant spin-offs, such as the Albigensians and Bogomils—gained wide popularity and were eventually seen by the church as a deviant threat. Finally, they were hunted down by mainstream Christians and were mercilessly slaughtered wherever they were found. Some historians have referred to this repression as the first genocidal campaign directed from Christian Rome but whether it was actually the first is debatable.

While suppressing Catharism, the medieval church began building defenses against the attractions of Catharism. The church retooled its wedding ceremony, coming up with an etheral Cathar look-alike, as a compensatory palliative for those attracted to Catharism. The wedding was brought from the home into the church building, and marriage was elevated to one of the seven sacraments, curiously the only sacrament without any specific roots in biblical texts. The best explanation that the medieval marriage liturgy could come up with to authenticate itself as a biblically based religious rite was to pronounce in its opening exhortation that Jesus attended a marriage in Cana of Gallilee. The Church authorities might just as well inaugurated a sacrament on the basis of Jesus embarking on a fishing boat. In elevating marriage to a sacrament, the medieval church imputed a special sanctity and otherworldly cast to marriage, actually quite alien to the biblical texts. But Cathar notions of otherworldly love did in fact appeal to a great many people. Thus marriage was given a new sacred aura, through the impact of Catharism, on the wider Christian culture.

The central cultural motif that spun off from the Cathars was the flowering of passionate romantic love, a sort of love so poignant that it cannot be sustained in this world and thus must be reserved to be consummated only in the next. Tristan and Isolde are such types. So are Romeo and Juliet, whose play is set in Verona, a Catharist center. The theme is passionate, heartrending romance, not to be consummated in this messy world but in the world to come. Thus the lovers always die just prior to the opportunity for physical consummation of their love. The Cathars were a peculiar challenge to the medieval antilibidinal juggernaut; it is difficult to measure which side was most out of touch with reality. Of the Cathars, Dennis deRougement says, in his own inimitable way: "The melodies in their distressing morbidity disclose a world in which carnal desire has become no more than an ultimate and impure apathy of souls in the process of curing themselves of life."[2]

But the Cathar movement did demonstrate, in a most idiosyncratic way, that the libido will not remain long in lockdown, regardless of who has the keys, and sometimes reemerges in the most bizarre forms.

Vestiges of Catharism linger in western culture today in odd manifestations, modern romantic love being the principal remnant. And at the very heart of this contemporary drama stands the bride. In other cultures a wedding typically has sexual overtones, as well as symbols of property distribution, two important physical components of any marriage. Nothing about a western Christian bride suggests anything of the marriage bed, sexual relations, or property distribution. Neither the groom nor anyone else can get near a bride, what with all her drapery, which is white, suggesting sexual purity, and also, by insinuation, readiness for the next world. In the church, white is the color of resurrection—and is also, in many churches, associated with death and mourning. Thus the modern bride, as did the medieval Cathars, prepares by innuendo for death, not for the messy pleasure of sexual intercourse or for the hard work of gender coupling in the real world, where sex leads to children.

None of the other rites of the church has been an object of such inflation as marriage: an inflation inherited from the Cathars. Hardly ever, in modern times, is any church as filled to capacity as for its weddings, and never does a typical contemporary family spend as much for any religious rite as it does on a young woman's wedding. The modern inflation of the wedding ceremony, far above all proportionality, is a posthumous partial victory for Catharism.

Adolph Hitler and his Nazis were also a twentieth-century incarnation of Catharist themes, albeit peculiar ones. In the church of the Cathars, "guides" were commissioned, rather than priests or deacons. (*Fuhrer* is German for "guide.") Hitler was, in authentic Cathar fashion, obsessed with cleanliness and purity. He allowed no one to smoke in his presence. He was a vegetarian. He reacted negatively and repressively to any evidence of sexual activity that came into his view, whether heterosexual or homosexual, the latter potentially incurring a summary execution. He treated Eva Braun, his consort, as an ethereal presence, kept pampered, unaware of calamitous events happening around her, a dweller already in the next world. If their relationship led to physical intimacy of any sort, they left no evidence of it, save their mutual suicide. In public view, Hitler was never paired with Braun. He also sought to clean up Europe of those social elements he and his followers considered socially unclean: Jews, gypsies, and the retarded or afflicted of any sort. In true Cathar fashion, Hitler married Braun just before they committed suicide, a bride and groom not for this corrupt world, but for the pure world to come.

The medieval church retained much of the religious content of Catharism, even as it crushed the movement politically. The church remained, in the spirit of Catharism, as oriented toward the other world as ever—in its catechism and ideology, if not in actual practice. The church elevated Mary as the perpetual virgin and queen of heaven, echoing the Cathars' theme of the heavenly woman onto whom they could project their suppressed libidos. The medieval church set up marriage more as an ethereal union of spirits than of physical bodies, and—in practice if not in theory—made marriage the highest of its seven sacraments. The Cathar movement may have been crushed politically, but it bequeathed to medieval European Christians a stronger, stranger dose of negativity—toward sexual pleasure and the physical body—than had been promoted prior to its emergence.

The medieval church, having cast its lot largely with the ethereal spirit of Catharism, prepared European soil for what was coming, namely for the earthy, sex-affirming Protestant reformers, who would define themselves sexually in radically different terms when the Reformation finally began in the sixteenth century.

CHAPTER 11

THE TWO FACES OF THOMAS MORE

The name Thomas More has evolved in modern times into a cultural icon symbolizing personal integrity as well as courageous defiance of authoritarian political power. In large part, Thomas More was catapulted into this morally elevated position by Robert Bolt's acclaimed 1960 play, *A Man for All Seasons*. In this play, More is portrayed as an inspiring figure, a resolute man of integrity and compassion. But any resemblance between Bolt's fictional account and the actual man is minimal. As Jasper Ridley put it, "There's only one thing wrong with the play; the upright hero shouldn't be named More."[1] Bolt's Thomas More is not the Thomas More of history.

Thomas More was indeed beheaded during the reign of England's King Henry VIII, and with the king's approval, but in light of the political mores of early sixteenth-century Europe, he received what he was due. Anyone who openly challenged a ruling monarch—as More directly challenged Henry—had reason to expect such a harsh fate. During those cruel times, no individual, even a socially prominent one, could expect to be granted the privilege of publicly dissenting from an important ruling of the crown. It didn't matter who sat on the throne. Respect for dissent in Europe did not attain any currency until the late eighteenth century.

Thomas More's modern reputation is that of a progressive figure of his time, born several centuries too soon. But in fact he was no such man. He was far more of a medieval man than a man of modern sensibilities. Whatever he was personally, when he was in a position of political power, he was as quick as Henry to crush anyone who publicly held opinions contrary to the views held by the authorities. He presided over the executions of quite a number of Protestants. Worse, he surveilled and entrapped them, even when they sought to stay out of public view. He imprisoned some in his own mansion but denied beating or torturing them, except for one alleged to have instructed children in heresy.[2]

In fact, King Henry was rather merciful to More, whom the court had ordered to be dragged through the streets on a hurdle, then hanged, drawn, and quartered—a procedure whereby the prisoner had his genitals severed and stuffed in his mouth, then was disemboweled while, it was hoped, remaining conscious. Henry's reduced sentence called simply for a less painful, more dignified, beheading.

Thomas More was the last great exemplar of the medieval imagination. He devoutly and rigorously subscribed to values and principles of medieval Christendom, and at a time when those certainties were losing credibility. The Renaissance and Reformation were in full blossom, and More did not appreciate what was coming into being. He fully subscribed to the old order, in which obedience to the pope was a basic, inviolable assumption—an order within which the pope even had the authority to depose kings. Thomas More saw Protestantism, which arose contemporaneously with his own life, as a threat to all he held dear. Further, he believed it left anarchy in its wake.

Darker still was More's florid sadomasochism, the evidence of which is amply available. Starting around age 18, he wore a hair shirt—and continued to wear it until a few days before his execution. Its chafing is said to have often broken his skin and must have been a source of constant pain. But he felt he deserved such pain because of the severity of his sins. Throughout his life, he also kept a lash handy, with which he regularly, alone in his room, beat himself. This was all part of a particularly medieval form of piety to which More subscribed. Perhaps less sadistic was a practice he imposed on his extended family. On holy days, everyone was rousted from bed in the small hours of the morning for liturgical services in the family chapel.[3]

It is impossible to verify, conclusively, which sins More was expatiating with his whip, his hair shirt, and his middle-of-the-night liturgies. Still, judging from his written works, there can be little doubt that sexual sins lay in the forefront of his conscience. Presumably they were sexual sins of the imagination. More's writings are peppered with erotic and scatological references. "Someone should shit in Luther's mouth," he is recorded as saying.[4] He invested considerable personal energy in an attempt to diminish his sexual urges. Though highly attracted to monastic life from an early stage, he declined the path to holy orders because he felt he would not be able to control his sexual drive. It is not clear whether he was most concerned with homosexual urges, heterosexual urges, or both combined. At any rate, he decided to marry and to pursue the law. He rose steadily in the ranks of political power until he assumed the penultimate position of Lord Chancellor, the chief lawyer in the land, and principal advisor to King Henry VIII.

Thomas More's approach to marriage was revealing. As a most medieval Christian, he viewed marriage as a cure for concupiscence, a safety net against sin. At 26 he married 16-year-old Jane Colt, although he was actually more attracted to her younger sister. Choosing a wife, Moore said, was "like putting your hand into a blind bag of snakes and eels."[5] He selected the less desirable sister, he said, out of "pity" and "a sense of propriety." This would not be the last time he made a self-defeating decision on matters of sexuality. When Jane died six years later, after delivering their fifth child, he married Alice Middleton, a wealthy widow of 42, a decade older than he was. The general testimony on Middleton seems to support More's friend Ammonius, who described her as "a hook-nosed harpy."[6] Even More himself confessed that he had told Alice that "if God gives her not hell, he will have done her great wrong."[7] More's friend Erasmus, an occasional house guest, thought Alice difficult. Both of More's wives seem to have been selected so as not to stoke the fires of his libido.

It is perplexing that a man with such a brilliant mind, able to rise to the pinnacle of political power, could at the same time be so self-defeating in the arena of his affective and sexual life. Thomas More left the impression that inner conflicts around issues of sex were more than he could manage. So it is hardly surprising that he chose to throw his weight on the side of sex-repressing medieval religion, especially during the heated emergence of the sexually liberating Reformation. For a man desperately struggling to control his libido, whatever form it took, his passionate commitment to medieval values was perhaps essential to the task of keeping his ego intact.

Thomas More became a committed warrior for medievalism. He had the fortune, or misfortune, to live on the cusp of a changing world in which the old medieval order was disintegrating. He worked feverishly to suppress the infiltration of Protestant liberationist ideas into England. As far as he was able, he blocked the spread of the new English translations of the Bible. As Chancellor, he had the political standing to search out Protestants of various stripes and personally saw to it that many were burned at the stake, including the great Bible translator William Tyndale. At burnings he sometimes mimicked their dying cries. In all this defensive work against "the new learning," as it was called, More initially followed not just his own wishes, but those of the king as well. But this was soon to change.

At the beginning of the Protestant uprising, King Henry was solidly on the side of Rome. He actually wrote an essay in defense of Rome, attacking Martin Luther and his theological position. Henry was unusually literate for a king. This essay earned him and his successors the honorific, "Defender of the Faith," awarded by the pope and still displayed today by the British crown. But that happy alliance was soon to go on the rocks. Henry was something of a Renaissance man, both as a writer and a composer of music. In the context of his time, he was no barbarian. He read and digested what the Protestants had to say; eventually they turned his head.

The famous Richard Hunne case got Henry's attention, and contributed, early in his reign, to softening Henry's allegiance to Rome. Hunne had got himself embroiled in an altercation with the church that cost him his life. In that era, church authority was not restricted to private religious issues as it is today. Church courts of that day had the power to indict, arrest, and punish persons who violated church law. When Richard Hunne's infant daughter died, he was expected to follow custom and donate the baby's baptismal gown to the church. When he refused, Hunne was arrested by church authorities; he died in church custody under suspicious circumstances. The speculation is that Hunne was a covert Protestant. Henry intervened and prohibited church authorities from exercising their usual prerogative of bypassing civil courts referring the scandalous case to Rome. Thomas More countered with the argument that the jurisdiction of Rome ought to be maintained. This difference between the king and More was a signal of more substantive differences to come.

The issue on which Henry's relationship with Rome was finally shipwrecked was that same issue of papal authority over English matters. It took the specific form of Henry's desire to divorce his wife, the very Catholic Catherine of Aragon. Twentieth-century popular historians tend to portray Henry VIII as a randy king who sought a divorce, only to be blocked by a pope who took the high moral ground in support of the sanctity of marriage. The facts are not so neat. Popes regularly granted divorces to the powerful, especially monarchs, disingenuously labeling the divorces "annulments." In an ordinary time, Henry would have received his annulment post haste. But the current pope was, at that moment, a captive of the army of Charles V, who was the Holy Roman Emperor and a nephew of Catharine. Also, Henry's new marrying eye was fixed on a cryptoProtestant, Anne Boleyn. Meanwhile, Protestants all over Europe were putting forward the proposition that the authority of the pope was an artifact of history with no further viability. This influence brought on Henry's decision to sever his nation's relationship with Rome. Thus England officially became a Protestant country, and Henry was freed to receive his divorce from the English Archbishop of Canterbury.

Henry went on to accumulate a total of six wives in succession, thus sealing his modern reputation as the testosterone king who hopped from marriage to marriage to satisfy his unquenchable libido. This, too, is a caricature. The facts of the case are that Henry's libido was not the salient factor driving him from wife to wife. As king, he could have pretty much any woman he desired, married or single; actually he was unrestrained in this regard. (He had already sired one bastard son.) But he sought a male heir to the throne, and this required that a son be born in wedlock. His wish was not so much a matter of personal pride as one of social stability. In those days, hardly anything was more fraught with danger to the social fabric than the death of a ruler who had no heir in place. Henry's string of wives was consistently unproductive of male issue. From his total of six wives, he garnered a single male, the sickly Edward, from Jane Seymour. Edward died at age 15 after a brief reign.

In those times it was not usual—though not unprecedented—for a girl or woman to be elevated to the throne. No one would have foreseen that both Mary, born of Catherine, and Elizabeth, born of Anne Boleyn, would one day reign successively as monarchs. That the latter became arguably the preeminent monarch in all English history is not a little ironic. The political success of his daughters, and especially of Elizabeth, would have greatly surprised not only Henry, but all his advisors.

Another misleading rap against Henry, and against English Protestants as well, is that he founded the Anglican Church. All over Europe, kings and princes were acting similarly, separating the church in their jurisdictions from the oversight of Rome. The notion of the separation of church and state was an idea that gained force later in history, not in the sixteenth century. When Luther defied Rome, he survived the church's order for his execution only because he was protected by the German princes, who did not think of themselves as creating a new church so much as severing Roman authority and offering protection for "the new learning" now known as Protestantism. So, too, did Henry in England put up barriers against Roman ecclesiastical authority and make it possible for Protestants to flourish. The subsequent English church was led by clerics under, to be sure, the watchful eye of the king, as was typical in that era. As could be expected, Henry appointed to leadership positions those clerics whom he favored. His appointment of Thomas Cranmer to the senior religious post of Archbishop of Canterbury, his first and only appointment to that post, was a felicitous choice, of immense historical significance. Cranmer authored the English *Book of Common Prayer*, a monument that made its beneficent influence felt on the language and thinking of the English-speaking world for more than four centuries. Cranmer was one of those giants in history, a man of constraint and conciliation in a violent time. He left the mark of his wide embrace on the religion of the English-speaking world. He was later burned at the stake in the reign of the very Catholic Mary I, or so-called Bloody Mary.

The concupiscence that Thomas More strove to bring under control, and which kept him from the "religious life," meaning monastic celibacy, may well have been specifically homosexual desire. In his life, he was consistently much closer to men than he was to any woman. The monastic life, to which he was strongly drawn but which he declined to embrace, would have presented more homosexual than heterosexual temptation, which may have been the basis for his refusal of the life that so attracted him. Thomas More was very close to Erasmus personally, though not philosophically or theologically, referring to him as his "darling," and in turn was addressed as "sweetest Thomas."[8] Thomas More was especially incensed when he learned that

Luther had married a nun, an act which More, in typical medieval fashion, labeled "incest."

When Henry VIII shifted his stance toward favoring the Protestant camp, creating by fiat an autonomous national church, Thomas More was destined to fall. But he was not destined to die. He brought that on himself by publicly scorning Henry's marriage to Anne Boleyn. The symbolic episode that brought about his demise was More's decision to absent himself from the coronation of Queen Anne. He did not accept her even as a lawful wife to Henry, much less as his queen. So More's fate was sealed. After resigning his position as Lord Chancellor, he was soon called to trial.

In martyrdom, More got what he seemed to have longed for throughout his adult life. To his executioner on the scaffold, he said, "Thou wilt give me today a greater benefit than ever any man can be able to give me."[9] Martyrdom was the ultimate extension of his asceticism and of his religious sadomasochism. His disdain for sexual pleasure, his hair shirt, his self-administered flogging, all seem to have led inexorably, in an almost perversely natural progression, to his beheading. In this sense, More lived out the medieval dream of religious obedience unto death. He was a man of singular will and commitment, even if the object of his commitment was undesirable. He may well have been the last truly great medievalist in England; the Vatican later declared him a saint and martyr.

In a few short years after More's execution, the medieval Catholic Church was permanently and radically deconstructed in England. The authority of Rome was voided. The monasteries were closed, and most of the yeasty ideas of the new learning were allowed to circulate with relative impunity. The requirement of celibacy was voided; clergy began taking wives, a cultural change of no small significance. Sexual pleasure gained, at last, a modicum of respectability among observant Christians. In England, the medieval era was over.

CHAPTER 12

The Reformation as Sexual Revolution

The man who formulated the theological and philosophical principles of medieval religion was Thomas Aquinas. Drawing heavily from Aristotle, he created a synthesis of Greco-Roman philosophy and Christian theology. Faith and reason were united in one system, each commensurable with the other, which is to say that faith and reason are each arrived at by the same mental processes and are measured by the same standard. Aquinas solidified Christianity's adoption of Greek and Roman views of the nature of human life and of virtue, a process that had begun in earnest eight hundred years earlier under Emperor Constantine. In this system, sexual pleasure had no substantive place.

Aquinas actually thought of himself as affirming the goodness of sexual pleasure against those who held otherwise. But he allowed pleasure in sex only on condition that it accompany the desire to procreate. Separated from the wish to procreate, he contended that sexual pleasure was a sin. Beyond that, Aquinas was also critical of the "animal-like" qualities of sexual relations, "untempered by reason."[1] He cites Augustine: "Nothing so casts down the manly mind from its height as the fondling of a woman and those bodily contacts which belong to the married state."[2] In the innocence of the Garden of Eden, he claimed, sex would not have robbed a woman of her virginity. Semen would have traveled the route of menstrual flow, but in reverse direction. Aquinas speculated that there were sexual relations in the Garden, but they did not include intercourse.

In brief, the theology of Aquinas was a spirituality of mental incorporeality. It represented the final victory of the philosophy of imperial Rome—and the defeat, in Christianity, of the biblical view both of human life and of virtue. The contemplative life became the highest moral path—a life of the intellect but not of the body. The needs and impulses of the body were considered demeaning.

Fasting was a virtue. And sexual pleasure was the ultimate antithesis to everything spiritual. Aquinas laid out a theological system in his magnum opus, *Summa Theologica*. This system included the most negative valuation of sexual pleasure of any significant culture in history, and it still stands, today, as the official theoretical position of the Roman Catholic Church.

But Aquinas is not quite so uncomplicated. Though he adopted Greek philosophy, he took Aristotle rather than Plato as his model, which meant that he valued empirical evidence over ideals, or Platonic "forms." Thus Aquinas laid the foundation for the scientific revolution to come, however unwittingly. He also exposed the conflict between faith and reason even while attempting to create a synthesis of the two.

While Plato understood the body as pulling the soul away from God, Aristotle, and Aquinas, saw the body and soul as inextricably one. They believed that the rational mind can only act on what it learns from the five senses, whereas Plato valued the imagination as the source of truth. Rational thought for Aristotle is the accumulation of empirical evidence. Aquinas was an Aristotelian, an empiricist, but the religious environment finally overwhelmed his empiricism. In the decades following his death, Aquinas was condemned by the church for his emphasis on empiricism and reason, but by 1323, he was acknowledged as a saint. The Catholic Church absolved him but remained wary of his Aristotelian empiricism.[3]

There was to be a critical difference in what theologians called the "doctrine of man" between the theology of the Protestant reformers and the medieval theology of Aquinas. A doctrine of man was supposed to define the sense in which persons were religious, or potentially religious. One of the issues explored was the meaning of the Torah's claim that we are created in the image of God. Aquinas defined the "image of God" in human beings as the intellect, the mind. This very platonic cast to the metaphor, image of God, carried evil portents for sexual pleasure in any construct of human values. Such a definition of the image of God was very restrictive but congruent with Aquinas's elevation of the contemplative life as the highest form of spirituality. Luther and his fellow reformers were more faithful to the biblical and Jewish assumptions about the image of God. They argued that the image of God in human beings is *relationship*. Humans do not exist apart from their relationships, and such relationships involve the whole body and therefore must include sexuality.

The death of Aquinas was a revelatory one. At age 49 he had some kind of breakdown, related perhaps to the opposition he was receiving from religious leadership. He may have realized that his empiricism, his use of evidence based reasoning, was a threat to orthodoxy. He was summoned by the pope to a Council at Lyon in 1274, where he may have been censured. He died beforehand. He is reported to have had some kind of emotional experience while saying mass. After that disturbance, he entirely ceased working on his almost completed *Summa*. When his friends asked what had happened, he was strangely aloof, as if in a stupor. But he did seem in full possession of his faculties and his physical health. One of his colleagues reported that Aquinas confided the following:

"Everything I have written seems to me like so much straw compared to the truths which I have seen, and which have been revealed to me."[4] An intriguing confession, no record exists as to what might have been revealed to him.

Exactly three months after the onset of his disturbance, on March 7, 1274, Thomas Aquinas died. Just like that. The cause was declared to be mental exhaustion, extreme lassitude and weakness, and lack of appetite. He had no fever. In his last days he celebrated mass with flowing tears. His manner of dying was viewed by Christians as a sign of his piety. The religiously observant assumed that God had called him to "a higher life." In fact, the manner of Aquinas's death was an expression of disdain for this world and this life. By comparison, Martin Luther, the preeminent Protestant leader, died of congestive heart failure while on a strenuous journey to mediate a conflict between two adversaries, striving to the end to create justice.

Both Aquinas and Luther were monks. The former died a monk and had no use for this world and its pleasures. He had prayed so devoutly in his youth that he had ridden himself altogether of sexual desire. The latter, who abandoned monastic life, exuberantly affirmed the pleasures of the world. A popular Lutheran ditty, not known to be from Luther himself, was "He who loves not wine, women and song, remains a fool his whole life long."[5] In an affirmation of his love of the created world, Luther said he would plant an apple tree today even if he knew he were to die tomorrow.

The Renaissance in Europe was a cultural upheaval of which the Protestant Reformation was merely an appendage, though a very important one. The Renaissance was an awakening of humanism, and was reflected in the culture at large, especially in art and literature. Spurred by such inventions as the printing press, it was an abandonment of the restrictions of medieval life—economically, politically, artistically, religiously, and sexually.

The Renaissance was a rediscovery of the human body and its pleasures. The plastic arts transformed themselves from two-dimensional, stylized forms to three-dimensional, more naturalistic ones. The beauty and sensuousness of the body, and of sexuality, were put on display as the Renaissance came into its own.

In 1983, Leo Steinberg published an astonishing work, *The Sexuality of Christ in Renaissance Art and in Modern Oblivion*,[6] a detailed study of forgotten early Renaissance treatment of Jesus through its paintings and sculptures. What Steinberg demonstrated was that the infant Jesus was often portrayed in vividly erotic displays, happily playing with the breasts of his mother, often while being genitally stimulated by her. Such representations would hardly have shocked the common people of that culture; they were familiar with such things. But it would have unnerved any clergyman who subscribed to the injunctions of Aquinas and the medieval church. Steinberg also found that representations of the resurrected Jesus in the plastic arts often portrayed him with a barely disguised erection. One might argue that the arts dragged the medieval church into the Renaissance as much as sermons did. And the arts succeeded, with a few key leaders emerging to affirm the blessedness of sexual pleasure, Luther being the most candid.

All of the significant Protestant leaders of the sixteenth century were Catholic priests who had defected from Catholicism and married. While a claim for the right of religious leadership to partake of sexual pleasure was not the defining issue for these dissenting priests, it was a significant issue and was the single Protestant issue that most troubled, and also most delighted, society at large. The Protestant Reformation was the religious dimension of the Renaissance, and as such was, as much as anything, a sexual revolution. Except for Luther, none of the principals recorded significant or extensive ruminations on sex or marriage. But he made up for the taciturnity of all the rest. John Calvin of Geneva, Luther's chief rival for the title of preeminent reformer, while no celibate, kept relatively bloodless in his posture toward sexual pleasure. He commissioned friends to find him a wife and seems to have viewed both sex and marriage as necessary distractions from the work at hand. When his young wife died after a decade of marriage, Calvin kept to his regular work schedule. He was scandalized to hear of a woman of 70 who still sought sexual relations, a reaction diometrically opposed to that of Luther.[7]

Any serious discussion of Luther must address two issues on which Luther continues today to receive bad press: his alleged anti-Semitism and his vivid and consistent use of scatological references.

Luther's invective against the Jews is the more serious matter, and rightly continues to trouble anyone who might otherwise appreciate him. The Nazis portrayed Luther as unabashedly anti-Semitic and one of their own, with evil consequences in Germany. They called him "the greatest anti-Semite in German history" and similarly misused Nietzsche. Lutheran bishop Martin Sasse of Thuringia spoke of the appropriateness of burning synagogues on Luther's birthday, November 10, 1938.[8] (It should be noted that the great majority of Lutheran leaders supported Hitler during his rule, as did the great majority of Catholic leaders, and that Pope Pius XII negotiated a mutually beneficial treaty with Hitler, the infamous "Reich Concordat.")

Luther is much more vulnerable to criticism than most simply because so much of his writing and speaking, including his letters and dinner table conversation, were preserved in print, far more than the remarks of almost anyone else in the sixteenth century. Moreover, Luther was garrulous, with an opinion on seemingly every subject. Also, as time passed, he changed his mind on many matters. It seems likely that there are many quotations in print that Luther, in retrospect, would prefer to have erased from the record. Furthermore, he was deliberately provocative, often irascible, skilled in the use of invective, and was both quite dialectical and not unwilling to contradict himself. He was a stout defender of the Jews at points and hurled curses against them at others.

Luther was actually approached by Jewish leaders in 1536, a decade before his death, because of his reputation as "a friend of the Jews." He was asked to persuade the Elector of Saxony, Luther's own patron and benefactor, not to follow through on his plan to expel Jews from his territory. Luther declined to aid the Jews at that point and in fact verbally attacked them.

In medieval Europe, anti-Semitism was virtually universal. Jews were marked as Christ-killers, with the words of the New Testament used to support the charge. No one seemed to recognize that the New Testament writings actually reflected not Jesus, but the open warfare between the emerging new religion of Christianity, born within Judaism, and mainstream Judaism, which rejected the notion that Jesus was the messiah. Even the use of "new" in juxtaposition to "old" Testament is a slur against Judaism. The New Testament documents were all written a generation or more after the death of Jesus. The early church that was represented in the New Testament texts was bent on discrediting "nonbelieving" Jews. (Even today, this seems not widely known.) This determination of the early Christians—themselves Jews—to portray those Jews who did not believe that Jesus was the messiah as malicious Christ-killers negatively shaped all subsequent Christianity.

Luther is hardly unique in excoriating the Jews verbally, but he went no further than verbal abuse. This was the era of the Inquisition, during which church and state jointly burned Jews at the stake simply for being Jews. In 1509, for example, 39 Jews were burned alive in Berlin by Catholic authorities. They were also burned in Rome, in mid-century, in the shadow of the Vatican. (Luther himself would have been similarly executed had he been seized by Catholic authorities.) This was the punishment due all who dissented from the authorized Christian doctrines of the time. Jews were perpetually under threat of execution simply because they were "unbelievers."

Luther actually considered himself "a product of the Jews."[9] Thus he held the view that Jews should have supported him in his dissent from Roman Catholic theology and practice. He expected the Jews to see his new biblically based approach to religion as the true biblical faith, common to both Christians and Jews. However naïve such an expectation seems today, Luther was not totally off base. He did not set himself up as the inventor of a new religion but, rather, as one who was reforming Christianity and restoring it to its authentic—and, it is not too much to say, Jewish—origins. His reform had a profound affinity with Judaism, even if Jews should not have been expected to see it. Furthermore, Luther sought allies in his personal life-and-death struggle and thought the Jews would be natural allies. But rather than supporting Luther, Jews kept their distance. Who could fault such reticence? Yet Luther felt abandoned by them.

Matters were made worse when some Jews, during this time, appealed to the Holy Roman Emperor, Charles V, for refuge—which he granted. Charles, who was as anti-Semitic as anyone, and who was also Luther's *bête noire*, played politics in offering the Jews this short lived protection. Charles never protested or rescinded the deeds of his grandparents, Ferdinand and Isabella, who had rendered the Iberian peninsular *judenrein*, or "free of Jews," in 1492. This alliance between Charles and the Jews did not give Luther, who already had a death sentence hanging over his head, much comfort. He could not have been expected to feel benevolent toward those who allied themselves with his mortal enemy.

Luther's reformed Christianity was a democratized religion. According to his interpretation, every man and woman with a Bible was the authority for his or her own life, canceling the alleged authority of the priestly hierarchy. Jews would typically have appreciated this, because Judaism has always been singularly nonhierarchical. And to promote a universal reading of the Bible, Luther translated its original Hebrew and Greek texts into vivid and poetic vernacular German, a major literary achievement that endures today. In refocusing attention on the texts, all of which were written by Jews of one sort or another, Luther certainly did the Jews no harm. In focusing the church back on the biblical texts, he restored much of the original Jewish character to the church. But that did not impress the Jews.

To make matters worse for the Jews, there was talk among Roman Catholics that Protestantism was the result of a perverse Jewish influence. Again, not a far-fetched notion. The successor to Charles V, his son Philip II, made a public statement, early in his reign, claiming that "all the heresies which have occurred in Germany and France have been sown by descendants of Jews."[10] Luther likely felt that he needed some distance from the Jews if he were to survive.

Luther was, in the long run, good for the Jews, as was the Reformation itself. Luther was the central figure in laying the foundation for religious pluralism in Europe. Jews typically prosper in pluralistic contexts, where there is no single authoritarian religious establishment. Early Protestantism generally did not promote the medieval notion of Jews as Christ-killers. Luther's own Wittenberg Hymnal, published shortly before his death, contains a hymn with the words: "the Jews we may not upbraid inimically, for the guilt is ours."[11] Jews would likely have suffered even more than they did, in the half-millennium since Luther, if no Reformation had occurred. Secondly, Luther restored a Jewish understanding of the nature of human personality to western religion. He restored a positive—let us say Jewish, or biblical—valuation of sex to the Protestant faction of western religion. This gave the Jews some philosophical common ground with a segment of Christianity. With the arrival of Protestantism, Jews were no long alone in Europe in permitting religious leaders the blessings of sexual pleasure. Jews were less conspicuous than in the context of a culture in which the highest moral vision was a renunciation of sexual pleasure altogether, the vision that the Roman ecclesiastical authorities had—and indeed still have—for anyone it brings under its authority.

Luther's invective against the Jews is abhorrent, yet it does not make him the kind of person who would have supported the twentieth-century Nazis—not one bit. Luther should be judged in the context of his own time and culture.

Luther is also diminished by his detractors for his vivid scatological language, a charge that wins points among modern prigs. It is quite true that Luther's religious experience, his journey toward personal integration, was inextricably associated with scatological images. The boundary between cleanliness and righteousness, on the one hand, and filth or sin, on the other, was associated by Luther with his bowels. His religion was rooted in bodily experience, not in cerebral speculations as it was for Medieval Christianity. For Luther, the devil was associated with filth and shit. His struggle with his own bowels, with constipation, was a representation of his struggle for salvation and peace of mind. His experience of salvation came with the recognition that he would not succeed in cleansing himself, that he would remain a sinful person—full of shit—seeking redemption. Purity was not achievable as long as his bowels remained to be attended to. Thus it should not surprise us that Luther came to his experience of salvation, or inner reconciliation, while sitting on the toilet. This fact has been flung at embarrassed Lutherans for five hundred years.[12]

Luther's strong scatological language, jarring as it is may be to cultured modern ears, was his weapon of choice in polemics against both Rome and the devil, who were, for Luther, much the same. When a cardinal lets wind in Rome, Luther said, the Germans believe a new article of faith is born.[13] However, it should be pointed out that Luther's chiding of Rome was potentially far less lethal than the death sentence Rome had levied against *him*.

The devil got the same scatological treatment from Luther that the church received. When he despaired for the future, Luther characterized the whole world as a shard of feces from the devil's anus. Such imagery does not sit well in polite twenty-first-century society.

When Luther nailed his now famous *Ninety-five Theses* to the Wittenberg Church door (in 1517, the date now considered the start of the Reformation), his message contained no mention of sexual issues.[14] Had Luther been interested in sexual purity, he might well have made sexual misconduct the focus of his *Theses*. The Catholic religious leadership, from pope to priest, had a long tradition of keeping mistresses and fathering children. Bishops in some dioceses were known to tax their priests who kept mistresses: one gulden a year. Rather than harping on sexual purity, Luther concentrated on the Catholic practice of indulgences, a method of raising money through selling coupons of credit against both past and future sins. By a stroke of his hand, Luther swept off the table the very notion of a debit and credit account in relation to the divine.

Luther's *Theses* was an attack on both the authority of the pope and on the notion of commensurability in the relationship between God and human beings that Rome was promoting, in the form of indulgences. That is to say, Luther argued that the relationship between God and human beings was not like that between a banker and clients, which must be an eminently commensurable relationship if it is to be successful. Indulgences eloquently testified to a commensurable religion. They also provided windfall profits for the church. Luther preached a religion of inner reconciliation, in which each person stood on his or her own before God, and stood unequipped with bargaining chips or religious lucre. In his democratized religion, the pope and his clergy were not only wrong, but irrelevant.

The principal claim of the Reformation was that salvation came "by faith alone," not via any sort of intermediary. True religion was a matter of each person's personal private grappling with God, or idea of God, through studying the Bible. The corollary was that the relationship between mankind and God was "incommensurable," meaning it could in no way be totted up or measured, at least not by man.

While the practice of bargaining with God using coupons purchased from the clergy was the substantive issue that sparked the Reformation, the most dramatic proposition of the Reformation in the eyes of ordinary people was the repudiation of the sexual values of the medieval church. Chastity and celibacy were, in the public mind, the chief Christian virtues. Of the three legs of monasticism—poverty, chastity, and obedience—chastity was the most drastic and the most demanding, requiring the most energy and resolve. The first leg of the monastic stool that the Protestants knocked off was obedience, but they got more attention when they knocked off chastity.

In the very early years of Luther's dissent, the baleful sexual rules of the medieval church got little or no attention from him. The authority of the pope and the claim of the pope to speak as God's intermediary was the focus of Luther's critique. In a very few years, however, sex became the *cause célèbre* of the Reformation. Obviously, the challenge to the authority of the pope, and to the requirement of obedience to the Roman magisterium, led quickly to questioning the requirement of celibacy among the clergy and monastics.

Eventually, Luther himself contributed to the focus on sex by teaching that medieval sexual rules lacked any support in the Biblical texts. Furthermore, he contended they were inhuman. Not one person in one hundred thousand, he said, possessed the ability to abstain from sexual pleasure.[15] The Reformation ferment led to a flood of priests, monks, and nuns leaving the monasteries and convents to seek marriage. A social problem developed, in that the fleeing women were vulnerable in ways the men were not. They needed husbands if they were to find social security. Luther responded to the crisis by converting his formerly Augustinian monastery into a halfway house, a veritable matchmaking and dating service for runaway nuns and monks.

In a later reflection, Luther wrote:

> God knows I never thought of going so far as I did. I intended only to attack indulgences. If anybody had said to me, when I was at the Diet of Worms [1521], "In a few years you'll have a wife and your own household," I wouldn't have believed it.[16]

At first, Luther made it clear that he was not himself a candidate for marriage. Nor is there any suggestion that he took a mistress of any sort. As for marriage, he rightly pointed out that his own life was too tenuous for him to take a wife. From 1522 on, he was living out in the open. Catholic authorities likely had the resources, if they had put their minds to it, to seize him at any time and deliver him to the Emperor for burning. In 1521, he said, "They'll never force a wife on me."[17] But at some later point he changed his mind. He married a runaway nun, Katharina von Bora, on June 13, 1525.

Katy, as Luther called her, was a sister of Johannes von Staupitz, Luther's mentor in earlier times. She came to Luther for sanctuary. A husband, Jerome Baumgaertner, was found for her; the two became engaged. Then Baumgaertner left on a journey, never to return. Why Luther decided to step into Baumgaertner's shoes, he never said, that we know of. He may have felt an obligation to Staupitz. Or he may have felt pity, seeing von Bora as damaged goods and difficult to place, as the couple may already have engaged in intercourse. In letters inviting friends to the marriage feast, Luther wrote, "I do not love my wife, but I appreciate her." He even viewed Katy as "haughty" and confessed that he had had his eye on another woman. But Katy later became "his beloved wife."[18]

That a priest would marry a nun was so inflammatory that even some of Luther's associates and supporters—the important Philip Melangthon, for example—were opposed to it. In the medieval world, sexual relations between a priest and a nun were classified as incest. Intercourse with a nun subjected one to the death penalty. Luther's supporters thought that this attention to sex would undermine the more substantive issues of the Reformation. Furthermore, Melangthon and others were still hoping for a theological settlement with Rome, to preserve the unity of the Roman Catholic Church. They knew that the marriage of a priest and a nun would make certain no settlement was possible. Luther was not unaware of the political ramifications of his so-called incestuous marriage. Yet he was undaunted, and even relished the thought of violating this taboo. He was already condemned to death for his ideas and his refusal to recant, as demanded by religious authorities. Now he had committed yet a second capital crime. He confessed that he married in defiance of the devil and that marriage had brought him so much contempt that he hoped the angels were laughing, and the devils weeping. This was the Luther who said that it was in living and dying and being damned that we are saved.

According to sixteenth-century custom, someone was required to witness the consummation of a marriage. For this task Luther selected Justas Jonas, who, oddly enough, would also witness Luther's death years later.

When Katy was pregnant with the first of their six children, considerable anxiety surrounded the wait, as folk wisdom held that the sexual union of a priest and a nun would give birth to a two-headed monster. Thomas More speculated that the child might be the antichrist.[19] The modern historian Heiko Oberman wonders what would have become of the Reformation if Luther's first child had by chance been born handicapped. Fortunately, the child was born healthy. Nevertheless, and just as Melangthon predicted, many Catholic scholars and polemicists attempted—and some still attempt—to reduce the Reformation to a product of Luther's lust.[20]

With millions of Luther's words preserved in archives, some of it rambling table-talk, one can, by careful selection, create many different portraits of Luther.

Many of his views were mere reflections of his time and culture. For example, a researcher might comb through Luther's collected works and make a case for Luther as a male chauvinist, but would this be accurate? When Luther says that girls grow faster than boys for the same reason weeds grow faster than cultivated plants, is he being a prankster or simply a man of his time?

> Consider when Luther writes of his own marriage: If I ever have to find myself a wife again, I will hew myself an obedient wife out of stone.[21]

Was he being serious, or funny, or a little of both? Undoubtedly, the Luthers had their quarrels. Katy was no retiring hausfrau. We read in the recorded table-talk that she participated in theological discourses and was not bashful about disagreeing with Luther. When he chided her for talking too much, she gave it right back to him. She seems very much his equal. Luther's letters and table-talk showed a couple who found immense satisfaction, and considerable intimacy, in their relationship. Luther added that he learned more theology lying next to Katy and her pigtails than from all the books ever written. This marriage of convenience in the course of time turned into a deeply loving and productive relationship. He once said he "would not trade Katy for France and Venice," and that he would die as "one who lauds and loves marriage."[22] In fact, the Luthers had a very modern marriage, in spite of the century in which they lived.

Luther was no cautious religious politician. He was unafraid to take positions that wounded him politically, once persuaded they were right. His approval of the bigamy of his benefactor, Philip of Hesse, was a case in point. Philip had wished to divorce his wife and marry a woman already his lover. Luther was opposed to Philip's divorcing his wife on the grounds that it would be damaging to her. (He opposed the English King Henry VIII's decision to divorce Catharine of Aragon on the same grounds.) When Philip then proposed to take a second wife while maintaining his first wife in the privileged state to which she was accustomed, an arrangement to which both women agreed, Luther decided to support him, stipulating that the plan be kept secret so as not to stir up the public (a predictably fruitless request); Luther absorbed much negative publicity as a result. Heiko Oberman rightly calls this "an exemplary decision" on Luther's part.[23] Luther had the courage to stand alone in a decision few would understand. But any other decision would have been hypocritical.

In the Luther corpus one can find a large amount of material that makes Luther sound like a typical minister or religious leader. He is opposed to divorce, adultery, prostitution, promiscuity, and everything else on the typical list for a moral authority. There is little question of his sincerity on these issues. Every item on the list is in some respects potentially destructive to human values. But this paints a one-dimensional picture of Luther, one which is encountered in virtually every popular, and even in many scholarly, biographies—the expurgated, bowdlerized Luther.

What is missing in the more conventional biographies of Luther is his willingness to make exceptions for anything. He embodied what came to be known in the twentieth century as situation ethics. Luther was, in fact, wonderfully contradictory and wonderfully resilient, willing to make exceptions in any sphere, provided they suited his own notions of justice and compassion. Consistency was not his concern. Thus when he gave Philip of Hesse pastoral approval for his bigamy, Luther knew full well that this was not consistent with his own preaching on marriage. There are many other instances where he took positions that were contrary to the ideals and standards that he, under normal circumstances, supported.

In one of Luther's dinner conversations, the subject of polygamy came up. Luther remarked that eventually polygamy would return to favor, as it had been in biblical times. His wife joined the conversation.

Katy: Let the devil believe that.

Martin: The reason, Katy, is that the woman can bear only one child a year, while her husband can beget many.

Katy: Paul said each man should have his own wife.

Martin: Yes, his own wife, and not "only one wife," for the latter isn't what Paul wrote.

Katy: Before I put up with this, I would rather go back to the convent and leave you and all the children.[24]

We do not have the context of this discussion, and more importantly, we do not have the affective content. Almost certainly this couple is playing with each other, and having fun in the process.

Luther reveals himself to be unabashedly positive about sexual pleasure. When he was asked whether it was "moral" for a young man to marry an older woman, beyond child bearing years, his response was, "Yes, indeed!"[25] When a Waldensian minister named Lawrence commiserated with Luther over having castrated himself for religious reasons as a youth, Luther responded, "I'd rather have two pair added than one taken off."[26]

Six months after the Luthers married, his dear friend Georg Spalatin was set to be married in another part of Germany, to a woman also named Katy. Luther regretted that it was not safe for him to venture on a journey to join the wedding party, given the numbers of authorities who wanted him arrested. So he sent Spalatin the following message:

I will calculate how long it will take my courier to reach you. The very night you receive this letter you penetrate your lovely Katy, and I will penetrate mine. Thus we will be united in love. [27]

Luther was approached by a man claiming that his wife had syphilis and could not engage in sexual intercourse. The man complained that he could not bear the burden of chastity. Luther replied that the man had one of two choices, adultery or bigamy. Luther recommended the latter, with the proviso that he see that his first wife was fully cared for and not abandoned.[28] Luther followed the same path here as he followed in regard to Philip of Hesse. He tried to balance security for the wife and the other woman with the man's sexual needs. And on this issue he was no male chauvinist. A woman who came to him with a similar dilemma received similar advice. Her husband was sexually impotent. She wanted to have children, and she also suffered from a lack of sexual satisfaction. Luther advised her to seek the permission of her husband to take a lover, preferably one of her husband's brothers. (Luther was undoubtedly thinking of the Torah's levirate law, requiring a brother-in-law to replace a dead brother.) He also advised the woman to keep any such agreement secret, so as to protect the dignity of the husband. In the event that the husband refused to negotiate, Luther advised the woman to find another husband and flee to another region. Thus he took seriously the sexual needs of both men and women.[29]

Luther was rare among Christian leaders in holding such views but not radical in the context of the culture generally. Common law in Westphalia, seemingly *unchristianized*, held that a man who could not perform his conjugal duty was required to seek satisfaction for his wife through a neighbor.

On his last journey, a visit to his birthplace of Eisleben, Luther died of what is presumed to have been congestive heart failure. To the very end of his life, he remained playfully ribald, as if to embarrass forever the succeeding generations of middle-class Protestants. During his trip, he wrote to his beloved Katy telling her that he had recovered from his illness and suffered "merely from the resistance of the beautiful ladies." He added that their resistance prevented him from any wrong or fear about his virtue. Certainly, he was attempting to be humorous, but one's choice of humor is revelatory.[30]

Luther's appreciation of sexual pleasure was shaped primarily by the generally positive attitude toward sexual pleasure in the Bible, especially the Old Testament. This freedom to take pleasure in sex, along with the subversion of clerical authority, led to the Protestant proclamation of "evangelical freedom." After getting out from under an authoritarian religious regime with an obsessive moral code, Protestants were energized by the notion of freedom, a notion not to be confused with bourgeois ideas of freedom. They preached that law was made for man, not man for the law. Luther himself even pressed, to its limits, the case for evangelical freedom. He taught those who had formed an overly scrupulous conscience as Catholics to stand unafraid of condemnation they might feel from their own long-reinforced consciences. Luther proclaimed that saying "yes" to God sometimes means saying "no," even to the conscience. As he put it, in Latin, *Pecca fortiter*, which is to say, "Sin boldly, or bravely."[31] Thus it was that many found sexual liberation under the sway of Luther and sixteenth-century Protestantism.

CHAPTER 13

THE SEXUALITY OF TERESA OF AVILA

In 1515, just two years before Luther nailed his *Ninety-five Theses* onto the Wittenberg church door, Teresa of Avila was born in Spain. A central religious figure of sixteenth-century Spain, Teresa founded countless convents and monasteries for her discalced—"barefoot" or "shoeless"—followers. (Sandals were not considered shoes.) In the context of a culture and church in which men controlled almost everything, Teresa's ability to wield such personal power was quite amazing. She was determined and aggressive, but she had a capacity to charm and to persuade as well. A splendid and judicious biography was published in 1999, Cathleen Medwick's, *Teresa of Avila: The Progress of a Soul.*[1]

Teresa is most popularly remembered for one particular vision, or "rapture," as it is called, which she described in some detail herself. An angel, who seemed to be on fire, appeared to her:

> In his hands I saw a large golden spear, and at its iron tip there seemed to be a point of fire. I felt as if he plunged this into my heart several times, so that it penetrated all the way to my entrails. When he drew it out, he seemed to draw them out with it, and left me totally inflamed with a great love for God. The pain was so severe, it made me moan several times. The sweetness of this intense pain was so extreme, there is no wanting it to end, and the soul isn't satisfied with anything less than God.[2]

Teresa stated that the pain was not physical but spiritual, though she added that the body "has a share in it—in fact, a large share."

Gian Bernini's famous sculpture depicting this rapture, made a century later and based on Teresa's written account, shows a woman with her mouth open, limbs akimbo, obviously in the throes of ecstasy. It sits in the Church of St. Maria Della Vittoria in Rome, and has sexual innuendoes galore.

No rational person knows quite what to make of this rapture of Teresa's, this amalgam of religious devotion and eroticism. Not surprisingly, some devout Christians see no problem. They would see nothing sexual in Teresa's rapture and assume that her vow of chastity would mean that she was sexually inexperienced. From their point of view, Teresa is simply having an encounter with God, and that is that.

Less credulous persons, and anyone who approaches Teresa's life from a clinical perspective, is left wondering. (Examining God's part in Teresa's life is out of the question, because God is not available for clinical examination.) But the unmistakable sexual overtones in Teresa's autobiographical account, seconded by Bernini, beg explanation.

Perhaps Teresa's rapture was the fruit of a sublimated sexuality, in which her pent up energy was diverted, in a general sense, toward other, perhaps higher, goals. Sigmund Freud claimed that sublimated sexual energy created culture. Thus it is plausible that Teresa diverted most of her sexual energy (which occasionally could not help erupting in visions and raptures) to her work of reforming monastic life. She does not explain herself in such terms, but this is one interpretation of her experience.

Another interpretation of Teresa's erotic dramatization views it as a neurotic manifestation of unresolved sexuality. This is the position taken by Jacob Breuer, a teacher of Freud, who concluded that Teresa was "the patron saint of hysteria."[3] Breuer's view of Teresa has carried the day among psychologists ever since.

Yet a third possibility is that Teresa was neither a hysteric nor one who entirely sublimated her sexuality. Her life did not have the marks of an emotionally unstable individual, which a diagnosis of a floridly somatizing hysteria would presume. Quite the contrary. Nor did she have the appearance of one who denies herself pleasure, sexual or otherwise. Teresa may well have been a sexually liberated woman, yet with enough political savvy to defend and protect her reputation in a tightly repressed social environment—and may well have appreciated how sexual innuendo can give impetus to religious commitment. This interpretation would remove her from the diagnosis of psychopathology and presume that she was psychologically healthy.

Teresa did not have Luther's option to speak openly about God's gift of sexuality and discuss sexuality's attendant blessings. Secular authorities protected Luther from being seized by Roman Catholic officials, whereas Teresa would have been burned at the stake by the officers of the Inquisition. Should she have had the vocation to promote the blessedness of sexual pleasure, no route other than the one she chose seems to have existed in sixteenth-century

Spain. Thus we can conjecture that Teresa used the religious rapture to give a sub-rosa religious blessing to sexual pleasure. This would have made her somewhat duplicitous in relation to the Catholic authorities, but then we know that her duplicity in relation to them was, in other instances, well-documented. Teresa was brilliant in the use of personal and political power, whatever her sexual experience may have been.

Among these differing views on Teresa's inner life, a clear winner is not likely to emerge. But the balance of evidence suggests that Teresa was psychologically a healthy, competent woman and a sexually liberated one who learned how to prosper in a dark, repressive culture in which gynophobic men controlled everything with an iron fist.

To construct a plausible portrait of Teresa, we should look for clues in her environment and in her various life choices. In Teresa's culture, the monastic life was the only option, aside from marriage, for a young woman who had any standing in society.

Teresa's family was well-off. Her father had a reputation for integrity and humanitarianism; he was known to have declined, out of conscience, to own slaves. When Teresa was 19, he arranged a marriage that would have been politically beneficial to all concerned. But Teresa refused to marry and made known her intention to enter a Carmelite convent called "Encarnacion." Her father objected to her choice of a monastic life, but objected even more to her choice of Encarnacion, as the nuns of that convent had a tawdry reputation.

When twentieth-century readers learn that Teresa entered a convent and became a nun, they assume a twentieth-century context and see her retreating from the world, seeking the safety of the cloister. Modern readers also assume that she would have been separated from society generally, and more specifically from men. But this was not the case. Teresa's monastic quarters hardly resembled the restrictive quarters imposed on a modern nun. At Encarnacion, Teresa had a two-story private apartment with guest quarters. This arrangement, which allowed her to entertain both men and women in privacy, was not the sort of setting we might expect would nurture sexual abstinence.

Modern readers also assume they know what the vows of poverty, chastity, and obedience meant in the context of sixteenth-century Spain. But social life and societal rules were not the same then as today. First, sexual trysts were commonplace among clergy and popes alike. Concubines, secret wives, and illegitimate children followed clergymen all over Europe. Today we may view that as corruption, but in the context of the times it was simply business as usual.

In the sixteenth century, not every leader of the Catholic Church was satisfied with the behavioral conditions of monastic life. Late in the century, the pope sent out representatives to promote "holy poverty, chastity and obedience." And in 1566 the pope issued a bulletin mandating that convents be enclosed, shut off from the public. But this directive was too late for Teresa, who by then was 51 and in her prime. Not only was she prioress of Encarnacion, but she was the founder of a new order, the Reformed Carmelites. In this capacity she traveled throughout Spain during her mature years, starting up new convents. She was so persuasive with certain key male authorities that she was even given permission to create new Reformed Carmelite monasteries for *men*. She used what biographer Cathleen Medwick calls a "guerilla approach" to these start-ups. She was aggressive, worked fast, then quickly moved on. As a married woman, Teresa would never have had the freedom to accomplish what she did as a monastic. It seems that Teresa's choice of a monastic life was not an escape from the world, but, in the words of Medwick, "a strategic defense against it." Perhaps it would be still more accurate to call it "a strategic *offense*."

In this context, Teresa begins to look more like a woman of the world, a deeply religious woman who at the same time refused to let life—or sexual pleasure—pass her by. The rules of poverty, chastity, and obedience (as conventionally understood today) do not fit her portrait. While Teresa had little or no personal wealth, she was born into wealth, which she presumably could fall back on. More to the point, as prioress of Encarnacion, she had access to considerable communal wealth, especially when her order of Reformed and Discalced Carmelites grew and prospered. In that sense, she was no pauper, even though she probably had, strictly speaking, no personal wealth. But poverty was not a condition that could appropriately describe her life.

As for obedience, Teresa was obedient to certain religious authorities but was famously and repeatedly disobedient to many others. The nuns of Encarnacion were at one point excommunicated en masse, though the judgment against them was later lifted. Teresa knew ways of setting king against pope, and bishop against bishop, in the service of her noble objectives. To suit such objectives, she was skilled at reinterpreting even direct orders.

As for chastity, Teresa does not look or sound as if she was a woman determined to deny herself sexual pleasure. Rather than a blanket denial of all sex, chastity has always carried a secondary meaning of careful and prudent *selectivity* in seeking sexual pleasure, as when a married person is described as "chaste." Teresa may well have been chaste according to that definition but at the same time been sexually active. Teresa had a reputation as one who spoke more with men than with women and more with angels than with men. She understood where power lay. To say Teresa was sexually abstemious does not correspond to what we know of her life.

Further evidence suggests, if it doesn't absolutely prove, that Teresa was indeed sexually active. Coming to the attention of the dreaded Inquisition for

alleged sexual immorality, she was interrogated but seems to have dazzled
her inquisitors. On the other hand, she did fail to impress some of her interlocutors. One papal nuncio reported back to Rome that she was an

> unstable, restless, disobedient and contumacious female who, in the name
> of devotion, devised false doctrines, leaving the enclosures against orders
> of the Council of Trent and her superiors, and teaching as if she were a
> master, in spite of St. Paul's order that women should not teach.[4]

The nuncio wanted Teresa to retire obediently and quietly to her convent
and then close the door behind her.

Teresa's alliance with John of the Cross further suggests that she was a sexually liberated woman. She appointed John to be confessor for the nuns at
Encarnacion. He protected them from reactionary and inquisitorial forces
that sought to undermine Teresa. John's life and work was, like Teresa's,
marked by powerful erotic themes and innuendoes; he created a luscious,
erotic recasting of the biblical Song of Songs.[5] His enemies accused John
of seducing all the women in the convent and also of being Teresa's lover.
When Teresa was away on a journey, a vigilante group of religious and political figures captured John of the Cross and took him away for confinement.
Immediately prior to his seizure, John burned most of his papers. Some he
could not burn he is said to have quickly eaten, difficult as this is to imagine. It would seem that he had something that he did not want ecclesiastical
authorities to see. Imprisoned for nine months in a dungeon in Toledo, he
was beaten repeatedly. Teresa begged for his release. A decade later, he died
a painful death in exile. But, as has so often been the case in Catholic Church
history, he was later canonized and made a Doctor of the Church.

John's writings are so unabashedly sensual, it's impossible to reconcile
them with medieval Christianity. No one can read his poetry without feeling
their incongruity with sexual innocence—at least, sexual innocence as we
presume it today. Here is the Campbell translation of part of a poem titled
"Songs of the soul in rapture at having arrived at the height of perfection,
which is union with God by the road of spiritual negation":[6]

> Upon a gloomy night, With all my cares to loving ardours flushed, (O
> venture of delight!) With nobody in sight I went abroad when all my house
> was hushed.
>
> In safety, in disguise, In darkness up the secret stair I crept, (O happy
> enterprise.) Concealed from other eyes When all my house at length in
> silence slept.
>
> Upon that lucky night In secrecy, inscrutable to sight, I went without
> discerning And with no other light Except for that which in my heart was
> burning.

It lit and led me through More certain than the light of noonday clear To where One waited near Whose presence well I knew, There where no other presence might appear.

Oh night that was my guide! Oh darkness dearer than the morning's pride, Oh night that joined the lover To the beloved bride Transfiguring them each to the other.

… Lost to myself I stayed My face upon my lover having laid From all endeavour ceasing: And all my cares releasing Threw them amongst the lilies there to fade.

Sixteenth-century Spain neither suffered the wounds nor enjoyed the blessings of the Reformation. Spain was the only significant European country to avoid the Reformation entirely. Throughout Spain, a great deal of invective circulated regarding "dangerous Lutheranism," yet Protestants did not penetrate the rigorous controls of the Spanish Catholic Church. First of all, the key sixteenth-century rulers, Charles V and Philip II, were very Catholic emperors, and Spain was their home ground. Secondly, the Spanish Inquisition was ready to burn any heretic as soon a candidate came into view. Spain was sealed tightly against the Reformation.

That does not mean Spain was bereft of social and religious ferment. Popes, bishops, and heads of the religious orders continually vied for power; some also advocated reforms of one sort or another. In policy decisions, popes and kings sometimes cancelled each other out. In this maelstrom, Teresa used her wit and charm to build a woman's empire under the noses of authorities who generally denigrated women.

Although she would likely have declined such a label, history should view Teresa as something of crypto-Protestant. While she could not have been a Protestant openly without getting burned at the stake, her reform movement promoted many of the same crucial human values as Protestantism.

First and foremost, Teresa promoted, as the source of her authority, her own idiosyncratic visions. Her claim is very close to the claims of Luther and other Protestants whose authority was *sola scriptura*. This "scriptures alone" slogan actually refers to the reader's right to interpret the scriptures in whatever way seems true to him or her. Both Luther and Teresa set themselves up as religious authorities independent of the proclamations of the church hierarchy. The basis of their authority was their personal revelatory experiences. This was a radical departure from, and a threat to, mainstream Catholic tradition, in which absolute authority resided in the pope and his clerical representatives.

Teresa was able to achieve some of her objectives by way of support from the Holy Roman Emperor, Philip II, in the same way Luther relied on the protection of local German potentates. Each simply made the pope's edicts void. The Holy Roman Emperor did this selectively for Teresa by limiting the pope's emissaries' power over her; German authorities did it categorically for Luther by closing the borders of the province to Catholic authorities.

Teresa was also a liberator of women, though in a somewhat different way from Protestantism. While Protestantism elevated women's status by giving them a place at bed and board with male religious leaders, Teresa's liberation of women was arguably more potent. Her convents were places of refuge for harassed and abused wives and daughters. Teresa's women determined their own destiny outside male control—or almost outside it, as male ecclesiastical authorities held the decisive cards in any showdown. But male power had its limits. Teresa's liberation, while more radical, was also short-lived. Once she died, male leaders were free to exercise power more freely against her less formidable successors. By contrast, the Protestant liberation of women, while less radical, was permanent.

Both Teresa and John of the Cross were thought to be Jews, but only genetically so. In Teresa's case, it is established that her grandfather, Juan Sanchez, was a *converso* in Toledo. During the Inquisition, *conversos* were Jews who converted to Christianity as an alternative to being burned at the stake. Sanchez elected to convert but later was convicted by the Inquisition of secretly practicing Judaism. His punishment was relatively mild: He only had to parade through the streets of Toledo in disgrace. Then he packed up the family and moved to Avila. John of the Cross was also reputed to be of *converso* stock.

Given the fact that Christianity had struggled for centuries, successfully, to obliterate the Jewish affirmation of sexual pleasure, the fact that Teresa and John of the Cross were both genetically Jews, and both marked by eroticism, is not a little ironic. It is similarly ironic that Encarnacion convent was built on a Jewish graveyard. These connections do not prove anything by themselves, except the appearance in history of another strange convergence of events and people. Whatever else they accomplished, Teresa and John, though not practicing Jews, carried forward in their own opaque ways the Jewish vision of the blessedness of sexual pleasure, a vision that subverted medieval Catholic teaching as much as Luther did.

Teresa came into her own just as the Roman Catholic Church was in the process of defending itself against Protestantism. A particularly hard right turn came when the Roman Catholic Council of Trent, meeting between 1545 and 1563, tightened controls and reinforced the church's central authority. An *Index* of prohibited books was issued by the Grand Inquisitor of Spain; it listed many of Teresa's favorites. Agustin Cazalla, a person who had some interest in Teresa, was burned at the stake in 1559; the substance of their relationship was never revealed. When church authorities turned their attention to Teresa, demanding the source of her visions and raptures, she asserted that Jesus Christ was the one who spoke to her. When they asked how she knew it was Jesus, her rejoinder was simple and brilliant—and circular: "He told me who he was."[7] That church authorities would defer to such idiosyncratic authority is a testimony not to the visions themselves, but to Teresa's personal and professional power.

Teresa and Luther suffered similar fates of being misunderstood and misused by their followers who came later—Luther by Lutherans, Teresa by the Catholic Church. One of the stunning twists of Catholic history came when Teresa was canonized, in 1622, a half century after her death—and was praised "for overcoming her female nature."

CHAPTER 14

FROM MARTIN LUTHER TO ANTON BOISEN

After the revolutionary ferment of the sixteenth-century Protestant Reformation, the various Protestant churches settled into a fixed system of sexual ethics that was distinguished from medieval Catholic ethics in one respect only: Protestant clergy were permitted to marry like anyone else. In other respects, sexual pleasure was, in both Protestant and Catholic cultures, treated with careful rationing and Platonic suspicion. The same uneasiness over sexual pleasure permeated both cultures. The Orthodox Christians of eastern Europe continued in their somewhat different—but similarly negative—posture toward sexual pleasure, allowing parish clergy to marry, but selecting bishops solely from among the monks.

In fact the one major reform movement in Protestantism's five hundred years—the Pietistic revival in the eighteenth century—actually heightened uneasiness over sexual pleasure, thereby creating more of an affinity with Catholicism. The Pietists sought purity of life and hardly anyone thought that religious purity and sexual pleasure were compatible, in spite of Luther and all his teaching. John Wesley, one of the major leaders of the Pietist movement, was as wary, both of sexual pleasure and of women, as any monastic. It seems likely he never had a successful sexual relationship in his life. (He experienced a number of failed courtships, and a brief, failed marriage.) Thus the achievements of Protestantism, in restoring sexual pleasure to a legitimate place in "the good life," were limited. Protestants who followed Luther never seemed able to adhere fully to his audacious work. (Protestantism did have more staying power in its efforts to reform its structures of authority and in bringing to Protestant Christianity a more democratic system of organization.)

In a paradoxical way, later *Catholic* cultures became somewhat more relaxed about sexual pleasure than did Protestant cultures. Prostitution, for example, has been consistently tolerated in Catholic cultures; Protestant cultures seem brittle by comparison. In much of the largely Protestant, English-speaking world, it is not unusual for a man to be arrested for patronizing a prostitute. By contrast, in most Catholic cultures prostitution is not only tolerated, typically it is monitored by the state for considerations of health. Similarly, extramarital sexual relationships have been treated with benign neglect in most Catholic cultures, this despite church teaching.

In the mainly Protestant, mid-twentieth-century environment in which I was reared, there were no state-licensed "boys' towns" as exist in nominally Catholic Mexico. In my Virginia hometown, police checked license plates at local motels, feeling it was part of their mission to expose extramarital liaisons. Compared to Mexicans of my generation, I was reared in a state and country that was flagrantly sex-phobic.

It seems likely that this paradox—of Catholic tolerance and Protestant rigidity—stems from the two-class system of religiosity in Catholic cultures. The Protestant notion of religious classlessness—the priesthood of all believers—has permitted only one ethical standard for sexual behavior. But in Catholic tradition the religiosity of the "religious" (celibates and monastics) has carried the moral burden, and the morality of the "nonreligious" has been, therefore, less strenuous, less demanding. The nonreligious have been expected to marry, and a certain level of permissiveness in testing the sexual boundaries has been granted them. In Protestant cultures, such "dual religious citizenships" has not existed. Both lay people and clergy have been judged by the same moral standards.

The sixteenth-century Anabaptists (the name comes from their practice of "re-baptizing" as adults those who were baptized as infants) were among the most radical of the groups that emerged under the Protestant umbrella. They called into question not only the authority of the Roman Catholic Church, but of every existing social institution. Unlike more mainstream Protestants, they disdained marriage altogether and practiced free love. They also practiced gender equality, placing women in positions of leadership, something unheard-of in religious groups of that era. The Anabaptists, and most of their teachings, soon went into eclipse. Their religious descendants, plain "Baptists" (even though *they* practiced re-baptism, as well), evolved into a denomination that has as conventional a position on sexual pleasure as exists anywhere in Protestantism. (Dropping the "ana-" prefix may have helped.) Twentieth-century hippies and communards have been more authentically heirs of the Anabaptists than the Baptists have been. Several singular figures among the Baptists—Will Campbell, Carlysle Marney, Wayne Oates, and Myron Madden, to name a few—brought something of the spirit of the Anabaptists into the present but have not been invited much on the stage of the twentieth-century Baptist Church.

A number of isolated challenges to traditional Protestant sexual ethics have emerged during the five hundred years of Protestant history, but none has been effective enough to trouble the Protestant status quo. One of the more interesting challenges came in the mid-nineteenth century, in upstate New York. The Oneida Community was founded by a renegade Methodist minister, John Humphrey Noyes. The community practiced free love, or what they called complex marriage, meaning everyone in the community was married to everyone else. Its members also practiced eugenics (the control of human mating), a custom that ceded authority to the leadership to designate which pairs were to procreate. The community's leaders made their decisions on the basis of physical attributes and perceived intelligence. Otherwise, sexual relationships were permitted within the community, according to individual preference. By common agreement, birth control was practiced by *coitus interruptus;* violations were considered very serious. The Oneida Community, which attracted and produced more than its share of creative people, was a dynamic enterprise for a generation, then declined in membership. It disbanded soon after the death of its charismatic leader, leaving no discernible dent in the Protestant culture from which it had sprung.

During the same period, the Mormons, led by another charismatic leader, Joseph Smith, sprang up, also in New York State. Though the Mormons had emerged from Protestantism, they established themselves as a new and distinct religious group, which developed its own particular scriptures, the Book of Mormon. Initially they advocated and practiced polygamy, flouting monogamy, which had become one of the bedrock principles of the rest of Christianity. The Mormons' motivation stemmed first from Smith's sexual promiscuity, but later was related in part to an urgency to multiply their numbers and expand rapidly as a community. A generation passed. When they migrated to Utah, it became clear that statehood would not be granted without state laws legislating monogamy. The Mormon leadership revised its marriage laws; mainstream Mormons have been monogamous ever since. In modern times they have generally presented themselves as more sexually abstemious than other Christians.

A number of isolated free-love, polygamous, or anti-marriage advocates have appeared from time to time to challenge normative Christian sexual ethics, but none have had significant influence on the mainstream. All remained, however brilliant, renegades and outliers. The central Christian thesis, only slightly less negative among Protestants than Catholics, that the "best" people have the least amount of sexual pleasure, remained well in force in the West. From Luther to 1950, nothing much changed.

Then the landscape shifted, with the eruption of the so-called "Sexual Revolution."

The Sexual Revolution was, for the most part, a revolution in the middle-class, Protestant, English-speaking world. Continental Europeans had already revolted against Christian middle-class sexual ethics. For some time, Protestant north Europe had lived its sexual life as if unaware of the sexual rules of Christianity. Southern Europe, mostly Catholic, had the dual class system of religious and nonreligious, as previously mentioned. The English-speaking world, largely Protestant, was the most conventionally "Christian" sphere in the way its laws and customs treated sexual behavior. (Exempted from these laws and customs have been, as usual, the aristocracy and the underclasses, who traditionally have lived by laws of their own.)

The Sexual Revolution, in the Christian West, should arguably have been called the Second Sexual Revolution, the first having been led by Luther and his fellow Protestants. In each of these "sexual revolutions," monasteries and convents were vacated with a stunning rapidity. Protestant leadership did not diminish in numbers, as did the Catholic leadership, but the kind of persons admitted into the clergy changed greatly. As late as 1960, in the Episcopal Church in the United States, the clergy was exclusively male, monogamous, and heterosexual. A divorced man stood a slim-to-none chance of being approved for ordination; an "out of the closet" homosexual stood no chance at all. Nor did a woman. After 1960, a homosexual person with multiple divorces could be ordained, as could women. Finally, with the ordination of women, the moral cornerstone of traditional sex values was removed. If the highest moral claim of medieval Christianity was a priesthood of men untainted by sex, but especially untainted by sexual contact with women, then the ordination of those same contaminators—women—had to be the death knell of medieval religious ethics. This is why the Catholic Church is unlikely, anytime soon, to permit the ordination of women.

The Sexual Revolution radically uncoupled sexual pleasure from the strict constraints of heterosexual monogamy. Prior to the mid-twentieth-century, premarital sexual relations would never have been acknowledged by a religiously observant Christian, either Protestant or Catholic. By the 1970s, premarital sexual relations were almost universally taken for granted. The notion of the bride as a virgin, walking the church aisle draped in symbols of her presumed sexual purity—*and* anticipating her first sexual experience on her wedding night—seemed to be facing extinction. (In the era of George W. Bush, frothy campaigns for the restoration of pre-marital virginity have picked up momentum and gained followers in high places, but it seems doubtful that they will achieve much success in the long term.) And for the first time, and in great numbers, persons claiming homosexual identities presented themselves publicly. These changes came with shocking suddenness. For most religious persons in the West, sexual pleasure had escaped the confines of monogamy. Only the Roman Catholic leadership and a few noisy Protestant leaders attempted to hold the line against such a juggernaut.

No one can say with confidence precisely what caused the Sexual Revolution. Like most events in history, it may well have been "over-determined," in the sense that the forces setting the revolution in motion were multiple, complex, and redundant. Certainly the sexual research of Alfred Kinsey in the 1950s made a monumental contribution. At the same time the discovery of the birth control pill reduced the risk of undesired pregnancy and made pre- and extramarital sexual relations less dangerous. I recall, as a college student in the early 1950s, listening to a woman lecture on the positive changes that were coming in premarital sexual behavior as a result of the pill. As I was then a divinity student who had learned the Christian catechism, I also recall that I was none too happy to hear of such changes. After all, I was a product of my own culture.

The sexual choices made by Karl Barth and Paul Tillich (see chapter 16 of this volume), though largely kept quiet, were nevertheless not entirely secret. The effects of their behavior added significant weight to the Sexual Revolution.

Likewise, the sex life of civil rights leader Martin Luther King helped push the sexual freedom movement forward. It's worth noting that FBI Director J. Edgar Hoover failed in his attempt to destroy King by exposing his sexual exploits. Hoover's evidence, put on film by undercover agents, was the sort that would have ruined a middle-class white religious leader but had no noticeable effect in the African-American community. For these Christians, strict monogamy had always been the white man's rule. Hence they did not and generally do not feel subject to the burden of middle-class morality, even when significant numbers of them started rising into the middle class.

The leaders of the various Protestant churches had to be dragged, for the most part, kicking and screaming into the Sexual Revolution. Though cautious and conservative as is typical of bureaucrats, Protestant leaders could not ignore (as Vatican leaders could) rumblings from below. For example, in the Episcopal Church in the United States, bishops remained obstinate in the face of widespread rank and file sentiment that favored ordaining women. The leadership declined to permit such an innovation. Then, in 1974, four renegade bishops performed irregular ordinations for a group of women, who were called the "Philadelphia Eleven."[1] The fact that this action was not legal (according to church law) turned out to be irrelevant. It was another instance of *de facto* trumping *de jure*. Two years later, Episcopal Church leadership capitulated on the issue of the ordination of women. Except among scattered atavistic[2] subgroups, the Episcopal Church has ordained women in great numbers in the years since.

Even if the Sexual Revolution was mainly a Protestant phenomenon, its effects carried over into the larger culture, and into other religious groups.

In the Roman Catholic Church, the summoning of the Second Vatican Council by Pope John XXIII, in 1962, coincided with the emerging Sexual Revolution. The Vatican Council offered the promise of profound changes, and hope was widespread for an institutional transformation. In fact, a great many changes were made by the Council, but none had much to do with the church's position on sexual behavior. Celibacy, birth control, and divorce were reserved as special subjects controlled by the Pope. These topics were not even allowed to be publicly discussed—a decision made by both John XXIII, who died before the Council ended, and his successor Paul VI.

The Catholic theologian Hans Kung was a major voice for change in the Catholic Church from the 1960s onward. Kung is a progressive liberal who has not equivocated in challenging the autocracy of the Vatican. He courageously attacked the doctrine of papal infallibility but, for whatever reasons, has not had much to say on sexual issues. In his monumental eight-hundred page tome, *On Being a Christian* (1984),[3] sex isn't treated with so much as a paragraph. In a religious community where sex is listed first on every moral agenda, such an omission is astonishing. Kung probably recognized that he had to pick his battles, always at the risk of being punished by Rome. Perhaps he saw the claim of papal infallibility as more important, more deserving of the expenditure of his capital, than the sexual issue. Which was the same position Luther took in the start of the Reformation. As it turned out, Kung was silenced by Rome anyway.

Among those who did speak openly and boldly for a change in the church's position on sexual ethics, the most articulate was Kung's contemporary, Jacques Pohier, a French Dominican priest. A more articulate protester than contemporary Protestants, he is an unsung hero of the twentieth-century Catholic Church.

Pohier spoke pointedly on the failure of celibacy: "An increasing number of priests and religious of both sexes no longer feel that to abstain from all affective and sexual life, or repress it, is a privileged means of achieving the goal."[4]

He described the plight of the many Catholics who felt their hopes dashed soon after the collapse of any prospect of sexual reforms by Vatican II. Progressive Catholics soon came to the awareness that, in spite of all the talk, little had changed. Especially on matters of sexual behavior, the Catholic Church remained more firmly frozen than ever in its posture toward sex. Pohier described aging Catholics who felt pain and bitterness and shame for having their sexuality, in his words, "stolen from them by the Church."[5]

With astonishing forthrightness and candor, Pohier contended that even non-exclusive marital relationships were compatible with faith:

Men and women of profound belief ... discover that an emotional monolith is not necessarily the ideal form for a marital relationship, and that while the existence of other emotional commitments can indeed break up their own relationship, it can sometimes further it, and at all events, enrich first themselves, and then their relationship, and their partner.[6]

He gleaned wisdom from psychology, from psychoanalytic theory, and from his personal experience of psychoanalysis and used his learning to criticize the Church practice:

> I have known very eminent religious who thought they had no sexual life because they had the sexual life of a boy of eight, working hard and well, and thinking of mummy every day.[7]

Pohier's trenchant critiques gained him considerable attention, and considerable heat, from the Vatican. When he was invited to address a meeting of sex educators in France in 1973, he told them that, as the requirement for a good math teacher is to like math and to want students to like math, so sex educators should like sex and wish for their students to take pleasure in sex, too. For Rome, this was the last straw.[8]

Pohier's brilliance did not impress the leadership of his church in a positive sense. The Vatican silenced him, forbidding him to teach, preach, or participate in any liturgical events. He has the distinction of being the first in a long line of Catholic theologians disciplined by Pope John Paul II. He had enough of a following to continue publishing books, and his voice continued to be heard by others, both inside and outside the Catholic Church. But leaders of the Catholic Church remained deaf to his wisdom. What followed was an exodus from convents, monasteries, and rectories—a reduction in force from which the Catholic Church has yet to recover. Pohier left the Dominican order in 1984.

Pohier was more than merely a dissident Catholic priest. Much more. Steeped in psychology and psychoanalytic theory, he spoke the truth about Christianity's peculiar approach to sexual pleasure, then suffered punishment at the hands of an authoritarian system. He gained no ground against the impregnable, negative artifice of Catholic teaching on sex, but he lived the life of a courageous prophet, a man who paid a price, in a dark time, for telling the truth.

Among Protestants only a few voices of sexual liberation made themselves heard, Rustum and Della Roy and James B. Nelson among the notable few. The large majority remained silent, or spoke negatively about sexual liberation. But a yeasty religious movement emerged early in the twentieth century that was to prepare the soil for the Sexual Revolution to come. It was the so-called "clinical pastoral movement," and it was to alter radically the environment in mainstream Protestantism in the United States in ways that prepared congregations to accept the basic tenets of the Sexual Revolution. No public announcement of this preparation was made; in fact, the preparation went on "under the radar." The preparation consisted of a radical shift in the way religious leadership was trained. Like medicine at the turn of the century, the professional ministry was reshaped by a radical new posture toward ministry, the so-called "clinical." This word derives from the Greek word for "bed" and is meant to connote a primary attention to the body (in bed) and to the data provided by the body, as opposed to primary attention given to ideas or doctrines.

Clinical training for ministers reoriented (as it did for physicians) their posture toward their parishioners. Ministers began to pay attention to what was good for the person, rather than relying solely on doctrines and theories. To paraphrase a saying of Jesus, "Religion was made for man, not man for religion."[9] Among the clinically trained, what was good for the person would now supplant what was "right thinking" or "correct" doctrine.

Clinical training was the twentieth-century route by which ministers became more competent pastoral counselors. The movement continues into the present. This training provides a strong alliance with psychology in general. Ministers become more knowledgeable psychologically. Many personally undertake psychotherapy or psychoanalysis. They are made more aware through clinical training that the principal tool of the minister is the *self*, a radical shift from the notion of a minister as the bearer of certain correct religious dogmas. This change has a liberating effect on a minister's approach to his charges, leading to a more humanistic posture in general, and to a more tolerant posture toward sexual behavior in particular. Thus it was that the clinical training movement, beginning in earnest in 1925, actually prepared the ground in the Protestant churches for the Sexual Revolution to come. It had a generation to do its advance work. The clinical pastoral movement effectively dismantled Christianity's long-standing repugnance for sexual pleasure. This is a story that has not received much attention in church literature.

The professional practitioners of the clinical pastoral training movement are called "clinical pastoral supervisors." They typically do their teaching in the context of general or psychiatric hospitals where they train other ministers in the skills of pastoral counseling and pastoral psychotherapy. During their heyday, in the mid-twentieth century, this was an especially eccentric collection of ministers. Their influence far surpassed their numbers, which never exceeded about eight hundred at any one time. Furthermore, sexual conventions were not all that was challenged by these clinically trained ministers. They challenged all three legs of the stool of conventional Protestant ethics: the prohibition against alcohol, tobacco, and sex. Nearly all the early clinical pastoral supervisors were drinkers and smokers and tended to be sexually liberated in one way or another. Many died of alcoholism, others of cancer; many suffered economic hardships for their protest against the principal ethical claims of Protestantism. But whatever their shortcomings, these men—and they were almost all men until the 1960s—trained most of the younger mainstream Protestant leadership in the United States. These clinical pastoral supervisors were widely seen by rank and file clergy as counselors, consultants, and therapists available for critical pastoral problems.

The clinical pastoral movement was sexually liberating because it sat at the feet of psychology in general, and of Sigmund Freud in particular. In addition, a great number of the early leaders of the movement were openly liberated in their sexual behavior. But it was not Freud's theories, or the field of psychology, which created the clinical pastoral movement; the movement was principally born of the efforts of an obscure Presbyterian minister named Anton Theophilus Boisen.[10]

In the late 1950s, by the time Elvis Presley heralded, in his inimitable way, the Sexual Revolution, the younger Protestant clergymen were ready for action, because they had studied under the sexually liberating spell of the clinical pastoral training movement. Thus in Protestantism generally, the Sexual Revolution had a soft landing.

The Sexual Revolution brought the fresh air of honesty into religious communities and laid an axe to the root of the tree of medieval sexual values. Protestantism changed its heart and changed its way of functioning in regard to sexual values but did not complete the task by formalizing a changed position on sex, at least not in ways people could understand.

Basic assumptions about what constitutes a moral sexual life must neither be passed over in silence, nor obscured by generalities. Until it deals with formalizing its positions on sex and morality, Protestantism will remain in danger of reverting, if only by implication, to the safe harbor of sex-phobic medieval teaching.

CHAPTER 15

ANTON BOISEN'S CONTRIBUTION TO THE SEXUAL REVOLUTION

The strong influence of Anton T. Boisen (1876–1965) on sexual ethics was both inadvertent and indirect. He would be surprised—probably amazed—to know of his contribution. And were he yet alive to witness it, he may not be entirely pleased by the result. Whatever positive assessment one could make of Boisen and his contribution, he personally never quite escaped the burden of sexual repression placed on him by his mother. The injunction stamped into his psyche, and fully absorbed by him, was that sex was a powerful and malignant drive. In spite of the restrictions he imposed on himself, Boisen was paradoxically the main original source of sexual liberation in American Protestantism. That is, to whatever extent it became liberated.

The clinical pastoral training movement that revolutionized American religion in the twentieth century was the creation principally of Boisen and his principal lieutenant, Helen Flanders Dunbar (1902–1959). She typically dropped "Helen" in professional usage so as to leave her gender undisclosed. She was defending herself against the denigration of women in professional roles that were presumed to belong solely to men. In addition to the stated purpose of revolutionizing the training of ministers, the clinical pastoral movement also overturned the basic sexual teachings of American Christianity. Boisen and Dunbar together, in fact, mounted the only significant and effective challenge to accepted Christian sexual ethics in the West since Luther.

They were an unlikely pair of religious revolutionaries. Boisen was a failed Presbyterian minister and sometime psychotic, and Dunbar was not a minister at all, but a psychiatrist by trade, a published literary critic, and a cosmopolitan polymath with academic degrees in medicine, theology, and literature.

Both Boisen and Dunbar were sexually unconventional, though polar opposites individually. Boisen's conflict over sexual pleasure took him into five psychotic episodes, including three hospitalizations, the first and most serious one lasting 15 months. Dunbar was a sophisticate in the European mold and part of the sexual avant guard of the early twentieth century. Dunbar was as sexually liberated as Boisen was sexually constrained. If Dunbar was later punished for her daring, Boisen punished himself for his wish to be daring. Dunbar's first husband, Theodore Wolfe, brought Wilhelm Reich and his orgone box to the United States, promoting sexual liberation in a quite courageous manner.[1] It is said by those who knew Dunbar that her breakfast table in the 1940s might be occupied by daughter, husband, and ex-husband, all breaking bread together in apparent harmony. Boisen probably never had more than the most fleeting sexual relationship his entire life and that with Dunbar herself. Dunbar's alliance with Boisen was a most unlikely one.

The personal sexual biographies of Boisen and Dunbar were not the material that changed the sexual landscape in the religious communities of the United States but, rather, the philosophical basis of clinical training for ministers that they jointly invented and promoted and the effect of this training on the life and work of the typical congregational minister. Nevertheless, the personal stories of Boisen and Dunbar, and more especially the former, are not irrelevant to their public accomplishments. In fact, their respective biographies are quite instructive. In this respect Boisen is unique in that he wrote his autobiography as if it were a case study. It was the "case" he knew best, as he put it. James Hillman calls it an "absolutely remarkable autobiographical account of a mental breakdown."[2] We have no autobiography of Dunbar, unfortunately, but we do know that her views about what constituted proper sexual conduct were quite counter-cultural and that she lived a life that appropriately would be referred to as "sexually liberated."

We learn from Boisen's autobiography that at barely four years of age his mother found him engaged, as he put it, in "sexual organ excitation which seemed beyond normal."[3] Notions of what was "beyond normal" obviously were his mother's, not the four-year-old Anton's. His parents did their duty. They rushed him off to a physician and had him summarily circumcized. The treatment, as Boisen himself confesses, failed to correct the problem. One year later his mother discovered him engaged in mutual exploration with a boy cousin a year younger. "The horror on my mother's face (after she washed his mouth with soap!) and her volunteered promise that she would not tell my father are impressions which still remain," wrote Boisen.[4]

These memories from Boisen's early childhood are stark ones. He took them to be key markers on his road to psychosis. In a peculiar and paradoxical way, Boisen seemed to have understood that his mother's teaching about sex was the beginning of his problems and the crux of his lifelong struggle for sanity and wisdom. Furthermore, Boisen appeared never to have recovered from the maternal assault on his sexuality. In fact he seems to have absorbed fully his mother's message, that sexual pleasure was something to be avoided, a message that he seems to have lived by for the rest of his life. But he did succeed in understanding that his inner conflict over sexual pleasure was the key to his psychological problems. That discovery was a critical breakthrough for him, limited as it was.

Whatever protection Boisen may have had from his father was ended when his father died of heart failure at age 37. Boisen himself was seven years old. He remembered with affection his father teaching him about trees and plants, memories that were to shape his later life.

Not long after his father's death, Boisen heard his grandfather speak of winking as a protective function of the eye, and he quietly resolved not to be defensive. In an altercation with some bullies trying to steal pears from a tree in his yard, Boisen faced the bullies and was threatened by the interlopers, who put a nail gun in his face. When the gun was fired, the nail penetrated Boisen eyeball without touching the lid, thus proving to Boisen himself that he was steadfast, because he did not blink. He spent the rest of his life as a one-eyed man, and a single minded one as well. In this strange, almost deliberate blinding of himself, and that so soon after his father's death, the associations with Oedipus are irresistible.

As Boisen grew older, he seldom engaged in peer discussions about sex, even with his close friends. But he had plenty that he would have liked to discuss with someone. He felt that his sexual interests could neither be controlled nor acknowledged for fear of condemnation, certainly a difficult spot for any adolescent.

In college Boisen first decided to major in languages and French literature. In reading a French novel by Emile Zola, he reported that he had several spontaneous orgasms "induced by fantasies of the opposite sex." He felt that he had crossed a line that he had determined he would not cross.[5]

The next troubling episode that Boisen reports in his autobiography occurred when obscene words jumped off the page of the Greek dictionary and hit him in the eye, presumably the one good eye. He was self-reflective enough to know by then that he was in some kind of psychological trouble. He did not know what to do about the problem, so he elected, like Oedipus, to talk with his mother, probably the worst of all possible choices. He did find her understanding. Later he talked with a professor he trusted, who told him that "it would always be necessary to fight for control of the instincts" and that he "must look to Christ for help, and to some good woman."[6] Boisen changed his college major to forestry, undoubtedly in memory of his father—and probably because trees would not arouse him sexually as French literature had.

In 1902, at age 26, Boisen met the woman of his life, Alice Batchelder, a YWCA secretary. It was a one-sided love at first sight. Alice was seemingly a moral replica of Boisen's mother. After meeting her, he promised to reward himself with the privilege of writing her, provided he could control his sexual urges for three months. When he finally wrote, she did not answer. He then followed up with a visit to her home and received a chilly response. After he wrote three more letters, Alice wrote back asking him to stop writing and thinking of her further. He describes his reaction as a "horrible sense of failure and guilt," followed by three orgasms without erections, in rapid succession. The suggestion here is that Boisen took some masochistic pleasure in being rejected by Alice.

Boisen next wrote to tell Alice that he was called to the ministry and would study at Union Theological Seminary in New York. She then agreed to meet with him. They prayed together. He kissed her proffered hand. When he wrote her subsequent to their meeting, she responded that her first answer still stood: There was to be no correspondence.

But Alice changed her mind when Boisen finally entered seminary, where he spent "the three happiest years" of his life, presumably in part because of his correspondence with Alice. She sent him a photo. She suggested they correspond in French. He continued in English, apparently without comment, undoubtedly remembering Zola. She visited him at seminary at Christmas, 1910, and told him that there was no other man in her life and that she would give her heart a chance. Boisen's roommate observed that Alice did not show Boisen the kind of affection that he would have expected. Then Boisen visited Alice in New Hampshire, after which she announced that it was God's will that the relationship not be continued. He wrote her begging, and by Christmas, 1911, she agreed to correspond again.

When Boisen wrote Alice, at the completion of his seminary studies, to tell her that he was soon going to take a position as pastor of a rural church, she replied that she was good at keeping house and making donuts. When he "replied accordingly," she answered back in a stinging rebuke, saying that she had never loved him and that the relationship must cease.

After several years and a couple of failed positions as a minister, Boisen went to Europe during World War I as a YMCA worker. On his return, he attempted to visit Alice, who was then living in Chicago. She refused to see him. Later, however, she agreed to correspond and even invited him to call on her at home when he was making his next trip through Chicago.

In October 1920, while living temporarily with his mother, Boisen was seized by six policemen and a physician and delivered to the psychiatric hospital in Westboro, Massachusetts, where he remained for the next 15 months, by far the longest of three psychiatric hospitalizations he experienced.

Once Boisen settled down and regained some rationality at Westboro, he began to think about the meaning of his delusions. One of his delusions was that he must go insane into order to get married. In another, he saw himself as a personal symbolic representative of the sex instinct and because of that deserved to die. He attempted suicide several times during the early days of his hospitalization. Another delusion was that he was called to break down the wall between medicine and religion. By that he meant that religious experience and psychosis shared common ground, and that the source of religious knowledge was often delusional, or appeared as delusions.

Each of Boisen's three delusions was profoundly true, an invitation to him to move deeper into self-awareness. The last of the three seems to have been the only delusion that Boisen reflected upon with great seriousness and perseverance. He spent the rest of his life following its injunction. It is noteworthy, however, that the first two delusions were not ones that Boisen explored, at least not in relation to himself. In retrospect, he seems the poorer for it.

In his lucid periods Boisen was thus a strong advocate of the view that delusions carried important content that must be taken seriously. He said of himself, many years later, "I was never more nearly right than at the very moment I was taken to the hospital."[7] The cure, Boisen believed, lay in the faithful carrying through of the delusion itself. He buttressed his conviction that psychotic delusions offer healing content to the soul. He referred to numerous historical examples of the experiences of religious figures, such as George Fox, who reached important religious knowledge through what appeared to have been psychotic experiences. Boisen's physicians, taking a strong and rigidly organic view of mental illness, were unsympathetic. One of the few physicians who would talk with him, by Boisen's account, suggested that Boisen's great mistake had been in not giving freer rein to the sex impulse. He had heard that bit of advice before, something that, as his mother's child, he did not want to hear. The physician's mistake was in giving Boisen advice in what to do rather than exploring the source and meaning of his sexual conflicts.

Boisen's ambivalence is obvious. He wanted to understand his own strange mental processes, but he appears to have resisted examining deeply his mother's contribution to his difficulties. He went only half way to the well. But he did go half way. All along Boisen was aware that he was psychologically troubled, but all along he was willing to work only on certain aspects of his disturbance. He had sought a course in psychology as a seminarian at Union Theological Seminary in hopes of learning something about himself. Only in his middler year did the seminary finally introduce such an innovative course, to Boisen's delight, and probably in part because of Boisen's insistence. But the course did not go into psychopathology, to Boisen's regret.

While Boisen was hospitalized, a good friend sent him Sigmund Freud's *Introductory Lectures*, a surprising gesture toward a patient in a psychiatric hospital, but also an indication of how seriously self-reflective Boisen was about his own mental processes. This book provided Boisen with his first contact with Freud. He was very excited to find Freud confirming his own independently-arrived-at ideas.

As Boisen put it:

Freud's conclusions are so strikingly in line with those which I had already formed that it makes me believe in myself a little bit more ... He asserts that neuroses, i.e., abnormal or insane conditions, have a purpose, that they are due to deep-seated conflict between great subconscious forces and the cure is to be found not in the suppression of the symptoms but in the solution to the conflict.[8]

As might be expected, Boisen could not accept one of Freud's views, one similar to Boisen's own physicians, that lowering the bars of inhibitions would resolve some of the conflict over sex.

Boisen consistently viewed his psychosis and his hospitalization as a vital and enriching experience, deepening his self-understanding without which he would have been a poorer man. He even held the view later in life, that if Alice had married him as he wished, he would have turned out to be a passably successful minister, living a relatively uneventful life, but would not have created the clinical pastoral training movement.

In January 1922, Boisen was released from Westboro Hospital. He felt like a traveler back from a distant country. In an amazing rebound, he was appointed Chaplain of Worcester State Hospital two-and-a-half years later. In the period immediately after his release, Boisen took courses at Harvard Medical School, where Dr. Richard Cabot taught him the case method for training physicians. Boisen was determined to apply this method to mental illness, his own and other's, and to train ministers for work with such patients. He was on his crusade to break down the walls between medicine and religion, the delusion he was willing to examine and pursue in detail. And apparently enough people were listening that Boisen was beginning to get attention. Cabot had taken a keen interest in Boisen and had supported him both morally and financially. He accepted a part-time teaching appointment at Chicago Theological Seminary while continuing to hold his position at Worcester State Hospital.

Then in the summer of 1925, Boisen organized his first clinical pastoral training course. Four students registered. One was Helen Flanders Dunbar, then a 22-year-old middler at Union Theological Seminary, who was simultaneously working on her Ph.D. in literature at Yale, and also on a Med.Sci.D. at Columbia. (She hired two secretaries to keep up with her course paperwork, one in New Haven and one in New York.) Dunbar was quick to see the significance of what he was doing. "I saw her as an instrument of the highest precision sent to help in the new undertaking," he wrote.[9] Dunbar returned to work with Boisen in the spring of 1927. Meanwhile his now annual summer training program grew in numbers. Boisen was on his way to transforming the work of training ministers and breaking down the wall between medicine and religion.

On his release from Westboro, Boisen had written to Alice, who agreed to resume correspondence. For two years he wrote her weekly letters that included daily diaries. It is not clear whether she wrote back, or if so, how often. When he suggested she join him in his new clinical undertakings, she wrote back withdrawing permission for him to write further. Even so, in the spring of 1924, while teaching at Chicago Theological Seminary, Boisen attempted to visit Alice. She refused to see him. He then wrote her a letter that is different from all the other communications he had sent her. The time had come, he said, to end this one-sided relationship.

But Alice herself reestablished contact in 1927 and agreed to see him the following year. This time her change of heart seems to have been related to the appearance of Dunbar in Boisen's life. The reappearance of Alice presented the inhibited Boisen with a conflict. He now had two women on the string, however thin the string may have been. Boisen began feeling troubled. "It was hard to see the way," as he put it.[10] The resolution Boisen came to was to ask both Alice and Dunbar to join him at the Hilton Chapel in Chicago, to kneel at the altar for a quasimarital covenant of friendship. Both women agreed, but Dunbar suddenly and sensibly left for Europe prior to the scheduled event. So only Alice showed up for this peculiar quasimarital ceremony, which took place on Thanksgiving Day, 1929. She was favorably impressed.

Boisen reported in his autobiography that the conflict he felt in trying to relate simultaneously to two women led to another psychotic episode in the fall of 1930. "The gracious shadow of another, younger woman" threatened his relationship with Alice, the primary object of his affection.[11] Though Boisen does not say so, it seems likely that his mother's death in June of that year contributed to his mental disturbance as well. He was hospitalized this time for only three weeks. Both Alice and Dunbar stood by him in this crisis. Professionally he hardly skipped a beat, running his usual summer program in 1931. But he did come close to losing his nascent clinical training organization. His principal benefactor, Cabot, turned against him, declaring him to be unfit for the ministry because of his mental status. Cabot was by then the president of the organization that Boisen and his lieutenants had founded to promote clinical training for clergy, the Council for the Clinical Training of Theological Students (CCTTS). Dunbar, who was Medical Director of that organization, remained loyal to Boisen and rejected Cabot's negative assessment. She then seized the books of the CCTTS, took them to New York City, and set up a new office there, out of the reach of Cabot. She in effect instigated a coup, distancing Cabot, and supporting Boisen in his leadership position. But a gulf now appeared among this small band of visionaries, and it centered on a differing view of the meaning and significance of mental disturbance.

In April 1932, Boisen left Massachusetts to take the position of Chaplain at Elgin State Hospital near Chicago, ostensibly to be closer to Chicago Theological Seminary, where he continued as a part-time professor. Being near Alice was a part of his motivation, as he declares in his autobiography. Putting some distance between Cabot and him may have been added motivation. In Chicago Boisen typically met Alice once a month for dinner and a concert or theater. Then in August 1935, Alice wrote that she was to have surgery and was going into retirement. She asked for no callers and no flowers. Apparently, without ever seeing Boisen again, she died in December of cancer. In her last weeks Boisen developed recurring psychotic symptoms and was spirited away by his colleagues to Sheppard Pratt Hospital in Baltimore, where news reached him of Alice's death. He was released after a two-week stay. Subsequently, for the next 30 years, Boisen apparently had no further psychotic episodes. Both his mother and Alice Batchelder were dead.

From one perspective Alice was the proverbial virago. From another she was the perfect match for Boisen. She was cut from the same cloth as Boisen's mother, and, as one might have predicted, she enthralled Boisen for as long as she lived. The relationship lasted for more than 30 years, but it is highly unlikely that Boisen ever got so much as a kiss from her. However, she met Boisen's psychological needs, reinforcing his maternal injunctions to control, with an iron fist, his sexual impulses.

Boisen wrote his autobiography to reveal the madness that led to his creativity. His mother had seemingly put a curse on his sexual impulses, and his choice of Alice as his life's partner was a fulfillment of his mother's curse. Boisen seemed to know the dimensions of his affliction, but he was powerless to escape them. His understanding of his inner conflict helped him to identify with others who were similarly conflicted, which likely includes just about everyone in one degree or another. He also saw with great clarity the convergence of inner conflict and religious experience. The astonishing aspect of Boisen's life is that he was able to turn his mental affliction into a source of wisdom and was able to point the way for many others to find personal integration. For Boisen, it was enough to know the source of his mental anguish. He did not seem to feel the need to explore or rethink his own constrained posture toward sexual pleasure. Thus he never had a satisfactory sexual life. (Freud felt somewhat the same way about himself, that he had liberated others sexually, but benefited little himself.)

Boisen did show the way for countless others to live a more rewarding life through a more liberated posture toward sexual pleasure. As Boisen so wonderfully put it, regarding sex education, and by implication regarding therapy in general, "It is not what the counselor says to the boy, but what the boy says to the counselor."[12] It was the kind of therapy that Boisen never found for himself, but he knew the need for it and its value. And he founded a movement that trained ministers to provide that kind of therapy. Boisen did dismantle to a considerable extent the wall between religion and medicine and thus pursued the content of one of his delusions.

By 1960, most of the younger mainstream Protestant clergy in the United States had had at least one summer's experience of clinical training from Boisen or one of the increasing numbers of his protegees. (Catholics and

Jews participated in significant numbers after 1960.) Consequently, most of the mainstream Protestant clergy came to recognize, earlier or later, the importance of at least minimal training in psychology. Furthermore, they also recognized the critical matter of their own personhood, their own sense of self, as the key to their work as religious professionals. This was a monumental achievement that is attributable to Boisen.

Some of the followers of Boisen from the 1920s onward became generally more devotedly followers of Freud than of Boisen. Psychoanalytic theory and sexual liberation permeated the clinical pastoral movement. (In the oral tradition there is a credible story of a ministerial protégée of Boisen's who drove around Texas with an orgone box strapped to the top of his automobile.) This love affair with the psychoanalytic movement occurred in large part because it gave allegedly scientific support for the same arguments Boisen was making. Boisen was a relative unknown and a simple preacher, not a Viennese physician. This was galling to Boisen in later life, because he felt that the movement was deferring too much to psychology and abandoning religion. After all, it was not psychology that saved him from madness. It was faith. Or both. Furthermore, Boisen remained rather abstemious in his own attitude toward sex and wary of Freud's libertarian views on sexual behavior. He strongly objected to the trend, as he saw it, in lowering the conscience threshold in regard to sexual behavior. The irony here is that the key figure in helping Protestantism enter the age of the Sexual Revolution without self-destructing was himself sexually repressed, and rather seriously so.

Freud the atheist and Boisen the theist did have much in common. They each sought to explore the inner life in an attempt to address the deeper meaning of life, whether religious or philosophical. The common ground between Freud and the clinical pastoral movement of Boisen is alluded to by Richard Schweder in a *New York Times* op-ed piece called, "It's Time to Reinvent Freud."[13] Schweder laments the wide dismissal of Freud in modern culture. He argues that psychoanalysis is a secular religion that tries to address the deeper meaning of life. The major interest currently in psychoanalytic theory, he asserts, is in schools of theology or on Broadway. Schweder calls for a remarriage of psychoanalysis with theology. The ghost of Boisen lends support to the claims of Richard Schweder.

The clinical pastoral movement itself became much bigger than Boisen, and it ran onward without him, especially as he aged. The movement also divided into several subgroups. Those in the Cabot camp, for example, created their own strong subgroup separate from the CCTTS. But Anton Boisen, with critical assistance from Flanders Dunbar, left an indelible mark on religion in the United States and provided the theological and theoretical framework that permitted the mid-century Protestant religious communities in the United States to participate in the Sexual Revolution.

CHAPTER 16

PAUL TILLICH AND KARL BARTH: SEXUAL OUTLIERS

By almost any assessment, the most influential Christian thinkers and theorists of the twentieth century were Karl Barth (1886–1968) and Paul Tillich (1886–1965). The marks these two men made on theological and ethical thinking crossed generational, national, and religious boundaries. Even Pope Pius XII characterized Barth, a Protestant, as "the greatest theologian since Thomas Aquinas."[1] He should probably have added that if Barth was the greatest, Tillich was the most influential, not only among Protestants but among Roman Catholics, Jews and even the nonreligious.

Each of these influential theologians demonstrated, by behavior especially, and to some extent by his teaching, his rejection of the established sexual ethics of both the Christian Church and the middle class, which (the established ethics of church and class) were about the same thing. The personal lives of these two men speak more loudly than their words. Each reached his prime in the 1920s and 1930s in Germany; each was influenced, to some extent, by European libertinism of the early twentieth century.

To state facts boldly, Tillich was a philanderer, or "womanizer," as one of his fellow theologians, Norman Pittenger, insisted on putting it.[2] And Barth was a functional bigamist who lived the entire second half of his 80 years in a household with two women, both of whom were sexually intimate with him.

Unfortunately for us, Barth left no autobiographical comment, at least for public consumption, on the subject of his personal sexual history. Tillich did share his thoughts and feelings on the matter of his sexual behavior but did so only privately with several close colleagues. He *published* nothing on the subject. In that respect, the challenge of each of these men to normative sexual ethics remains muted, but a challenge nevertheless.

The parallels in the biographies of these two men are striking.[3] They were both born in 1886, Barth on May 10 and Tillich on August 20. Tillich was a Brandenberger German, Barth was a German-speaking Swiss. Each was sympathetic to the socialist movement early in the twentieth century. Barth came to be known as the "red pastor" in his first parish, partly due to his support of unions over the objections of factory owners who were parish members. Both men taught in German universities in the 1930s; Barth taught in Bonn, and Tillich taught in Frankfurt. Barth, born in Switzerland, later took German citizenship. Both men were among the small cadre of Christian leaders who criticized Hitler and Nazism. Each was targeted for dismissal early in the Nazi era. When Tillich was dismissed, as soon as the Nazis came to power in 1933, he immigrated to the United States; Barth was dismissed from his teaching position two years later.

Initially Barth thought he could continue working under the new regime. He even gave substitute lectures for a teacher named Karl Ludwig, whom the Nazis had suspended. Barth, however, was under suspicion from the beginning. Among other things, he adamantly refused to open his lectures with the required salute, "Heil Hitler!" At first, Barth showed no particular sensitivity regarding the Nazi assault on the Jews, which began during the first month of their rule. Later he expressed regret that he had not done more to protest. Only when Hitler moved to nazify the Protestant churches did Barth come into direct conflict with the government. When the Nazis attempted to install "Reich Bishop" Ludwig Muller as a pro-Nazi authority over Protestants, Barth assumed leadership of a minority pan-Protestant counter-government movement, which called itself the "Confessing Church." It was a shadow church, which developed first out of Martin Niemoeller's "Pastors' Emergency League." The League was founded in November of 1933 to oppose Hitlerite authority over the Protestant churches. Hitler was slow to punish Niemoeller, who had been a submarine hero in World War I. Niemoeller survived World War II, albeit in prison.

In May 1934, the "Confessing Church" organized itself around the Barmen Declaration, a document drafted by Barth. The Barmen Declaration provided a theological rationale for renouncing the pro-Nazi "German Christian" movement among Protestants. In November of 1934, Barth refused to sign the Nazi loyalty oath; the next month he was dismissed from his teaching post. Just prior to his dismissal, Barth preached a sermon entitled, "Jesus Christ was a Jew." That this was a brave gesture on his part was reflected by the fact that some members of his congregation walked out in protest. Barth fled to Switzerland, where he lived and taught for the rest of his life.

After taming most of the Protestants, Hitler had virtually all of German Christianity under his thumb. The Pope had earlier made his peace with

Hitler, in the infamous treaty called the Reich Concordat of September, 1933. In retrospect, it's shocking to see photographs of Nazi Youth Day in 1933 Berlin; they show a number of Catholic cardinals and bishops on stage, offering the Nazi salute.[4]

Barth met Charlotte von Kirschbaum after he'd been married ten years, and about the time his wife Nelly was pregnant with their fifth and last child. Charlotte—or "Lollo," as she was called—was an attractive, vivacious 25-year-old, six years younger than Barth's wife Nelly. Lola had been a Red Cross nurse in World War I. She developed a keen interest in theology and a special interest in Barth, with whom she soon became sexually involved. He got to know her more intimately when she visited his mountain cabin at Bergli. He later visited her in Bamberg, in "wonderment." With a wife and five young children, Barth was now clearly smitten by "another woman."

In a stunningly audacious move, in 1929, Lollo joined the Barth household as a new member of the family. It was an undeclared *ménage à trois*. For the rest of her life, Lollo functioned as Barth's theological student, his secretary, and eventually his unacknowledged coauthor. Late in life she became a respected theologian and lecturer in her own right. In Barth's words, she became his "faithful fellow worker ... stayed by [his] side and was indispensable in every way."[5] She shared his work and shared much of his relaxation away from work.

We will probably never know what the Barth family experienced in this *ménage*, because no one on the inside seems to have left any testimony behind. According to Eberhard Busch, who, in Barth's final years, succeeded Lollo as private secretary (and became Barth's official biographer), the relationship caused the two women, and Barth himself, unspeakable suffering. (Although one does get the impression that Barth's followers suffer far more now than Barth's family did then.) In Busch's words, "Tensions arose which shook them to the core."[6] With the arrival of Lollo in the family home, Nelly retreated into a background of domesticity and child-rearing. Barth's mother, among other people, took offense at the arrival of this "other woman," and took her son to task on the matter. In the face of such interpersonal tension, Barth remained adamant and insisted that he was not negotiable on the subject of Lollo's presence in the family. Probably in an effort to relieve some interpersonal tension, he and Lollo regularly retreated to Bergli for summer vacations, a move that doubtless made Barth's relationship with Lollo even more transparent. The pair also traveled throughout Europe on numerous occasions, often with another couple, the Pestalozzis. A revealing family snapshot, taken in 1930, shows Barth in the center, with Lollo to his immediate right and Nelly on his far left, three children interposed between them. Busch's authorized biography merely implies that the relationship between Lollo and Barth was a sexual one. Barth's followers didn't wish to touch the subject of Lollo; even today they are generally taciturn on the matter.

But a Barthian theologian, Martin Rumscheidt, is an insider who was one of the first to discuss the matter openly. At some point after Barth died, Rumscheidt interviewed one of Barth's sons, who confirmed that the relationship with Lollo had been sexual. The son said that Barth acknowledged this in a family meeting soon after Lollo moved in. According to this account, Barth promised to end the sexual aspect of the relationship.[7] Whether the promise was actually made—and if made, was kept—Lollo remained in the Barth household for the rest of her life, continuing to work, travel, and vacation with him. She also accompanied him on his only trip to the United States in 1962. Whatever the continuing sexual dimensions of the triangular relationship, Lollo remained under the Barth roof, and, for four decades, continued as the central woman in Barth's life.

While Nelly stayed in the background as far as the world of theology was concerned, and perhaps even in terms of Barth's primary affection, she seems to have been content within the limitations of that arrangement. Hardly a wounded recluse, she is said to have kept a warmly hospitable home. It should also be noted that Nelly had the best part of Barth's last years. Then, when he was working less, Nelly could claim more of him. After Barth's second prostate operation, in 1964, he wore a permanent catheter. He wrote that Nelly looked after him "as well as a nursing sister, or even better."[8] The perhaps unconscious comparison of Nelly with a nursing sister is noteworthy, because Lollo had originally been a nurse. During these final years, Barth and Nelly grew much closer. He dedicated his last book to his wife, "with whom I am now able to celebrate a really harmonious 'evening of my life.'"[9]

While Barth was recuperating from his surgeries, Lollo was diagnosed with an unspecified chronic brain disease. She moved to a residential nursing home in January, 1966. Even in his decrepitude, Barth did not neglect Lollo during her hospitalization. Visiting her regularly on Sunday afternoons, sometimes he sang to her, especially when she was unresponsive. "But we had a good time, didn't we," she said to him once as he was leaving. Her dying took a decade. In her invalid state she outlived Barth by seven years.

To charge Barth with abusing Nelly, as some have done, would imply also that she was willing to be abused, and on a prolonged basis. More likely she made peace with the destiny that seemed to be hers. Some of Barth's followers clearly wished Barth would divorce Nelly and marry Lollo. Divorce would have provided both Nelly and Lollo with more dignity in middle-class social circles, but one can almost hear Barth railing scornfully against any such efforts to gain "middle-class respectability," one of his favorite epithets. That Barth managed to integrate a household of two women and five children, each of whom seems to have been grateful to have participated in his life, is impressive testimony to his skill, wisdom, love—and, not least, his audacity.

Barring the disclosure of some unknown document—which is not a far-fetched scenario, as his archives are said now to be tightly controlled—we have no record regarding how Barth understood his sexual and marital behavior. In certain writings, he was a strong proponent of monogamy, of the importance of one man with one woman. However, Barth was, like both Abelard and Luther, a dialectician. For every question there was both a "yes" and a "no" response. Even if one must say either "yes" or "no" in a particular context, as when Barth said "no" to Nazism, the dialectical context remains. Barth's voluminous writings reflect his dialecticism. Unassailable absolutes in the human sphere did not exist for Barth.

At many points in Barth's writings, one can hear his own marital and extramarital relationship commented on, however obliquely. Barth attacked romantic, idealistic notions of love and marriage. The whole relationship between man and woman is manifested in its creatureliness, he says. "We must leave them on earth under heaven."[10] Furthermore, to swear eternal love is a sentimental blunder. "The so-called marriage altar is a free invention of the flowery speech of modern religion," he wrote.[11] He thought the church should get out of the business of marrying people and leave the matter to the state.

"The command of God," Barth said, "requires no liberation from sex. Nor does it require any denial or repression of sex."[12] Barth followed Luther in criticizing the discrimination against eros in Christian tradition, calling it a very old mistake. He clearly, unambiguously rejected the supposed "higher perfection of celibate life," which, he maintained, "menaces the whole sphere of male-female relationships."[13] Furthermore, an asexual or neutral humanity is a rejection of creatureliness. Barth called these "evasions," tempting for some, a form of disobedience toward the God who made us as male and female creatures.

Barth went so far as to define the sexual union itself as the "image of God" in humankind. God exists only in relation, not in isolation, particularly in relationship with the wholly other. Male and female are commanded to relate, the basis for the Hebrew requirement that everyone should marry. Barth argued that this requirement is only loosened for Christians, not removed.

Barth was so radically heterosexual (not, however, in an antihomosexual sense) that he criticized all single-gender institutions. Man and woman, he said, must give account to each other for their humanity. Regarding single-gender groups such as men's clubs and women's circles, he chided, "Who commands or permits them to run away from each other?"[14]

Barth may have been speaking mostly about his own life when he commented, dialectically, on relationships which cannot flower in *regular* marriage:

they are not mere sin and shame ... they do not wholly lack the character of marriage ... They simply cannot stand in the face of God's command ... they are simply a heap of ruins. They can be good only on the basis of God's sin-forgiving grace and within its limits. They can be regarded as relatively good only through faith. But we must not forget that the arch of the divine command spans the whole reality ... there is here no one who is not struck by the divine judgment [and] ... no one who is not reached by the divine mercy and in his own way held and comforted. Thus even where man does not keep the command, the command keeps man.[15]

Barth was certainly thinking in his dialectical way either of Nelly or Lollo (or both) when he wrote:

and if there is no perfect marriage, there are marriages which for all their imperfection can be and are maintained and carried through, and in the last resort not without promise and joyfulness, arising with a certain necessity, and fragmentarily, at least, undertaken in all sincerity as a work of free-fellowship ... *There is loyalty even in the midst of disloyalty and constancy amid open inconstancy.*[16] (author's emphasis)

Barth was surely speaking for himself when he wrote, "As God's creatures, we are possibly nowhere so much on our own as in respect of our sexuality."[17] And in the midst of a discussion of sex ethics, he said, with surprising candor, "Things could be totally different from what they seem."[18]

Unlike Barth, Paul Tillich had very little to say, in his published works, about sexual behavior. Also unlike Barth, Tillich did share—with his most intimate friends—thoughts about his own sexual life.

Tillich's writings are congruent with what we have come to know of his private life. His published work contains nothing that could be construed as supporting traditional Christian sex ethics. For example, Tillich used human sexual development as illustrative of the journey from "dreaming innocence," symbolized by the Garden of Eden, to personal self-actualization and the guilt that accompanies it. The actualization of one's potential, he wrote, results in "experience, responsibility, and guilt."[19] The human predicament, like that of the adolescent, is one of being caught between the desire to actualize oneself and the wish to preserve a dreaming innocence. No one wants to lose either innocence or the potential for actualization. Anxiety, therefore, is experienced in either direction. The loss of innocence was for Tillich a reenactment of "the Fall," the exile from the Garden, as Tillich correlated Platonic and biblical metaphors. The Fall, however, was a "fall upward," as Tillich put it. He also registered his critique of Augustine, whom he claimed "never overcame the Hellenistic and especially the Neoplatonic devaluation of sex."[20] He wrote that Augustine tended to identify sexual desire with sin, even though he knew that spiritual pride, not sex, was the basic human sin.

Tillich shared with his intimate friends his concern about the countercultural character of his personal life. First, he feared that his personal life would become a public relations and political problem, thereby discrediting him as a theologian. Given the public mood and mores in the 1940s and 1950s in the United States, such a concern was certainly appropriate. Princeton theologian Seward Hiltner, who personally shared Tillich's sexual dilemma to some extent, has also suggested that knowledge about Tillich's sexual life was the cause of "a stony silence" that followed proposals to appoint Tillich to teaching positions at the University of Chicago in the 1930s and 1940s. (In 1962, he did win a Chicago appointment, after several years of a distinguished appointment as "University Professor" at Harvard.) Undoubtedly, many of the ministers, priests, and nuns who flocked to hear him late in his life (myself included) would have been shocked to know of his sexual history.

Tillich was also concerned about his personal sexual life from a moral perspective. He was aware that he was treading dangerous uncharted ground, and that such a transgression of the social code carried psychic risks. He was aware that the inevitable human journey from innocence to guilt was more than theoretical. And he did experience genuine guilt. The highly esteemed theologian and psychotherapist Rollo May, who had been Tillich's student and was later his friend, reported that Tillich had asked him, "Was my erotic life a failure, or was it a daring way of opening up new human possibilities?"[21] This question was not just academic or rhetorical on Tillich's part, but a deeply felt expression of existential anguish and uncertainty.

The facts of Tillich's sexual life remained for the most part safely below the surface, at the level of gossip, during his lifetime. In 1973, the matter appeared for the first time in print. His widow, Hannah, published an account of their life together, titled *From Time to Time*. Simultaneously, Rollo May published a brief biography called *Paulus*, which was Tillich's given name in German.[22] May's work seemed to be an attempt to neutralize Hannah's account.

In May's book and in the subsequent reaction, we can see the theological community's wish to deny the troublesome facts of Tillich's personal life. Hannah disclosed a lifelong pattern of countless sexual adventures on her husband's part, as well as details about her own sexual adventures, including experimentation with bisexuality. Both she and her husband had also participated in "swinging" (spouse-swapping) with other couples.

Hannah circulated her manuscript privately for some time prior to its publication; most of her friends advised against publication. Rollo May, a longtime friend of the Tillich family, may very well have seen the manuscript. Seward Hiltner and others assumed that May's book was an attempt to mollify the impact of Hannah's book on her late husband's reputation.

May's alternate account of Tillich's sexual life was embarrassingly naïve, especially as it came from an individual who had in other ways shown such good sense. Although he never argued explicitly that Tillich was entirely innocent of the stories about him, May did suggest as much, going to great lengths to distinguish between the "sensual" and the "sexual" in Tillich. May wrote:

> His letters to his women friends were filled with such words as touch, light, warmth, glow, and other terms which express sensuality rather than sexuality.[23]

May also recounted an afternoon Tillich spent in the park with May's fiancée, during which Tillich enchanted the young woman with erotic fantasies. May felt some pangs of jealousy but "knew" the encounter was innocent. He argued that another man might easily have turned the spiritual seduction into a physical one, but not Tillich. May believed that Tillich was genuinely devoted to a sensuality that was distinct from sexuality. May then proceeded to explain Tillich's behavior on the grounds that he, Tillich, was continually seeking his lost mother, and that his sexual mores were inherited from German intellectual society between the wars, which was in rebellion against middle-class values. Finally, May discussed Tillich's own guilt feelings about his sexual life. May seemed to want it both ways. But the overall impression he presented of Tillich was of a man whose bohemian sexual life was mostly in the realm of the imagination. Within the theological community, *Paulus* was generally accepted with a sigh of relief. *The Expository Times*, a British theological journal, pronounced May's account to be a welcome correction to Hannah's distorted rendering, in which she:

> lays bare, in the most distressing fashion, details of his private life damaging to his good reputation ... How much do we need to know?[24]

Many in the religious community reacted similarly, as though Hannah had maligned her late husband. Some even accused her of disclosing fantasies rather than facts. Word circulated in theological circles that the book was no more than a bitter widow's act of personal revenge. Hannah's book, however, had the advantage of springing from firsthand knowledge. Her personal account devastated May's thesis for anyone still rational on the subject.

In spite of characterizations to the contrary, Hannah's account in no way communicates ill feelings toward her late husband. The story itself, unconventional as it was, simply derailed many conventional readers. The information was plainly indigestible to some. But rather than an assault on her husband, the book is in fact a poignant testimonial to their mutual devotion, particularly in their final years, when their love grew deeper. No one can read the chapter on their last years in Chicago, and especially their time together when he was dying, without being deeply moved by their devotion to each other. Their relationship had been shaped by plenty of difficulties and, at

times, unspeakable suffering, betrayal, and intense emotional turmoil. Without doubt many religious people would just as soon not have heard of those
aspects of Tillich's marital relationship, particularly its bohemian sexuality.

Tillich had appointed his close friends and fellow theologians, Wilhelm
and Marion Pauck, to serve as his biographers. They came to Hannah's defense, supporting the accuracy of her account. Because the facts are now
well-substantiated, Tillich is often simply forgiven these days for his particular "sickness" and thereby is discredited by innuendo. As the seminary
dean Urban Holmes once put it, with a too-facile gloss, "Tillich was simply
defenseless in the face of seductive women."[25]

Seward Hiltner, on the other hand, is one of the few theologians who
took seriously Tillich's challenge to conventional sex ethics. His assessment
was that Tillich's challenge, though serious, was not serious enough. As he
poetically puts it:

> I am a little less sure that a fresh flower, even in a crannied wall, every day,
> is an effective way to break the unduly prurient and legalistic bonds of our
> own theological past.[26]

Hannah seemed to echo Hiltner. She had characterized her marital experience as providing a liberating "break with the whole concept of monogamy."[27]

For all his sexual adventures, no evidence suggests that any of Tillich's
many women friends were abused by him. In the 1950s, a woman friend of
mine was assigned the task of interviewing Tillich for an article. She re-
calls that Tillich clicked the lock on his office door after she entered, which
sparked her curiosity. He then, without hesitation, proceeded to make her a
sexual overture. She declined his offer; her response was accepted graciously.
Without further ado, they got on with their interview, which went quite
well.[28] One instance hardly proves a pattern, but the vignette sounds very
much like Tillich, erotically charged and bold, but gracious and humane in
his relationships.

In the examples of their lives—no small matter in religious traditions—
both Barth and Tillich presented the twentieth-century religious community
with a disruptive challenge to its conventional notions of sex and marriage.
More importantly, they mounted a challenge to basic Christian teachings
on sexuality. In their private lives they signaled, however obscurely, the
approaching Sexual Revolution, which arrived as their time was ending.
The challenge they presented consisted not of private indiscretions, but of
consciously made life choices that went against the stream of the religious
consensus in the West, as well as against the mores of the modern middle
class. Each of these theologians in his own way demonstrated in practice a

radical critique of the fear of sex and veneration of monogamy and celibacy. Most theologians still remain mute and perplexed before the biographies of these two theological giants of the twentieth century. The sexual lives of Karl Barth and Paul Tillich may have been incomprehensible for their own generation but need not be to any generation that has lived through, or lived after, the Sexual Revolution.

The two most creative and influential religious thinkers of the twentieth century lived private lives that, had they been publicly disclosed, would likely have ended their ability to work. Fortunately for them and for us, they were not born too late to be given a certain respectable degree of privacy for their private lives. It is no small irony that, had they lived into the post-Sexual-Revolution era in the United States, when everyone's privacy seems subject to public scrutiny, they would have been mercilessly excoriated.

CHAPTER 17

SEXUAL DISARRAY IN THE LATE TWENTIETH CENTURY

The latter decades of the twentieth century were marked by an odd paradox of sexual liberation on the one hand and fiercely anti-sexual impulses on the other. The Sexual Revolution had brought real cultural changes that were radical. Pre-marital sex became commonplace. Homosexuality became acceptable in many contexts; it certainly moved from its prior position of abject public disgrace, even as it became the *cause celebre* of reaction. Extra-marital sex was widely tolerated. Divorce was treated with less public shame than previously. Pornography became socially accepted in ways that would have traumatized American culture as recently as 1950. One can imagine the repercussions if one could have plopped a *Playboy* magazine down in an American social context in 1950, a time when it was illegal to possess an unexpurgated edition of D. H. Lawrence's *Lady Chatterly's Lover.*[1] The Sexual Revolution was a real social revolution.

Following quickly on its heels came a counterrevolution fueled by negative feelings about sexual pleasure generally, and exacerbated by radical feminism's resentment toward men in particular. The Sexual Revolution and its counterrevolution produced a kind of "perfect storm" in public values as they related to sexual pleasure. The national culture was at once obsessed with, and terrified by, sexual pleasure. To a limited extent, this obsession extended to the entire English-speaking world: Canada, Australia, New Zealand, and parts of Europe, as well as any regions where American influence dominates.

The impetus of feminism on the face of it was not to abolish sexual pleasure, but to assert, rightly, equality for women. But feminism in part devolved into a war against men generally, particularly male heterosexuality. Thus "sexual harassment" entered the language in 1975, according to Jeffrey Toobin.[2] The expression became a feminist weapon. While it has significantly denigrated and diminished male prerogatives, in many cases appropriately so, aspects of feminism have had, and continue to have, a negative influence. It has revived pre-Freudian amnesia regarding childhood sexuality. And it has demonized male assertiveness, sexual and otherwise. If the late twentieth century became a safer time for women to express their sexuality, and for persons engaging in premarital or extramarital sex (whether homosexual or heterosexual), it also has become a more hazardous time for some, specifically for heterosexual men, and for both genders who work intimately with children, especially child care workers.

At present, a heterosexual male who makes any sexual overture, however subtle or oblique, runs some risk of being charged with predation. In the current environment, any male courtship gesture may be grounds for complaint. The usual theoretical basis for such a complaint is the claim of a discrepancy in power between the two parties. Thus any male who has personal or professional power of any sort may be charged with a misuse of power simply for initiating a courtship. But in the real world, hardly any two people have precisely equal power on all matters. Consequently, almost any sexual overture may be labeled predatory (at the discretion, almost exclusively, of the female). Such options place extraordinary new power in the hands of women generally. Some see this as just recompense for generations of patriarchal abuse. By this accounting, men today should pay for the historic sins of their gender.

No one doubts that some men (but also some women!) have used, and continue to use, positions of power to extort sexual favors. Nor does anyone doubt that men generally, or at least white men in Europe and America, have possessed a balance of power over everyone else in the social order—power they have often abused. So the issue is not entirely spurious. A man demanding sexual favors of his unwilling subordinate is clearly making use of power in a reprehensible manner. However, the current counterrevolutionary response to the problem—like most popular solutions to problems—has exacerbated what has been a problem for a few and made it a problem for many. An automatic determination that any man in a position of power must be guilty in any sexual dispute is a draconian solution that voids any responsibility on the part of the woman. It dictates an orthodoxy of male culpability and female innocence. In almost any failed courtship (no small number), the man is now *prima facie* guilty, leaving the woman with a free hand to inflict penalties on him.

One of the prime slogans of the counterrevolution is, "There shall be no unwelcome or undesired sexual attention." This clumsy, heavy-handed, anti-male decree seeks to repeal the traditional rules of courtship, particularly the duty of the male to persist and press. ("Faint heart never won fair lady.") Men do not ordinarily find a welcome mat at the door to courtship. When they do, the woman is considered suspect. Her role is to play hard to get, but not *too* hard to get because she risks losing her suitor's interest if she makes the conquest too difficult. At the same time she risks embarrassment if she falls prey to the judgment, "Methinks the lady doth protest too much."

Most people understand that courtship is, consciously or unconsciously, a ritual act. It is difficult to see how anyone familiar with world literature and the arts could be oblivious to the persistent pattern, during courtship, of male pursuit and female resistance. More difficult to fathom is why anyone would attempt to abolish such primal behavior patterns. In the new counter-revolutionary order, the problem for men is that the rules of courtship have been challenged. Every courting man is now subject to indictment for sexual harassment.

In any ethical reflection on specific sexual behavior, we must keep in view our solidarity with the rest of the creature kingdom, particularly in respect to the nature of gender. David M. Buss in *The Evolution of Desire*[3] examines this matter in scholarly detail. His work challenges the wish, religious or otherwise, to elevate human beings from their place in the animal kingdom and place them on some more ethereal plane.

In the animal kingdom generally (including insects), males are dissemi-nators of seeds, while females are nurturers of the far fewer viable eggs or embryos. A profligate waste of male seeds stands in opposition to the conser-vation of the female. This is a matter of biology, not ethics; it is an aspect of what is given in creation. And it is a general characteristic of the animal and insect kingdoms to which human life belongs.

In human sexual behavior, as with animals and insects, we must not expect males to behave like females. Or *vice versa*. Each gender begins with a differ-ent biological agenda, and this difference has implications when it comes to determining human morality. In the human species, a woman produces roughly one egg a month over a period of several decades. The man, on the other hand, produces enough spermatozoa in the course of one monthly female cycle to reproduce the entire current population of planet Earth. This extraordinary redundancy of male sperm determines, in part, who the male is in relation to the female. This biological difference in sexual objectives be-tween the seed scatterer, with all its superfluity and waste, and the nurturer of the few eggs, with all its pressure to conserve and protect, shapes males and females in profound and unconscious ways. Females look to males for protection and assistance in nurturing their few eggs, while males look to females for multiple opportunities for disbursement of *their* sperm. Even in the presumptively high social order of the human species, these biological facts make themselves felt in every sexual interaction. Whatever social controls or ethical standards are in place, persons should make allowances for these facts.

The radically contrasting biological interests of the genders does not mean that human beings are wholly determined by biology. But it does mean that biology has a voice in any moral calculus. It is neither accidental nor capricious that females are generally "hard to get" and that suspicions arise when females are "too easy." It is no indication of immorality that males are more assertive sexually, are prone to seek sexual variety, or are egregiously competitive with other males. Women generally seek longer courtships, with the heaviest investment possible by the suitor. Men seek sexual gratification as early as possible, with the fewest restrictions, and at the lowest possible cost.

As far as reproductive capacity is concerned, the world needs only a few males. Every male knows this—not consciously, perhaps, but deep in his bones. Lopsided gender ratios exist in the barnyard, where very few sexually competent males are kept alive as males, the remainder being castrated for use as beasts of burden, or eaten. Such facts are not irrelevant to male identity and selfhood in the human species. Every barnyard is a reminder, to men, of their biological redundancy.

The biological makeup of the genders cannot be deleted from consideration in any attempt to weigh the moral character of a particular sexual transaction. In this connection it is ominous that China, with a quarter of the world's population, is consistently bringing more males into the world than females, aborting female fetuses and murdering female infants. India is showing the same trend. This is a prescription for an increased male redundancy and a reduction of the numbers of conservators. Given male competitiveness, it is also a prescription for war. In war, redundant males become expendable as cannon fodder. War becomes, even, a biological necessity.

David Buss also points out the superficiality of widely accepted notions of current gender conflict, such as the claim that men are united in the common purpose of oppressing women, and that women are now uniting against men to reclaim their share of available resources through gender equality. Buss calls this a simple-minded view of same-sex conspiracies. In fact, he says, men viciously compete with each other in the high-stakes gamble to make themselves more desirable to women. Women, likewise, compete for access to high-status men. Buss draws a startling conclusion: the dominant control of resources worldwide, by a select few men, can be traced in part to women's preferences in choosing a mate. For the most part, women do not join with one another to create equity for themselves and men. Rather, they more often compete with each other for a place beside the man who has the greatest resources.

The Platonists and Stoics of ancient times, and their later Christian followers, strove mightily to expunge the sex drive from humanity as animalistic. They sought to elevate the human species to a higher plane, the plane of the mind and soul. It was a grievous error to emphasize the mind and soul at the expense of the body and its pleasures. It was an error that has been the source of much confusion, mischief, and suffering for generations on end, including the present one. Human solidarity with the animal kingdom is the best antidote for the pernicious effects of Platonic and Stoic—and Christian—idealism.

Scratch the surface of any civilized male, and you will find a being who competes with other males, all of whom seek—or perhaps only wish—to inseminate a host. Scratch the surface of any civilized female, and you will find a being who competes with other females to provide the best resources for her brood (or prospective brood). Even those who have passed the years of reproduction continue to experience this biological drive.

Rape is a heinous offence, the act of forcing someone to accept sexual intercourse against his or her will. Such an assault may indeed occur on a date. Males are typically bigger and stronger than females, and some may succeed in raping even without resorting to weapons or drugs. However, we need not call such an act anything but rape. The covert purpose of the category *date* rape is to serve notice to overly aggressive males that they are vulnerable to extreme sanctions if they disregard the word "no." The concept of date rape actually seeks to repeal biology and the common and unwritten laws of courtship, in which the male pursues, and the female demurs, a dance that by design is full of purposeful deception and ambiguous communication. Some believe that the term and consequent repercussions following an accusation of date rape only serve as a platform for women who have second thoughts the next day about events of the night before. Date rape proponents naively seek to make courtship a national process in which parties mean precisely what they say.

Date rape as a concept tilts the scales against males and portrays them as brutes: a poisonous generalization. That males are sometimes brutes is indisputable. However, males generally arrive at their sexual identity through a process of trial and error, which, under the best of conditions, can be comical, but which is bloody and painful at first occurrence for a woman. The sexual counterrevolution has made this complex task more difficult even for the wisest of young males.

Defining rape simply as the use of physical force in sexual intercourse will not quite suffice either. Sexual intercourse often requires some physical force, even when two persons are both willing and eager—especially if they are inexperienced. Sometimes willing couples have been unsuccessful in their first attempt at intercourse, among other reasons because they may have failed to use sufficient force. Sexual intercourse is not a tea party. A naïve observer (e.g., a child) who happens to see a man and woman engaging in sexual intercourse might take it to be a dangerous physical assault. The satirical newspaper *The Onion* used this fact of life to elicit laughs. Under the banner, "Study Finds Sexism in Nature," its editors printed the photograph of a male lion roughly straddling and biting his mate. *The Onion*'s caption for this photo read, "One of the millions of lionesses trapped in an abusive relationship."[4]

Johnathan Prevette, of Lexington, North Carolina, could be the poster boy for the insidious assault on, and impugning of, biologically driven male sexual assertiveness.[5] In 1996, when he was six-years-old, Johnathan was suspended from school for an entire day for the transgression of kissing a girl classmate on the cheek. He was warned that if he ever again was caught kissing, hugging, or hand-holding, he would be suspended again. School officials defended the dismissal as consistent with federal definitions of sexual harassment, which all schools are required to follow.

Adult sex with minors foments rage in the souls of righteous Americans, as well it should when a young child is prematurely sexualized by an adult. But the righteous indignation is often blunt and heavy-handed. The current absence of subtlety on the subject is the product of an unawareness of, or repression of, pedophilic instincts. Children are oftentimes objects of sexual urges, however well these interests may be sublimated or redirected. We love them. We want to touch them, embrace them, and kiss them. Out of consideration for children, responsible persons control their libidinal feelings. The relatively few who do not or cannot control these urges, and who gratify themselves sexually with young children should be restrained and punished. At the same time, however, in the words of the great Southern Baptist theologian Myron Madden, "none of us will be well until we recognize our own basic pedophilia."[6]

There are socially accepted ways in which limited forms of pedophilia are expressed in various cultures. Earlier in the twentieth century, it was almost *de rigueur* for parents to photograph their toddlers in the nude. Later in the century, that practice became high-risk behavior; child protection personnel were empowered to use such photographs as evidence of child abuse. In certain cultures, mothers and grandmothers are known to genitally stimulate their male children at a very young age, a practice that has led to great difficulties for some immigrants to the United States when these women have unwittingly come in conflict with over-reactive child protection services. In some cultures, genital stimulation of young children is thought to be health-giving, leading to a more vigorous sexual life later.[7] No evidence except intuition is available to prove or disprove such conclusions. But this activity is certainly not in the same class as adult exploitation of children for the purposes of an adult's own sexual gratification.

The lack of wisdom and subtlety in response to charges of sexual abuse of children in the current environment is troubling. Not only are false accusations too readily accepted, but degrees of abuse are rarely weighed. A child of four is very different, sexually, from a child of 16. The 1953 play by Robert Anderson, *Tea and Sympathy*, is a poignant story of the sexual education provided to a late adolescent boy by a mature woman.[8] (The boy had been taken to a prostitute by his peers, where he became so upset he vomited. Subsequently he became uncertain of his manhood.) In spite of more recent concerns about homophobic innuendoes in the play, it stands as a work of art that explicates a very human theme. A sexually healthy culture will value, or at least tolerate, such amatory relationships, off the beaten track as they may be. Many an adolescent, and particularly many an uncertain male, has greatly benefited from such mentoring. To consider such encounters by definition as abuse is a judgmental overreaction. But in our current culture, any such encounters risk arrest and felony conviction if the adolescent is under the statutory threshold for adulthood. This is the work of a culture held hostage by moralists, infected by Christianity's ancient loathing of sexual pleasure.

In September, 2005, Sandra Beth Geisel, a 42-year-old mother of four and an English teacher at the Christian Brothers Academy in Albany, New York, pleaded guilty to a charge of third degree rape in a plea bargain that eliminated the possibility of her spending years in prison.[9] Geisel admitted to sexual relations with several teenage boys. One happened to be 16. His age made it possible for officials to prosecute the case as statutory rape. The judge, Stephen S. Herrick, showed great wisdom in his sentencing of Geisel, giving her only six months of time served. He also stated at the sentencing that the 16-year-old boy was "a 'victim' in the statutory sense only."[10] The judge had the grace to add that Geisel herself was victimized by the boys, who took advantage of her and spread their exploits with her to their peers. Geisel was fortunate to have found herself under the jurisdiction of Herrick.

Representatives of the family of the boy who had been "raped" were outraged that Geisel got off so lightly; there was even talk of civil suits to be filed by the boy against the Catholic school and Geisel. Some of the popular talk shows classed the case as child rape. Although the 16-year-old was a minor, he was not a child in the same way that a younger student would be (e.g. an elementary school student). Some would say that to label his affair with Geisel as rape is a slur against all the women and men who have experienced true rape. The notion of Geisel as a rapist, a convicted felon who deserved time in prison, and a continuing danger to the community requiring a decade of supervision as a sexual predator, illustrates the extent of our skewed cultural perception of some sexual behaviors.

Sandra Beth Geisel is not the last American woman, or man, who will engage in some form of "tea and sympathy" with an adolescent, some of whom may be younger than the statutory threshold of adulthood. Such relationships will continue to take place but at enormous personal risk to the adults who take part in them. It should go without saying that the risks males take when engaging in such relationships with adolescents are dramatically higher than the risk taken by women.

In the mid-1980s, in Roanoke, Virginia, I was involved with a group of mental health professionals—social workers, physicians, clergy, and others—who attended to issues of sexual abuse of children. I found that the majority of these professionals believed children generally were, and should be, sexually unaware and uninterested. I found this viewpoint extraordinarily naïve. The truth is that children are generally fascinated with anything sexual, even if the depth of their interest and their attention span is limited. In the Roanoke group of professionals, it seemed as if Sigmund Freud had never existed. Indeed, many of the participants clearly wished that he hadn't.

On one occasion a case was presented to us in which two grade school boys were found in the basement of one their homes; each had his pants down. One boy was a few years older than the other, but they had been playmates for some time. The parents, on discovering the boys in this compromised predicament, did what counterrevolutionary, law-abiding American citizens are expected to do: they immediately called the police. The resulting involvement of the police led to the case being brought for consultation to our child protection group.

My own consultation on the matter was that the police should never have been involved, that their involvement was highly inflammatory, and that the only serious question was whether the two boys might be too far apart in age to be appropriate playmates. I expressed the view that the parents, other than rethinking the age-appropriateness of the two playmates, should drop the matter entirely. No one else in the group of a dozen or so professionals—therapists, social workers, and physicians—openly agreed with me. Everyone else, of those who expressed an opinion, said that calling the police was the appropriate action. One participant in the group sent word to my administrator that I promoted sexual abuse of children.

In another case an eight-year-old girl, trapped in the crossfire of a custody battle between divorcing parents, complained of mistreatment by her father during her time spent with him. She was allegedly locked in a cold basement, deprived of food, and threatened with bizarre and extreme sorts of punishment. Her complaints continued for many months but were treated as exaggerated by Virginia's child protection agency. Finally, when she reported that her father had fondled her *sexually*, the state agency responded with lightning speed, severing the father's relationship with the child. The truth may never be known about either the child's charges of physical cruelty or of sex abuse against her father. Suffice it to say that the girl may have discovered what it takes, in our twisted culture, to get attention from the authorities. If she didn't know then, she certainly does now.[11]

A particularly malignant result of the sexual counterrevolution has been the epidemic of charges made against innocent persons who were accused of sexually abusing children. Many of these charges were made in the context of day care centers. The common feature of the charges was the astonishing irrationality that characterized the evidence presented in the trials. The public motto became "Believe the Children." Many of the accused went to prison, and some are still there, based on charges no rational person could accept as accurate. From roughly 1980 until the end of the century, the American public engaged itself in a series of witch hunts comparable to witch hunts of the fifteenth through the seventeenth centuries.

Freud's now century-old contention that children are sexual beings had inflicted a narcissistic injury on the stodgy keepers of late Victorian public morals, who promoted the notion that children were sexual innocents. Now the counterrevolution was effectively repealing Freud's claim. This was one of the major victories for those who wished the Sexual Revolution had never happened.

The restoration of pre-Freudian obliviousness to—or denial of—childhood sexuality created the soil in which countless irrational accusations of sexual abuse of children sprouted. These cases were fed by sexual hysteria; and "hysteria" is not too strong a characterization. In the process, enormous suffering has been inflicted on a great many innocent persons, mostly, but not exclusively, males.

Prosecutors who abused their offices in pursuing such cases were usually rewarded rather than punished. Janet Reno, then the Dade County (Miami) District Attorney, was rewarded by President Clinton with the office of Attorney General. In Florida she had compiled a record of relentless and irrational pursuit of Bobby Fijnje and Francisco Fuster. She lost the case against Fijnje but succeeded brutally against Fuster. Later, Reno's debacle at Waco, the black mark on her tenure as Attorney General, was reported to have been inspired by her belief—unsubstantiated, as it turned out—that the children in the Branch Davidian commune were being sexually abused. Reno put an end to the imagined abuse and to the lives of the children as well.[12]

The bulk of fanciful child abuse cases has occurred in the United States; with few exceptions such cases have been limited to Anglo-Protestant cultures. Britain, Australia, Canada, and Finland have experienced a few cases. All of the accused in high-profile cases have eventually been exonerated, their convictions overturned in the appellate courts, or pardoned. However, many obscure victims in similar cases of injustice—the lesser known, unpublicized, and poor—remain incarcerated. Often they are denied parole even after serving long sentences for failure to "confess their crimes," a classic instance of a double bind.

This general hysteria was given a forensic assist by psychiatrist Roland Summit, who provided what he alleged to be a scientific basis for assessing the evidentiary reliability of child witnesses in such cases. In 1978, he came up with a concept he termed the "Child Abuse Accommodation Syndrome." His thesis was that children never lie when disclosing episodes of sexual abuse; and his corollary was that when they *retract* such "disclosures," child witnesses *are* lying, accommodating themselves to parental pressure. This "syndrome" achieved the status of an established truth and became a useful tool in getting convictions. It gave impetus to the popular ironic slogan, "Believe the Children."[13]

Mindlessly accepting Summit's thesis, many therapists and social workers who interviewed children often lured them, and subtly or unsubtly browbeat them, into "disclosing" that they were abused by adults. When a child later tried to retract the fabrication, the child was judged to be acting according to the "accommodation syndrome," which made for an airtight, circular theory, establishing as a "fact" that children never lie about sex except when denying it.

With Summit's theories to back them up, and armed with newly designed "anatomically correct" dolls, sex therapists could discover abuse wherever they chose to peer. They talked sex with children, offered rewards to them for joining the conversation, and eventually lured many "victims" into whipping up stories of their own. This was not a difficult assignment. Any relatively uninhibited six-year-old, presented with an anatomically correct doll (which was *incorrect* in that its genitalia invariably were much larger-than-life), could be expected to demonstrate curiosity about such a surprising phenomenon, very much unlike any doll he or she had seen before. A child's curiosity about the explicit, shockingly large genitalia was considered evidence of abuse. Summit has since gone out of favor, but some of his most diehard followers persist.

Anyone who knows children knows they will lie about anything, and knows, further, that children often will tell adults anything they feel the adults want to hear; and children's willingness to lie only increases when they are coerced. Stephen J. Ceci, a developmental psychologist at Cornell University, demonstrated, through tests carried out under laboratory conditions, that young children are quick to spin elaborate sexual tales when encouraged by sympathetic interviewers. He also proved that children, when encouraged by adults to lie, usually show an awesome facility for invention.[14]

In 1989, accusations were made against the staff of the Little Rascals Day Care Center, owned by Robert and Betsy Kelly, in Edenton, North Carolina. The accusations came on the heels of a Roland Summit seminar, which had been held in eastern North Carolina the previous year. Therapists and social workers were on a heightened alert for cases of sexual abuse of children, purported by the seminar to be taking place in epidemic proportions.

The Edenton case evolved in typical fashion. It began with a complaint from a disgruntled mother, miffed by a misunderstanding that was unrelated to anything sexual. When this grumbling parent was not satisfied, she added sexual innuendo to her complaint, at which point sex abuse experts were drawn to the case like filings to a magnet. Naturally, these "experts" were predisposed to find evidence of sexual abuse. And find sexual abuse they did, in virtually every child they interrogated. Seven adults in Edenton were arrested. Twelve pre-schoolers were enlisted to testify in court as to how fundamentally they had been abused. It was not a rational investigation but a witch hunt. The family of one Little Rascal's child, unconvinced of the charges, relocated to Charlotte, North Carolina, to avoid the frenzy.

As these alleged sex therapists continued their work with the children, the so-called evidence reported by these "witnesses" became more and more elaborate and fanciful. The children's imaginations extended to arenas far removed from the sexual. They reported swimming with sharks in Albemarle Sound, raising sharks in backyard ponds, carrying out magical acts, participating in witchcraft practices that involved murdered babies and ritual sacrifices of various sorts of animals. Satanic practices and symbols were a recurring theme in the Edenton case and in many other such cases. No one, among all the public prosecutors, defense attorneys, psychologists, or clergy seemed competent to distinguish between flights of imagination and truth-telling. No corroborating evidence was ever found to substantiate any of the children's tales, sexual or nonsexual.

The irrationality that attended these charges infected the entire community, including the press and the defense attorneys. In the courtroom of Robert Kelly's trial, for example, every seat was taken on the prosecutors' side of the courtroom, but no one, except a few reporters, sat on the defense side. The atmosphere was much like that at a sports event. From time to time the audience broke out in applause at the highly prompted testimony of a child, to be shushed by the judge, only to repeat such outbursts later.[15]

Dawn Wilson, the day care center cook, was the second of the seven Edenton defendants to undergo a trial. On one particular day, the subject was the evidence supporting a five-year-old girl's claim that Robert Kelly had had vaginal intercourse with her, Wilson being an alleged accomplice. From a slide projector in the courtroom, a color reproduction was displayed for most of the day, showing the girl's hymen, labia pulled back by a pair of unidentified thumbs for better viewing. The camera revealed an obviously intact hymen, covering about three-quarters of the vaginal opening. The day's discussion consisted of explanations by the prosecutors and their expert witnesses as to how the highly resilient hymen in young girls actually springs back into position after intercourse. With pointers, the prosecutors noted stretch marks in the hymen. Long discussions followed, concerning the meaning of the stretch marks. The scene was surreal. Never did the defense attorneys effectively challenge the bizarre reasoning by pointing out that an obviously intact hymen was good evidence that the five-year-old girl had experienced no sexual intercourse, particularly with an adult male.

At the beginning of the Edenton trials, all the media personnel present seemed to presume the guilt of the accused, although later most of them changed their views. *Frontline* offered the first rational perspective on the case, in a series of television broadcasts (directed by Ofra Bikkel) over the course of several years.[16] In response to *Frontline*, hundreds of persons from across the nation joined the Committee for Support of the Edenton Seven (CSES). The committee provided moral and financial support and assisted in moving the appeals process along to its successful conclusion.[17]

In addition to *Frontline*, several other rational voices exposed the widespread hysteria over the sexual abuse of children. Freelance journalist Debbie Nathan and Dorothy Rabinowitz, an editorial writer at the *Wall Street Journal*, were among the most prominent journalistic voices of reason. They gave special attention to the Kelly Michaels' and Amirault family cases. Elizabeth F. Loftus, psychologist and distinguished professor at University of California, Irvine, was a strong voice of reason. Columbia University psychiatrist Richard Gardner, another lonely voice of rationality, testified for the defense as an expert witness in a number of cases across the country. He was treated with scorn by many of his colleagues for his willingness to oppose popular opinion.[18]

Congress's well-intentioned but misguided Mondale Act (The Child Abuse Prevention and Treatment Act, CAPTA), signed into law by Richard Nixon in 1974, provided additional impetus to prosecute these alleged crimes against children and to punish imagined offenders. First, it provided immunity to reporters of abuse, thereby unleashing an unlimited supply of unsubstantiated charges. Second, it provided funds to assist children who were abused sexually, funds permitting so-called victims to receive state-financed therapy immediately, even prior to any adjudication. Thus the numerous victims in the Edenton case received extensive counseling, at government expense, for "abuse" that had never occurred. Four "sex therapists"—who were themselves the de facto abusers—got all the business from the Edenton case and in the process received many thousands of dollars in reimbursement from the government in a case that was eventually overturned by the courts. The financially rewarded therapists were not motivated to suppose that the charges might be bogus. Public officials acted as if the charges were substantiated before any trials took place.

In a similarly unwise expenditure, the insurer carrying the liability insurance for the Little Rascals center also paid out one million dollars to the alleged victims prior to the reversals of the cases.

Many district or state's attorneys, like Janet Reno, North Carolina Attorney General Mike Easley, and Massachusetts Attorney General Scott Harshbarger, rode the wave of public hysteria by pushing or failing to restrain prosecution of the falsely accused. But Alan Rubenstein, District Attorney of Bucks County, Pennsylvania, followed a different drummer. When the Breezy Point Day School in Langhorne, Pennsylvania, was subjected to an elaborate skein of charges of satanic and ritualistic sex abuse, Rubenstein mounted an immediate, aggressive investigation of the evidence supporting each allegation. He took up the rug at the school where rabbits were alleged to have been ritually sacrificed and sent it to the FBI lab for analysis; no rabbit blood was found. He sifted the school sand box for evidence of allegedly sacrificed and mutilated animals; no traces were found. He had the children who were alleged to have been raped and beaten interviewed apart from their frenzied parents and without the assistance of the ubiquitous Summit-trained "sex therapists;" none were found to have been abused. One of the child "victims," whose videotaped "disclosure" was key to the original allegations, actually objected to being transferred to another school, claiming she "liked Breezy Point." Rubenstein firmly resisted hysterical parents and the public clamor for arrests. As a result of his courage and integrity, and his thorough, timely, and scientific investigations, all the charges of abuse at Breezy Point quickly evaporated. The owner of the Breezy Point Day School, Doug Wiik, in turn assisted other victims of false charges and subsequently became a key leader of the Committee for Support of the Edenton Seven.[19]

It has become commonplace since the onset of the counterrevolution for parents to be required by insurance companies to sit in as observers in their children's private tutoring sessions, such as piano lessons. This innovation is designed to protect children against sexual predation by adults, as indeed it probably does. But the cost of such protection is high. The special bonding that one might hope would occur between teacher and pupil (a bond that is the very soul of a mentoring relationship) is inhibited or eliminated by the presence of an adult observer. Even more worrisome is the unstated message communicated to the child, that they are sexually defenseless. When the child finally comes to understand why such an observer is invariably present, right up until that child's magical "age of consent," the message given that child about the nature of sex will be an exaggerated one, and thoroughly negative.

When the child becomes an adult at 17, or whatever age the state determines, such observers will exit. Or will they? Why shouldn't 20-year-olds be protected from their mentors' sexual predations? Twenty-first-century American culture has reinstituted the medieval chaperone system to guard the sexual purity of its children, this time not only of girls but of males as well.

A major theoretician of the sexual counterrevolution was Peter Rutter, author of the widely read *Sex in the Forbidden Zone*. He was a secular evangelist who sought out and attacked all vestiges of male heterosexuality in the workplace. Rutter saw himself as a defender of abused women. He argued that women do not have the ability to defend themselves from sexually predatory males. For Rutter, sex abuse begins with the words, "You know, you're very attractive."[20] Among other villains, he scurrilously condemned John F. Kennedy for his sexual history. (While he was at it, Rutter could have also condemned Washington, Jefferson, and Franklin.) Rutter's objective was to "spare women another destructive act of sexual invasion."[21] He had no ear for the possibility that a woman might sometimes relish such an "invasion."

Though Rutter crusaded principally against sex in the workplace, he so over-stated the problem that he appeared to rage against the phallus generally and to view heterosexuality, wherever it was found, as a kind of virus. He sought liberation from what he called the endless cycle of sexual pursuit. We can conjecture that Rutter spent his life in a neurotic struggle to surmount the connotations of his own name.

The invention of the concept of sex addiction is another example of the counterrevolution's war on sexual pleasure. It creates more problems than it solves. The metaphor of addiction has been applied to a number of activi-ties that are not literally addictive, and the metaphor is often inappropriate. When Wayne Oates invented the category *workaholic*, he created a metaphor from alcoholism for those whose lives revolved entirely around their work.[22] But it was only a metaphor. Work, after all, is not a true addiction. More recently, new kinds of addictions (e.g. eating addiction) have also entered the therapeutic vocabulary. But neither work nor eating can be understood as addictions in any literal sense. Substances like alcohol, nicotine, and heroin gain a powerful physiological hold on the body that the addicted person is powerless to break. No moderating use of such substances is effective be-cause of the body's metabolism demands the addictive substance, in increas-ing amounts. For so-called workaholics or eating addicts, no such control-ling substance exists. It is neither necessary nor possible to give up work or eating altogether. Unlike drug or alcohol addiction, one need only moderate one's attention to work to remove the label workaholic.

The recent invention of sex addiction is even more problematic as a meta-phor. But the sex-addiction industry has found receptive soil in an American middle class stubbornly influenced by Christianity's well-established goal of restraining all but the most conventional sexual behavior. Those miserable souls diagnosed as sex addicts are encouraged either to give up sex altogether or to restrict sexual activity to the most conventional and limited contexts.

Many people have—to one degree or another—disordered sexual lives and are therefore potential customers for sex therapy. The sex-addiction therapist (who could possibly be called a programmer) enters the picture, promoting a highly restrictive reordering of sexual choices and making no allowance for any choices that deviate even slightly from the Christian or middle-class canon. When a colleague of mine disclosed to her therapist an extra-marital sexual liaison that she had participated in, not the first in her life, the therapist immediately classified her as sex-addicted. Such summary judgments are as common as they are inappropriate. There are many good reasons—and also some poor ones—for someone to undertake one or more extramarital affairs. The problem of deciphering the reasons, and the appropriateness of these rea-sons, is not something that can be done in a cavalier fashion or by a summary judgment. An affair may be a means of acting out against one's spouse or may have other ulterior or unproductive motives. But an affair may also be a free choice made by a person determined to experience life's blessings to the full-est, a choice made with no ulterior or destructive intent.[23] Of all the blessings of human existence, sexual pleasure is surely near the top of the list. Or as the ribald saying goes, "if sex is not the greatest pleasure in life, it runs a close second to whatever is." Deciding whether a particular extramarital liaison is moral or immoral is not always a simple matter.

The misleading notion of sex addiction should be deleted from our vocab-ulary. We can speak only of good and bad sexual choices. Even so, we ought not listen to anyone who is too sure he knows in advance what is good or bad. Sexual choices are often clouded by conflicting goods. Often no simple process exists for determining the morality of a particular choice in seeking sexual pleasure.

Certainly, sexual desire feels like an addiction or a disease during certain phases of one's life. Most everyone has had the experience of not being able to think of anything else, which is among the popular definitions of addic-tion. This is especially true in the adolescent and young adult years, when hormones are churning at full throttle. However, sexual desire is not really a disease. (Or if it is, it is a disease from which no one in his or her right mind would wish to be cured.)[24]

Many ill-advised persons through history, some long before the notion of "sex addiction" was devised, attempted to cure themselves of sexual desire. Origen, the famous third-century Christian theologian, had himself castrated in hopes that this radical course would effect such a "cure." He was neither the first nor the last to make a very poor decision about sexual desire.

Those who work with the terminally ill know that even the dying often long for sexual pleasure, although they probably find it rarely. The journalist Mar-jorie Williams, who died at age 47 in 2005, chronicled her last years of dying from cancer. Among other things, she described her final days of chemotherapy. Whether the bad time lasted just five days or five weeks, she wrote, some inner voice eventually said, "Never mind. Today is a ravishing day, and I will put on a short skirt and high heels, and see how much of the future I can inhale."[25]

If sex is an addiction, then long live addiction! And let us grieve for those who have lost, willingly or unwillingly, their sexual desire.

The culture war currently being waged between the children of the Sexual Revolution and its opponents in the counterrevolution is not over. It remains to be seen what our children and grandchildren will do with the weapons we leave behind when this conflict winds down. Amid the continuing war of sexual values, some manage to persevere in claiming the blessings of sexual pleasure. The search for sexual pleasure is basic to our experience of being human. We reject it at our peril. It is tragic that Christianity has mostly been on the side of those who hold sexual pleasure in disdain, to their great loss.

CHAPTER 18

CAUSE CELEBRE: FROM MASTURBATION TO HOMOSEXUALITY

As a result of the Sexual Revolution, masturbation was largely released from its former special status of moral opprobrium, a status that it had held for several centuries, and was permitted a new measure of public acceptance. Homosexuality was then put in its place in the public imagination.

In a very enlightening article, the Princeton Theological Seminary professor Donald Capps traced modern religious, scientific, and philosophical views of masturbation.¹ Capps discovered that even the most progressive thinkers in the modern West have generally considered masturbation to be harmful to health and sinful. He also discovered that no other sexual issue rose to the level of importance, in modern times, as masturbation. Of all sexual concerns, masturbation was *the* most central in modern Western religious thought, but also in scientific and philosophical thought, from about 1700 until the Sexual Revolution of the 1960s. After the 1960s, the focus of public attention shifted to homosexuality. Public disapproval of homosexuality supplanted masturbation as the sin *de jour*, in Capps words.

It is hard to imagine any person interested in his or her own sexuality who has not masturbated. Masturbation provides knowledge of one's sexual responses that could not be discovered any other way. It seems an almost essential part of sexual self-discovery.

From Christianity mainly, but also from secular wisdom, we have inherited two alternate but inherently humorous labels for masturbation: "self-abuse" and "self-pollution." The satirical weekly newspaper *The Onion* appropriately exploited the humor of "self-abuse" in a 2004 issue, in which it reported that approximately 95 percent of all self-abuse went unreported.² It cited Sister

Hatchette, whom *The Onion* described as a "self-abuse counselor," as being dismayed by the fact that she was always forced to release self-abuse victims "back into the hands of the same persons who had abused them."

As one who reached puberty in the 1940s, I can recall being impressed by various adult authorities with the serious consequences of masturbation. Homosexuality, on the other hand, was mostly unmentioned. On the menu of sexual transgressions, masturbation always loomed large in ways that defied logic, even to my adolescent mind. My own teenage years were dominated by a relentless struggle to resist masturbation, especially as one who felt called to the ministry. So I took seriously the religious line that claimed such an act was an offense against God. Through Herculean will power (if my memory serves me reliably), there *was* a period of a couple of years when I managed to refrain from bringing myself to orgasm. But perhaps it just seemed like a couple of years. In my late teens, I gave up the struggle against masturbation, which seemed a hopeless crusade. (I had noticed too that any significant number of weeks spent successfully resisting the temptation resulted in a wet dream.) So I learned from experience what Martin Luther had written in 1522, that the semen will out, whether in a woman or in the sheets.[3] Unlike his Catholic teachers—and unlike the *Enlightenment* scientists, physicians, and philosophers who followed—Luther seemed to view the occurrence of wet dreams simply as a natural phenomenon. As usual, he was far ahead of everyone else.

In my early adult years, I came to believe that there was nothing immoral or unhealthy about masturbation. The only thing wrong with it was, I decided (to steal a line from Haim G. Ginot), one never meets any nice people that way.[4]

In the modern world, since the Enlightenment, the attention given to masturbation has been a most curious cultural development. If celibacy was (and still is) the highest sexual calling in Catholicism, then resisting the temptation to masturbate correspondingly became the sexual *cause celebre* for Protestants and secularists. All three traditions—Catholic, Protestant, and secularist—sought to suppress the attitude that masturbation might be a benign undertaking, or even a victimless crime.

The medical profession led the way in this religious-and-scientific assault on masturbation. *Onania or the Heinous Sin of Self-Pollution* (1716), penned by an anonymous physician, went through 80 editions. In 1756, Samuel Tissot, a Swiss physician, took up the same crusade in *Onania or a Treatise upon the Disorders Produced by Masturbation*. Later in the same century, Samuel Tissot, a renowned Swiss physician, took up the same cause. Tissot claimed that masturbation was the cause of insanity, moral degeneracy, and all manner of diseases, a claim that stuck well into the twentieth century.[5]

The radical psychiatrist Thomas Szasz, author of *The Therapeutic State* (1984),[6] pointed out that by 1800, medical dogma claimed that masturbation caused blindness, epilepsy, gonorrhea, priapism, constipation, anemia, insanity, melancholia ... and suicide! Physicians tried preventing the habit by use of restraining devices, as well as by such surgeries as circumcision, cauterization of the genitals, and even, yes, "clitoridectomy" for girls, and for boys, castration. Some of these extreme treatments continued into the middle of the twentieth century. Some popular nonmedical "experts" held to a view that seminal fluid was partly *brain tissue* that ran down the spinal cord and out (a view no more unscientific, after all, than the more widely embraced belief, clung to by a number of physicians, that masturbation led to blindness and other afflictions).

The great philosopher Emmanuel Kant went along with the view that masturbation was "an abuse of one's sexuality." Strange as this might seem in hindsight, Kant and other philosophers shared the position of the Vatican, that the sole and proper purpose for sexuality was the continuation of our species.[7]

During the latter nineteenth century, American culture underwent a broad public campaign to discourage masturbation. Even the government got into the act, encouraging parents to bundle their young children in such a way that their hands couldn't reach their genitals during sleep. Kellogg's Corn Flakes (and Graham Crackers!) were invented specifically as anti-masturbatory food, the thought being that the ingestion of whole grains, rather than the partaking of animal flesh, would lower sexual desire.

In 1883, the *Boston Medical and Surgical Journal* published an article, by Dr. Timothy Haynes, describing a surgical procedure to treat "hopeless cases of masturbation and nocturnal emissions." The surgery eradicated sexual appetite without the extreme act of removing the testicles, hence was considered a gentler alternative to castration. Haynes added his own recommendation of marriage—and even the highly "immoral" indulgence of taking a mistress—over the perverse habit of masturbation.[8]

Sigmund Freud held the view that his addiction to smoking was a consequence of the repression of his masturbatory impulses. In spite of Freud's immense contribution to sexual liberation generally, he reportedly considered masturbation a perverse habit, in the sense that it thwarted reproduction. And so (according to Donald Capps), this towering figure Freud, who did so much to liberate the world sexually, was unaccountably irrational on the subject of masturbation.

Even the super-rational analytical philosopher William James, famous at the beginning of the twentieth century for his tome *The Varieties of Religious Experience* (1902),[9] was convinced that "self-pollution" led to insanity.

In the nineteenth and early twentieth centuries, psychiatric hospitals were commonly thought to be overflowing with men who had masturbated their way to insanity. One estimate claimed that 32 percent of the inmate population was insane due to "self-abuse."[10]

Early in the twentieth century, progressive Methodist theologian and widely read author Leslie Weatherhead (1893–1976), debunked some of the wild and unsubstantiated medical claims that masturbation brought on horrendous health consequences. As well, Weatherhead debunked the very negative prospect of "going to hell" as a consequence of masturbation. But Weatherhead did concur with the "abuse" abhorrers to the extent that he felt adult masturbation was due, always, to maladjustment regarding sexual matters. The continuance of such a habit, he intoned, "maintains such maladjustment." Weatherhead recommended physically focusing on a picture of Christ whenever one's mind tended toward thoughts of masturbating. In addition, he recommended circumcision as a practical way to reduce the stimulation to masturbate.[11]

As Capps's research shows, even the more progressive physicians, philosophers, and clerics in modern times could find no way to separate themselves from the widely accepted assumption that masturbation was a serious, dangerous disorder. Capps himself speculates that the dramatic increase in circumcision, in the late nineteenth and early twentieth centuries, was driven by the hope of reducing masturbation. Certainly no mass conversion to Judaism was in the making. The emergency circumcision of Anton Boisen (discussed in chapter 15) lends support to Capps' findings.

As far as Capps could ascertain, the only authoritative modern figure to take a benign view of masturbation, in public, was Mark Twain. Twain delivered a brief, satirical talk on masturbation in 1879 to a group of American expatriates in Paris. His address remained unpublished for 85 years. Here is an excerpt from Twain's remarks, as quoted by Thomas Szasz:

> Cetewayo, the Zulu hero, remarked, "A jerk in the hand is worth two in the bush." The immortal Franklin has said, "Masturbation is the mother of invention." He also said, "Masturbation is the best policy." Michelangelo said to Pope Julius II, "Self-negation is noble, self-culture is beneficent, self-possession is manly, but to the truly grand and inspiring soul, they are poor and tame compared to self-abuse."[12]

Donald Capps's research led him to conclude that homosexuality supplanted masturbation as the principal sexual issue in our culture subsequent to the Sexual Revolution. Each of the presumed sins share in sexual pleasure that is not procreative. The participation of the "other" gender is not required. Capps believes that the requirement that male sexuality be expressed heterosexually is motivated by the need to assert the importance of the male role in procreation and is thus driven by anxiety. This can be supported by the obvious redundancy of men and their seeds, as pointed out by Buss and elaborated upon in the previous chapter.

The late war against masturbation, and the current campaign against homosexuality, both qualify as taboos rather than as ethical judgments, because each has been driven by a kind of logic that is impervious to reason. Evidence for this can be found in the fact that masturbation and wet dreams (also known as "self-pollution" or "nocturnal emissions") were equally demonized. Yet wet dreams are involuntary physiological events, and, as such, should hardly be considered morally reprehensible.

If masturbation and homosexuality are problems of taboo rather than ethics, it might be useful to explore the unconscious sources of the taboo. The equating of wet dreams with masturbation suggests a concern over wasted semen—which is to say, semen not directed toward conception. Wasted semen is also characteristic of many objections to homosexual relations. By contrast, it is intriguing to note the relative lack of negative public reaction to *female* homosexuality, where no semen is wasted.

On the other hand, this taboo may be overdetermined and related to anxiety about non-reproductive sexual pleasure, an unconscious fear that sexual pleasure separated from the burden of child-rearing will disrupt the social order with its siren song. The taboo also may represent an anxiety that men and women may lose each other and consequently jeopardize the perpetuation of the species. Perhaps both masturbation and homosexuality symbolize, somewhere in the recesses of the male psyche, a fear of a failure of generativity.

Since the Sexual Revolution in the 1960s, masturbation has been more or less accepted as a fact of modern life, and, as such, has lost much of its taboo character. Even the playful words of Mark Twain wouldn't shock middle-class listeners these days. In the 1980s, President Jimmy Carter's sister, Ruth Carter Stapleton, announced that "the Lord wants us to experience whole, complete lives, and He offers this gift (masturbation) to each of us as we surrender to Him."[13] Even though the statement came from a woman, the lack of any serious negative public reaction to her remark is probably evidence of the change brought about in the 1960s. All of the public fascination with masturbation has now been redirected toward homosexuality—or, more specifically, toward *male* homosexuality.

CHAPTER 19

SEXUAL DISARRAY IN THE CHURCHES

By the beginning of the twenty-first century Christian churches in the United States, just as the surrounding culture, were in disarray on the subject of what constitutes proper sexual behavior. The churches were both influenced by the Sexual Revolution of the 1960s on the one hand, and swept along by the hysteria over an epidemic of sexual misdeeds (and imagined misdeeds) on the other. The more conservative churches—particularly the Roman Catholic Church, and various Protestant evangelical churches—had generally if not entirely resisted the tenets of the Sexual Revolution and supported the broad sexual negativity of counterrevolutionary elements in American culture. By contrast, the more liberal churches generally embraced the tenets of the Sexual Revolution. But paradoxically, they also embraced many of the agendas of the sex-phobic counterrevolution. The liberal churches began ordaining women and homosexuals in great numbers in the 1960s. However, the United Methodist Church and the Presbyterian Church, two of the more liberal churches, demonstrated their ambivalence by ordaining large numbers of female clergy while at the same time forbidding the ordination of any active homosexual.

The Episcopal Diocese of New York has been one of the most liberal Episcopal dioceses of a fairly liberal denomination. For example, it was the first diocese to declare publicly, as early as the 1970s, under the leadership of Bishop Paul Moore, that it would ordain practicing homosexuals. Moore's action was not tokenism; he ordained homosexuals in large numbers. Yet by the 1990s, Moore's diocese had also succumbed to the widespread frenzy over alleged sexual abuse, which was directed almost entirely against heterosexual men. Under pressure from the counterrevolution, in 1994, this diocese put in place a peculiar document, entitled *Policies and Procedures for Responding to Sexual Misconduct in the Episcopal Church*. The committee that created this document consisted, curiously, of nine women and five men—this in a diocese where the ministers were mostly men. In the leadership's attempt to halt what was alleged to be widespread sexual exploitation by *male* ministers, the committee created a monstrous set of definitions and rules. These rules resulted in conditions that effectively outlawed, as far as the male minister's behavior was concerned, almost any manifestation of sexuality.

These *Policies and Procedures* seemed to place every Episcopalian off limits for sexual relationships with any Episcopal minister. Such rules dictated that a minister avoid sexual contact with anyone with whom he had a pastoral relationship—which, in theory, include every Episcopalian, because a minister is a minister twenty-four-hours a day. Further, it would be difficult to demonstrate that a cleric is not "in a pastoral relationship" with any other Episcopalian. The prohibition could also be construed to include even those who are not Episcopalians, because pastoral relationships (according to Episcopal practice) are not limited to Episcopalians.

The *Policies and Procedures* document defined "sexual abuse" as "sexual molestation of any person," a definition with wide enough reach to criminalize sexual behavior categorically. Further, it defined "sexual harassment" as "sexually oriented humor or language," "questions or comments about sexual behavior or preference," "sexually oriented conduct that is unwelcome, or undesired physical contact." Because it is virtually impossible to know whether a sexual overture is welcome or desired until it is made, such definitions have a very wide reach. Sexual harassment occurs, the committee declared, between colleagues of equivalent or equal stature *as well as* in relationships where one person is in a position of relative authority. Furthermore, the committee defined sexual "exploitation" as "a sexual relationship, or an attempt at one, between a cleric and a person with whom the cleric has a pastoral relationship, *whether or not there is apparent consent from the individual*" (author's emphasis). Thus the policies infantilized everyone in relation to a minister, depriving any lay person of her competence to make a choice to become sexually involved with a cleric.

The *Policies and Procedures* document provided examples of sexually suggestive behavior, such as, "unwelcome bawdy or suggestive conversation or jokes," and "unwelcome and persistent flirtatious or showing of pornographic materials." (In that definition, the qualifying word "persistent" gave the definitions a rare semblance of rationality. In other sections, qualifying words like "persistent" were not included.)

The committee repeated the radical feminist mantra that sexual harassment is not about sex, but about the abuse of power.

But at the same time, the *Policies and Procedures* document, injecting an additional sense of reality, recognized that ministers seeking spouses would inevitably (as they have all through church history), court other Episcopalians, often members of their own congregations. So a rule was devised whereby clerics intending to court persons in their sphere of pastoral influence were required to seek prior permission from both the bishop and the senior officer of the relevant congregation. (Presumably such permission would nullify the previous strictures.) That such a requirement was laughably unrealistic and would smother any prospective courtship in its crib seems not have concerned the authors of these policies.

The *Policies and Procedures* document went on to include another decree even more draconian than this previous ones, establishing a rule that, in instances of miscommunication, the benefit of the doubt would always go to the accuser. Thus if a parishioner were to interpret an embrace or a handshake as sexual, it would be considered sexual. In this peremptory ruling, the policies made it virtually impossible for anyone falsely charged to defend himself. (And it is, in fact, almost always *him*self.) In this act the policies overturned centuries of due process, particularly the right to defend oneself against one's accusers. This ruling was particularly grotesque in a church within which, during religious services, all participants are requested to make physical contact with those seated around them. This so-called "kiss of peace" is shared in the community's religious services, and customarily ranges from a real kiss or embrace to a formal handshake. The clergy regularly participate in this kiss of peace, embracing each other and members of the congregation as well.

This sets up a paradox that is more than a little peculiar. To promote a practice whereby strangers as well as friends touch each other physically—while simultaneously ruling that any recipient of a physical contact is declared the absolute arbiter of the "sexual" content of that contact—is nothing short of bizarre. It prepared the ground for a criminal charge against which no man could defend himself. Combined with its kiss of peace, its new policies on sexual abuse made the Episcopal Church a forum within which every religious service became a combat zone in the war on sexual pleasure.

More was to come. Two years later, in 1996, the New York Diocese ordered all its clergy, vestry members, employees, and volunteers to sign a *Statement of Compliance* explicitly requested by the Church Insurance Company. The document was clumsily entitled "Sexual Misconduct in the Church—What Are the Rules and How It Is Handled." Such tortured syntax seemed to project, consciously or not, the unraveled edges of the document's basic content. But in general the document seemed to back off from the most severe dimensions of the previous diocesan position. For example, the new document seemed to say that sexual liaisons are prohibited only between clerics and persons who are under their direct pastoral care or spiritual guidance. And the qualifying adjective "persistent" is used more often in defining sexual harassment. However, the document nowhere stated or suggested that it was revising the previously published *Policies and Procedures.*

The diocese at the same time also began a practice of sexual "background investigations" into the personal histories of clerics prior to ordination and prior to the assumption of any new position in the diocese. These investigations cast a wide net in their attempts to uncover any historical evidence of sexual misconduct. The background investigations made inquiries about a wide range of sexual misconduct, defined as "including, but not limited to, sexually oriented humor or language." It inquired whether the referenced person had engaged in "unwelcome sexual advances" in the past ten years. In this tautology a sexual advance must be welcome to be ethical, but if such an advance is known to be welcome, it hardly qualifies as an advance. (If such a question were put to a 20-something-year-old single man seeking ordination, and the response was "no," one could plausibly argue that he should *not* be ordained on grounds of social retardation.)

These demands for compliance statements and background checks communicated clearly that the church leadership was interested, to the virtual exclusion of everything else, in one moral issue only: sex. The documents also showed with unmistakable clarity that the diocese, like most Protestant jurisdictions, was floundering in the face of the winds blowing in the wider culture in regard to proper sexual conduct. And, to make matters more bizarre, even while this sexual policing was taking place, the married bishop of the diocese, Richard F. Grein, was rumored to be involved in a sexual liaison with one of his employees, a married minister herself. The bishop was soon publicly charged, by his wife, with adultery and soon married the alleged adulteress, who had in the meantime sued for her own divorce.[1] It should be said that the bishop should have the right to change wives, just as anyone. However, the disconnect between his behavior and his directives on sexual conduct was juicy in the extreme—and in its *extremity*—and was more than a little ironic.

The Episcopal Church was not alone in this frenzied pursuit of sexual misconduct. All the major Protestant churches climbed on the bandwagon and, up to the present time, are still bouncing miserably along on it. As time passes, each new version of sexual behavior standards for the clergy becomes a bit more peculiar than the last.

In 1993, the Baltimore-Washington Conference of the United Methodist Church instituted a new policy statement similar to those of other Protestant churches. A choice section reads: "Because of the imbalance in power and trust in a relationship, the person(s) being ministered to by the pastor shall be presumed to be unable to give meaningful consent to any sexual activity."[2] Such a baldly exculpatory claim for women is an invitation to mischief. Especially in a church where a great number of its ministers are married to persons whom they met in their congregations.

Undoubtedly, there are some persons whose idealization of ministers, or psychological transference, is so inflated as to lead them to act against their own interests, but this is hardly a typical characteristic of most members of most congregations. Any brokenhearted woman, disappointed in love, is invited to pose as a victim. All churches have liability insurance.

The New York Conference of the United Church of Christ (UCC), falling in line with the trend, in 2005 required a mandatory two-day training regimen for all its ministers on the subject of "Professional Boundaries and Ethics." It was a replication of the kinds of program now existing in virtually all denominational groups. In principle it doesn't seem a bad idea, until one considers the irrationality of its content. No mandatory training programs exist for other kinds of moral issues, only for the problem of sex.

In one particularly odd judgment, the UCC statement proclaims "The Myth of the Seductive Woman as the Evil Temptress."

> A woman who offers herself sexually to her pastor is wounded and very likely is a survivor of incest or other form of sexual abuse. She measures her worth in terms of her sexual value. She may have avoided punishment or been rewarded for sexual compliance.[3]

This judgment has the advantage of neatness. Any woman with sexual interest in her pastor is by definition emotionally troubled, and because of being in such a state (due to previous abuse), she is also, by definition, innocent. Any woman's sexual overture to a minister is by fiat categorized as a manifestation of psychopathology—any sexual proposition, or more specifically, any heterosexual overture, made to a minister is identified as the result of a disease. The UCC repeated the standard shibboleth, that no meaningful consent can be given when a power imbalance exists.

The sexual conduct document produced by the UCC made these curious additions to its list of definitions of sexual abuse:

> personal discussion of a sexual nature between a pastoral counselor and one of his or her clients.
>   personal discussions of a sexual nature between a pastor and a single member of the congregation.[4]

As to why it might make a difference whether the congregation member were single or married is a mystery.

Like the Episcopal Diocese of New York, the UCC gave the benefit of the doubt to all accusers. In its definition of different sorts of sexual harassment, the UCC document's list includes the offences: "Touching someone intentionally or accidentally in ways that they consider to be sexually suggestive." The document follows with a note, in bold print: **The interpretation of the nature of the touch is according to the perception of the person**

touched, not the state of mind of the person doing the touching."[5] Just as in the Episcopalian camp, any offending UCC member—almost always male—who is charged with sexual harassment has no basis for defending himself. Sex abuse is wherever and whatever the alleged victim says it is.

At least to some extent, the attitude of the American religious community's terror of sex has been exported abroad. According to a recent report in John Worrell's newsletter, *Nevertheless,*[6] the Anglican Diocese of Sidney, Australia, sent out an extensive questionnaire to all applicants for ordination, including the following questions:

> Is there any information from your past or present that may result in allegations being made against you of sexual conduct which would be regarded by *right-thinking* (author's emphasis) members of the Church in this Diocese as disgraceful and inconsistent with the standards to be observed by a Christian?
>
> Have you ever engaged in any of the following conduct, even though never having been charged? Sexual contact with a parishioner, client, patient, student, employee or subordinate; sexual contact with a person under the age of consent; illegal use, production, sale or distribution of pornographic materials; conduct likely to cause harm to a child or young person, or to put them at risk of harm?[7]

This all serves to illustrate that a fine net is also being cast abroad, with the intent of uncovering by "right thinking people" of every trace of any but the most conventional sexual behavior.

A dramatic moment of counterrevolutionary activity occurred at the Association for Clinical Pastoral Education's 1992 annual conference, in Breckenridge, Colorado. The academician Karen Lebacqz, a featured speaker at this 1992 conference, used the opportunity to upbraid male clinical supervisors for their "decades of sexual misbehavior." She spoke of their notorious reputations as persons who violated ethical norms of sexual conduct; she cited bizarre and atypical examples of abuse perpetrated by certified clinical pastoral supervisors; she reported on the male supervisor who asked a female trainee to divulge her sexual history, and who, once his overture was deflected, spoke to her of his own erection. Whether such an episode occurred or not, such an occurrence was hardly characteristic behavior among male members of the profession.

Lebacqz went on to recommend that the organization certify more women, on the grounds that one did not hear of sexual exploitation by women. She also parroted the radical feminist assault on due process, claiming that women were more likely to tell the truth about sexual abuse than men. Lebacqz focused exclusively on male heterosexuality and made it clear that she had no concern about sexual misbehavior by lesbian ministers in relation to their parishioners. To clarify this point, she stated that female ministers were not corrupted by patriarchal power.

In the face of this scurrilous attack, no man—and men made up the majority of those attending the meeting—rose to respond. Most seemed to take masochistic pleasure in this assault on their gender. At that same meeting the presidency of the organization passed for the first time to a woman, Cathy Turner. Turner declared in her presidential address that her principal focus during her two years of office would be sexual exploitation. Her listeners understood that she meant exploitation *by men*.

The insurance industry forced Protestant churches and religious groups to take drastic steps to curtail the amount of litigation over sexual abuse, and the Reverend Marie Fortune provided the theoretical underpinnings that implemented the counterrevolution in churches.[8] Fortune had more influence on Protestant churches, in the waning years of twentieth century, than any other individual. She created the Seattle Center for the Prevention of Sexual and Domestic Violence and from that headquarters made her influence felt throughout American Protestantism.

But if Fortune had not come along, the churches would likely have found someone else to perform the same task. The problem was what to do about increasing numbers of allegedly improper sexual liaisons and the flurry of lawsuits that followed—and how to calm the insurance industry. Churches felt increasing pressure from forces in the wider culture, as the definitions of what constituted abuse were expanded. The easy way out of the dilemma was to follow the simplistic solution offered by Fortune and expunge from the churches any trace of heterosexual courtship by its leaders.

And so Marie Fortune became, to the Christian world, what Peter Rutter was to the secular. She spouted many new protocols on sexual conduct and promoted the thesis that a clear and unambiguous boundary must be established between sexuality (meaning *heterosexuality*) and congregational life. *Not in My Church* and *It's Never Okay* are her unambiguous slogans.[9] Some of Fortune's claims were: that from a female viewpoint, sex with a male minister was not about sex, but about power; that ministers were in a power relationship with those to whom they ministered; that "dual" relationships (meaning a minister who was also a friend) were immoral; that adults who befriend children should be suspected of intentions to abuse children sexually; that most pedophiles were married heterosexual men; that children and adults who make charges of sexual abuse by a minister should always be presumed to be telling the truth; that one-third of all females are introduced to sex by being molested by a trusted family friend; that in prosecuting or adjudicating accusations of sexual abuse, "beyond a reasonable doubt" was an unnecessarily stringent legal standard; that heterosexual relations in all its forms are degrading to women, requiring them to submit to male authority; and that homosexuality was more to be preferred than heterosexuality. Under close scrutiny, many of these claims could not hold up, but, toward the close of the twentieth century, Fortune's blame-mongering nevertheless carried the day among American Protestants.

Thus Marie Fortune and her adherents have provided a theoretical framework for Protestantism's anti-male retrenchment in the face of the demands of the insurance industry. That the mainline Protestant churches have bought her thesis—hook, line and sinker—exposes the disarray in a religious tradition that originated, ironically, as a sixteenth century protest against sexual repression.

Women do fall in love with ministers, just as they fall in love with physicians or lawyers. In each romance, the question is how much psychological "transference," so-called, or what could be called "interpersonal distortion," might have been at work at the outset of the infatuation. But such questions apply to all romances and in relation to all kinds of professions. Contrary to Fortune's tightly sealed world-view, some women do become sexually involved with their ministers in a manner that is not pathological. Some of these romances have even led to long and satisfactory marriages.

Until recently, it was customary for a congregation to work at finding a wife for a newly ordained minister. Congregations would customarily delight in providing a wife, one of their own home-grown women, for a newly ordained minister, fresh from seminary and newly assigned to some small town or country church. According to the ideology of Marie Fortune, such women of the congregation lack the moral and/or psychological capacity to assent to a dating relationship with their minister. And since the recent assault by the insurance industry, and the campaign by Fortune, this practice cannot be continued without enormous risk both to the minister and his future. Should a courtship turn sour, such a woman now has the statutory basis for filing a sexual abuse complaint against the minister, with draconian consequences. Courting by single ministers seeking wives continues but has gone further underground.

Marie Fortune's claims of an insurmountable power differential between a male minister and a female church member are gross hyperbole. She caricatures male ministers as authoritarian representatives of God, whose requests or demands (particularly their sexual requests) female members of the congregation have little or no power or personal authority to refuse. Fortune is supported in her ridiculous assertions by Peter Rutter: "Even sophisticated women can have difficulty resisting an argument put forward by a minister that sex with him was part of the divine plan."[10]

The truth is, Protestant ministers do not have anything like the power over people that Fortune and Rutter contend. Obviously, there are some extraordinarily dependent persons, and a relatively small number of emotionally disturbed individuals, who might so idolize a minister as to submit themselves sexually on demand, or after some period of skillful seduction. And there are persons who are psychologically mesmerized by the aura of a minister's alleged divine authority—persons who might lay aside their own best judgment to accede to a minister's sexual requests or powers of seduction.

But such naively credulous persons are the exception, not the rule. This kind of dependency, and this kind of inflation of the authority of the minister, is not the general practice in mainstream Protestantism. Most Protestant ministers spend at least some time and energy wondering if their pastoral positions are secure, when they aren't wondering if they have any real authority at all. It would be the rare woman who could fall into a sexual liaison with her pastor solely on the basis of his charismatic request for sexual gratification. But on the basis of such a rare woman, Fortune constructs an ethical code that deprives every woman of the moral capacity to consent to a sexual relationship with any minister.

Marie Fortune inveighs against so-called "dual relationships." To be sure, dual relationships can be complicated. It can be disadvantageous if your physician, lawyer, or auto mechanic is also a good friend (or lover). The presumption is that tasks requiring a great deal of clinical objectivity are best performed without the distractions of other agendas, such as friendship. For example, one might not want one's brain surgeon to be a close friend. But dual relationships are not always harmful or corrupt.

Ministers, in particular, routinely develop special friendships with certain members of their congregations. One might even postulate that becoming "friends" is the proper objective for everyone in a congregation, including the minister. Every minister's spouse is by definition in a dual relationship, as a member of the congregation and as the pastor's spouse. No one ever suggests that the minister's spouse ought to participate in a congregation different from the congregation of the person he or she is married to, though such a strategy would indeed have some hidden benefits, as well as liabilities. A dual relationship, while complicated, is not necessarily corrupting. Nevertheless, as this argument progresses, the belief grows more widespread that a sexual relationship between a minister and a member of his congregation is categorically unethical. Such a relationship is judged to be a "boundary violation," an "improper relationship between persons of unequal power."

Marie Fortune also holds the peculiar view that homosexuality is morally superior to heterosexuality. To her, heterosexuality is a cultural or developmental perversity, inescapably linked to abusive patriarchy. While inflammatory in her attacks on heterosexual male behavior, Fortune has nothing to say about homosexual abuse in any form—nor about *any* abuses perpetrated by women. If a female minister were to become sexually involved with a male parishioner, the man, in Fortune's view, rather than the female minister, would be the culprit. As the possessor of patriarchal power, the man has free rein, whip in hand, to commit aggression. The essence of the Fortune crusade is found in her strong antipathy for male heterosexuality. She seeks to cleanse the churches of it.

In 2004, "Crazy for the Rev" wrote to "Dear Abby," stating that she had a romantic interest in her minister but was in a quandary as to how to proceed.[11] The columnist understood very well the current environment in which Fortune has become the moral guru. She advised "Crazy" to join another church, after which she and her former minister would be free to date. However, such a legalistic, devious approach would be hypocritical in a religious congregation that poses as an advocate of the highest standards of morality. Secondly, should the relationship turn sour, the minister in question would not likely have any protection in the event the woman turned on him and charged him with using his pastoral authority in a seductive manner.

A personal note may be in order here. In 1962, as a newly ordained Episcopal cleric, I was assigned to serve as assistant minister for a well-to-do suburban congregation in Virginia. The most startling aspect of my new assignment came when I experienced how many lonely wives came on to me sexually. Most did this subtly, although some made their advances in quite dramatic fashion. As far as I was aware, none of these women demonstrated any malicious intent; there were no wives of Potiphar[12] among them. (Undoubtedly, I must have communicated subliminally my own attraction to these women and was, therefore, hardly an innocent bystander. All animals emit pheromones.)[13]

I remember one woman, who remains a dear friend after all these years, when she begged me to take her to a motel—today. (In retrospect, I still admire her candor and audacity.) I maintained the strictest boundaries in each of these incidents, but not, often, without perspiring in the process. The seminary had not prepared me for such experiences. At the four seminaries in which I had studied, there hadn't been a whisper, not a hint, of the sexual temptations I would face once I was set loose in the world. The fact that I kept strict boundaries in this baptism by fire was not due to any concern that I might have damaged the woman or myself in any intrinsic or irreparable way. I doubted then, and doubt even more now, that such a liaison, complicated though it would certainly have been, would necessarily have been intrinsically destructive.

I was simply afraid of exposure, humiliation, and shame and knew that secrets seldom remain secrets for long. I knew enough to know that a sexual scandal would end my job at that particular location, if not my professional life. Looking back, I can see that it would have been very easy to become sexually involved with a number of young, attractive women in that context, especially if I had been somewhat more malleable and less stubborn. Thus I

have little sympathy with the likes of Fortune, who characterize male ministers who deviate from the sexual norm as psychopathic predators.

The Roman Catholic Church has also retreated in response to the sexual
counterrevolution, although the sexual travails in that church have taken
quite a different twist from that of the Protestants. The winds of change
have made themselves felt by the Catholic Church but in a very different form. Marie Fortune's program has had no relevance for the Catholic
Church. That church would be receptive neither to her radical feminism,
nor her promotion of homosexuality. Catholic problems for the most
part have not been heterosexual ones, but homosexual problems between
priests and young males. Ironically, some of Fortune's arguments about
the inflated authority of male ministers, and the willingness of a church
member to abdicate personal authority in relation to these clergymen, are
actually more relevant to Catholics than to Protestants. But Catholics are
not listening to her.

Conventional Catholics have found the sexual counterrevolution in line
with their own already-held values (except for its feminist elements). Premarital and extramarital heterosexual relations do not conform to traditional
Catholic teaching any more than such behavior is accepted by Protestant
counterrevolutionaries. But conventional Catholics have no truck, as we say
in Tidewater Virginia, with either feminism or homosexuality.

The Catholic Church long ago created a double bind for itself. It created
a monosexual—not to say homosexual—community; to which priesthood,
for the very reason of its monosexual nature, many homosexuals have found
themselves attracted. Homosexuals historically have always been attracted
to monosexual institutions, such as the YMCA. No one knows, or ever could
know, how many priests are homosexual. Estimates vary widely; some have
the number well above 50 percent.[14] The heart of the Catholic Church's problem lies not in its number of homosexual priests, but in its repression and
secrecy surrounding the subject of sexual pleasure in *any* form.

For, having created a monosexual community, the Catholic Church forbade sexual gratification in all forms whatsoever. The Catholic leadership
expects its priests to have "overcome their sexuality" in the words of a November 30, 2005, document from the Vatican on the topic of the problem of
homosexual priests.[15] This statement beautifully exposes the Vatican's official view that sexual desire is a kind of disease. This has had the effect that
even when homosexual priests have found each other, they have been forbidden from pursuing intimate relationships. The one sexually gracious posture the Catholic authorities could have taken—even if they felt compelled
to do it *sotto voce*—would have been to tolerate instances of adult-to-adult
homosexuality in its ranks. There have been some episodic and circumstan-
tial signs that those in the highest ranks of the Catholic clergy actually do

look the other way on this matter, but such grace does not trickle down to the clerical grass roots. (Nor up to the current Pope.)

Such a brutal, inhumane discipline as celibacy is destined to be ignored by some, perhaps even by most. Revelations of priests luring children, mostly boys, into sexual liaisons should have surprised no one. The Church is being hoisted on its own petard. If a priest breaks the rule of total abstinence from sexual pleasure, and is discovered, he makes himself a potential pariah. Therefore, he is less likely to pay much attention to laws and customs that rightly protect minors. And minors are both more attractive generally, and more amenable to seduction, than adults. This is what happens when you drive out nature with a stick. It returns with a club.

The Catholic Church leaves the impression that it has been recently and sensibly less concerned about priests' sexual involvement with women than it has been with its pederasty problem. As well it might be, because there are no civil statutes prohibiting Catholic clergy from sexual involvement with women. A joke currently making its way around the Church claims that priests who become sexually involved with boys will be defrocked; those who have liaisons with women will be elevated to monsignor.

An active, self-aware, and discreet homosexual priest would be no disgrace to any church, except among narrow moralists. The Episcopal Church has been ordaining openly-practicing homosexuals for a generation now, and no evidence suggests them to be any worse morally than heterosexual priests. However, rather than a course of grace and tolerance, the current Catholic regime has begun something of a witch hunt, furthered by the new pope, Benedict XVI, to smoke out any active homosexuals in hopes of controlling the current epidemic of abuse of boys. The campaign is so self-defeating as to be laughable. Already suffering from a scarcity of leadership, under this new pope, the Catholic Church seems headed toward decimating its leadership even further.

The wish of Catholic leaders to protect their children is commendable; their wish to stop the hemorrhaging of money in lawsuits is understandable, as well. Any civilized group protects its underage children from sexually predatory adults. A minor who has been sexually approached by an adult may well have cause for complaint. On the other hand, the current frenzy of criminal and civil suits against priests of the Catholic Church appears to have garnered some of its momentum (on the part of some of the alleged victims) from the prospect of instant wealth. The Catholic Church does have deep pockets, and it seems that some of its accused priests are victims of persons who think they have won the lottery without buying a ticket.

Many of the reports of abuse are a bit over the top. Can anyone really believe that so many lives were actually ruined by a sexual overture or even by a seduction on the part of a priest? The sexual seduction of a six-year-old child by an adult would seem to be a cruel derailing of the developmental life of that child and ought to be anathematized. But the notion that an average 16-year-old boy would be marred for life by a homosexual experience with an adult should be examined with skepticism.

Man/boy love has never been my cup of tea, but in recent times its harmful effects on personality development have been exaggerated beyond reason or evidence. The tears of some of those who contend that their lives have been ruined by sexual overtures from priests, or from other adult males, are not persuasive to me. If man/boy sexual relationships are so utterly perverse, so unambiguously destructive, how did it happen that Greeks in classical times, who widely practiced pederasty, have come to be so admired today? Since Socrates, Plato, Aristotle, and the other Greek inventors of democracy all tolerated pederasty to some degree, and may well have engaged in it personally, we might turn down the volume a bit, today, on the evils of pederasty.

On the other hand, the Catholic Church continues to invite trouble— possibly even its own demise—by its pretense that healthy persons, committed to high moral values, will be content with a lifelong deprivation of every sort of sexual pleasure.

Postscript

Sexual liberation was the likely scandal of very early Christianity. Jesus himself behaved scandalously, and except for his disturbance in the Temple in Jerusalem, some of his most boorish behavior involved his disturbing relationships with women. He was in his context sexually liberated. Twenty centuries later, sexual liberation in Christianity is yet again a scandal, however inadvertently.

The alleged originating texts of Christianity that make up the New Testament provide no congruent sexual ethics. Every appearance of the word "fornication" in the English Bible is a mistranslation of the Greek word, *porneia*, which in the Palestinian Jewish context simply means "illicit sex." But what the first century Palestinian Jews considered sexually illicit was a far remove from what later Christendom meant by it. Furthermore, the New Testament texts show no interest in the sex-phobic ethics of Stoicism and Neoplatonism, the central philosophy and quasireligion of imperial Rome.

Neither do the words and actions of Jesus leave us with a clear sexual ethics. Elusive as he was, historically speaking, some aspects of his life are not disputed. Certainly, he was a rabbi, or something like a rabbi, and was committed to obedience to God's commandments as expressed in the Torah, the Jewish law. And yet he was a radical interpreter of that law, and in that respect he found himself at odds with the established guardians of moral and religious standards. Jesus was such an innovative interpreter of the Torah that he appeared to some to be a religious outlaw. His conflict with the Pharisees—probably his fellow Pharisees—hinged on his daring and innovative interpretations. He violated Sabbath rules, for example, but claimed he was still keeping the Sabbath. "The Sabbath was made for man, not man for the Sabbath." Jesus claimed to be a unequivocally obedient to the Torah, but his interpretation about how the Torah should be obeyed was quite radical.

In matters of sexual behavior Jesus appears to have been similarly radical and humanistic. He traveled with women disciples and allowed women to relate to him and touch him in ways that were considered gauche in the Jewish context. He talked with strange women in public places, which was prohibited. He allowed tainted women to massage his body with oil and tears. Even his own disciples were uneasy about his approach to women. Mary Magdalene in the texts seems to compete with Peter as his principal disciple. Some of the extra-canonical texts portray Jesus and Magdalene as lovers or possibly even married. (In the Jewish context the two are equivalent.) More than any other issue, Jesus' words and deeds in the arena of sexual behavior were the most likely offenses that led to his public disgrace and execution.

After Jesus was gone, his disciples traveled with their wives, or "women" (the Greek word being the same for both), following Jesus' example in that most un-Jewish practice. And Paul the Apostle addressed his wife in one of his letters, a fact that Christendom has managed to cover up.

Some of the early congregations of Christians (who also understood themselves to be Jews) exhibited sexual behaviors that were liberated and sometimes excessive. A generation after Jesus' death the congregation at Corinth was excoriated by Paul in his letter to them because of their sexual excesses. The traditional interpretation of the admonition from Paul is that this was a community that simply went off the rails in its sexual behavior. However, I conjecture that the Corinthian Christian-Jewish congregation was in fact a sexually liberated community that simply went too far for Paul's very rabbinic sense of propriety. A man was reported to have married his father's wife, something "even the gentiles would not tolerate," says Paul.[1]

Thus Jesus appears to have been, in modern lingo, something of a sexual liberationist. One point is unambiguously clear: for all of Jesus' radical critiques of marriage and rules about men's relationships with women, no data shows him to have supported monogamy, much less celibacy. Nor does he specifically attack polygamy or plural marriage. The negativity toward sexual pleasure that characterized imperial philosophy of his time, and was certainly not unknown in Palestine, received no support either from Jesus or the earliest Christian texts.

The absence of a distinct sexual ethics in the New Testament suggests that the Christian-Jews who created the documents were more or less in accord with prevailing Jewish sexual values, which would mean that the very first Christians would have more or less subscribed to prevailing interpretations of the Jewish law. "More or less" is an important qualifier because of the ambiguity of Jesus himself, who claimed to support the law but at the same time showed willingness to make radical and humanistic interpretations of it that some found objectionable. Jesus and the early Christians were, we can believe, tolerant of plural marriage, or polygamy.

Subsequent generations of Christian leaders gradually turned away from Jewish sexual values and looked increasingly to the Stoicism and Neoplatonism of the empire for their sexual teachings. More and more they became advocates of virginity and sexual abstinence except for purposes of procreation. They also adopted the imperial standard of monogamy. To accomplish this, they needed to choose carefully which of the many texts available they would canonize. Then these Christian leaders needed to manhandle and mistranslate (into Latin) the texts that they did canonize. Furthermore, they needed to extricate Jesus the rabbi from Judaism and make him a divine being in the Roman manner, masquerading as a human being. For all of the early church leaders' efforts at imposing Neo-platonic and Stoic fear and loathing of sex on the canonical texts—the New Testament—they were never able to make their case without manipulating the texts.

The early Christian movement adopted the symbol of fish for reasons that are lost to us. The fish seems to have predated the cross as a central Christian symbol. We do know for certain that fish was a symbol of sexuality, both in the empire and in many other cultures the world over. Thus the use of the fish symbol is suggestive of a sexual liberation movement. So too is the wide use in the early churches of the kiss of peace, or kiss of love, which was pointedly a mouth-to-mouth kiss.

The Jewish Pharisaic tradition in the meantime evolved into the Mishnaic—Talmudic tradition, continuing the values of Palestinian Judaism. Unlike later Christianity it continued to tolerate plural marriage and a positive view of sexual pleasure. Highly scrupulous—even obsessive—in its approach to behavior, the Talmudic tradition nevertheless continued to hold sexual relations in high esteem. It was as if the Jews so valued sexual pleasure that they felt the need to protect it with intricate rules and boundaries.

The evolution of Christianity from a radical Jewish movement into a new world religion was expedited by the polemical discrediting of Judaism by the Christian leadership in the generations after Jesus. The very earliest of the followers of Jesus had debated among themselves how much of the Jewish law they should be expected to follow. We see from Paul's writings, and the Acts of the Apostles, that these radical Jews were willing to forego circumcision and Jewish dietary laws even as they remained identified as Jews. Such liberties made these early Christian-Jews a problem to the more conservative Jews. The backlash from these conservatives helped fuel the polemic further and finally led to a full break from Judaism, and Christianity as a discrete new religion. This also set in motion what became 20 centuries of Christian anti-Semitism. By the fourth century Bishop Ambrose and others were calling for violence against Jews and the burning of their synagogues.

Jesus was a radical Jewish rabbi who so offended the Jewish religious leadership that they conspired with the Roman occupying authorities to have him put him to death. Clearly, Jews conspired against one of their own. But the gospel of John, the last to be written—in about 150 C.E., three to four generations after Jesus' death—leaves the impression in places that Jesus might not even have been a Jew. The bald statement that "the Jews killed him ..." is misleading by innuendo. Because he lived and worked as a Jew among Jews, who else would have killed him? The Roman occupiers actually did the dirty work but with the compliance of the Jewish population and leadership. The innuendo in the Gospel of John is that Jesus himself was not a Jew.

The Gospel of John was the beginning of the fabricated extraction of Jesus from Judaism that was promoted by Christianity. This revisionist portrait of Jesus reached its culmination in the eighteenth-century German philosopher, Johann Gottlieb Fichte, who claimed that Jesus was not really a Jew at all.[2] The twentieth century theologian Karl Barth countered Fichte, preaching a sermon in 1933, during Hitler's first year, entitled "Jesus Christ was a Jew." Some in the congregation walked out in protest. His rejoinder: "Anyone who believes in Christ, who was himself a Jew, and died for Gentiles and Jews, simply cannot be involved in the contempt for Jews and ill-treatment of them which is now the order of the day."[3]

Having extracted Jesus from Judaism, the early Christian leaders extracted him from humanity as well, making him a divine being who landed on the earth and walked among human beings until he returned to the godhead. That is, he was made into a god in the Roman imperial style. The Imperial Church in the fourth century officially declared Jesus fully God and fully man. This claim was touted as a "mystery" because any person who would be fully God could hardly be said to be a true mortal.

Having transformed Jesus into a Roman-style god in mufti, interacting with human beings as if one of them, it was easy to attribute to him Roman-style sexual values of abstinence and purity. All this was alien to Judaism. Paradoxically, the Christians continued to revere Jewish religious texts— what they called the Old Testament—but they reinterpreted these texts to suit the Christian agenda. This transformation did not occur overnight. It took ten centuries to become fully established. But established it was. The medieval period was the full flowering of this new religion of Christianity, born in Judaism, but so radically different from it, and so persecutorial of its religious origins.

The burden of the theoreticians of this new religion was to recast Jesus and Paul into sexual celibates, a calling never explicated in the New Testament texts. The word *celibate* is never even mentioned. They accomplished this feat only by twisting and reinterpreting the textual record to suit their objectives. The sexually liberated Jesus, almost certainly himself married, and the twice married Paul, both rabbis, were morphed into celibates by mistranslations and misinterpretations of the texts. It took a millennium to complete.

The Christian leaders in the early centuries did not universally hold to a view of Jesus as a sexually celibate divine being. Some held to the understanding of Jesus as a human being, a Palestinian rabbi. In the third century the dissenting group was centered in Antioch, Theodore of Mopsuestria being the central figure. Theodore and all others with such views were crushed and declared to be heretics. They were run over by the juggernaut of the first millennium, Augustine of Hippo. Augustine was the one most likely to have known better, but he was hobbled by an incestuous relationship with his mother that left him, for all his brilliance, deeply and irreparably conflicted about sexual pleasure. Thus Augustine, almost inadvertently, laid the theological foundation for what became Christianity's ultimate negative posture toward sexual pleasure.

The monastic movement that flourished in the Dark Age added its cumulative weight to a negative assessment of sexual pleasure. In the eleventh century the entire ranks of the clergy in Catholic Europe were monasticized, finally outlawing clerical marriage in the West. In the face of such a juggernaut, even the Jews of Europe were forced to disavow polygamy and adopt monogamy as a religious obligation. Their survival was at stake. Outside of Catholic Europe, Jews of course continued to tolerate polygamy.

Medieval Europe was on the face of it an airtight culture as regards sexual pleasure. There were counter-cultural persons and movements, but they were under pressure and were all crushed before they got very far. The homosexual flowering of the eleventh century had its day in the sun but was driven underground eventually. Various individuals dissented from the prevailing sex-negative ideology but were silenced. Peter Abelard, one of the brightest dissenting lights, was castrated and harassed his entire life. Other sexual dissenters were harassed, like Teresa of Avila, or exiled, like John of the Cross, or burned at the stake like Jan Hus.

In the sixteenth century Martin Luther, the monk who married Katy the nun, sent shock waves throughout Europe and inaugurated a revised Christianity called Protestantism. While he criticized the authoritarianism of Rome and its idolatry and mechanistic approach to religion, his unabashed embrace of sexual pleasure was "the shot heard round the world." Protestants gained a large following that continues today. Their major accomplishment was ending celibacy, along with the authority of the Catholic pope. The victory was only partial, however. Even Protestants continued to understand Jesus as a celibate divine being. Thus the Protestant Reformation was at best a piecemeal achievement.

The dissenters gained ground in the twentieth century. The 1960s Sexual Revolution revived the tradition of many silenced voices in Christian history, not only relatively successful ones like Luther, but also those who were either silenced or hemmed in by those who held power in the church—Theodore of Mopsuestia, Abelard, Teresa of Avila. In the twentieth century the seemingly settled Christian view of sexual abstinence as the highest moral value came under increasing attack. The sexual lives of the twentieth century's two preeminent theologians, Karl Barth and Paul Tillich, also helped undermine the established Christian veneration of sexual abstinence. Anton Boisen's clinical pastoral movement reasserted the importance of the self, allied itself with psychoanalytic theory, and helped Protestantism recover an affirmation of sexual pleasure. Boisen prepared Protestantism for the Sexual Revolution.

By the end of the twentieth century, the Christian West was in wide disarray, swept by contradictory voices. The liberation of women—and the ordaining of them as ministers—and the coming out of homosexuals signaled a new era. At the same time dark forces arose. An angry male-hating faction of feminists, hysteria over an imagined epidemic of sexual abuse of children, and a virulent homophobia provided major counter-currents against the Sexual Revolution. In the heat of that conflict, no major voice spoke with clarity of sexual pleasure as a great gift of God and that everyone was entitled to an ample share of it, which has always been the basic Jewish position.

Having evolved into the world's most sex-negative religion, Christianity has some serious and difficult changes to make if it is to survive as a credible world religion. It arguably made a critical error in distancing itself from the Judaism that gave it birth. Certainly, it erred in jettisoning Judaism's appreciation for sexual pleasure as God's great gift to human life. In electing to adopt the sexual values of Platonism and Stoicism, Christianity made a fateful choice that has poisoned the lives of countless persons for two millennia.

Christianity as a world religion is in profound crisis on the matter of what constitutes the proper ordering of sexual behavior. The medieval Catholic achievement, celibacy and total abstinence from sexual pleasure for the most religious, is no longer tenable. The evidence of the disintegration of that view of the world is all around us. Protestants are in a similar state of disintegration as they fight among themselves, not over celibacy, but over the proper boundaries of sexual pleasure. The partisans who sanctify heterosexual monogamy as the strict boundary within which sexual pleasure is permissible are losing ground, but the end of the warfare is nowhere in sight.

Christianity in all its manifestations—Catholic, Protestant, Orthodox—has only one good option, to return to its Jewish origins, and to the Pharisaic-Talmudic rabbi who started it all, and away from whom everyone seems to have drifted. The Pharisaic-Talmudic tradition has two important features that Christianity has lost sight of. All behavior, including sexual, is subject to the biblical call to love and justice. And furthermore, specific ethical judgments are always subject to a second opinion. No final or absolute answers to specific and concrete human behavioral dilemmas are envisioned. The basic biblical teaching, especially that represented by Jesus, is that all behavior—including sexual—is judged by the demands of love and justice, a teaching that is both rigorous and liberating.

A serious and determined commitment to justice and love offer not only the best hope for good in the world, but also the least likelihood of continuing Christianity's long campaign to inhibit its adherents from experiencing the best of God's gift to humankind, the pleasure of sex.

NOTES

EPIGRAPH

1. Nathaniel Hawthorne, *The House of the Seven Gables* (New York: Bantam Books, 1981), p. 139.
2. Paul Ricoeur, "Wonder, Eroticism, and Enigma," *Cross Currents* (Spring 1964): 133.

SERIES FOREWORD

1. Leroy Aden and J. Harold Ellens, *Turning Points in Pastoral Care: The Legacy of Anton Boisen and Seward Hiltner* (Grand Rapids: Baker, 1990). Anton Boisen was at the University of Chicago for decades and developed models for understanding the relationship between psychology and religion, as well as between mental illness, particularly psychoses, and the forms of meaningful spiritual or religious experience. Seward Hiltner was one of a large number of students of Boisen who carried his work forward by developing theological and psychotherapeutic structures and modes that gave operational application to Boisen's ideas. Hiltner was on the faculty of Princeton Theological Seminary, in the chair of Pastoral Theology and Pastoral Psychology for most of his illustrious career. While Boisen wrote relatively little, Hiltner published profusely and his works became notable contributions to church and society.
2. J. Harold Ellens, *Sex in the Bible: A New Consideration* (Westport, CT: Praeger, 2006).

FOREWORD BY DONALD CAPPS

1. Raymond J. Lawrence, *The Poisoning of Eros: Sexual Values in Conflict* (New York: Augustine Moore Press, 1989).

INTRODUCTION

1. Edward Gibbon, *The Decline and Fall of the Roman Empire*, Vol. 1, ed. Hans-Friedrich Mueller (New York: The Modern Library, 2003), chap. xv, pp. 237–38.

2. Personal communication with author, at New York Presbyterian Hospital, Columbia University Medical Center, January 14, 2005.

3. Raymond Lawrence, *The Poisoning of Eros: Sexual Values in Conflict* (New York: Augustine Moore Press, 1989).

CHAPTER 1

1. "The Gospel of Philip," in *The Nag Hammadi Library*, ed. James M. Robinson (New York: Harper & Row, 1988), p. 138.

2. Philip Culbertson, "The Pharisaic Jesus and His Gospel Parables," *The Christian Century*, January 23, 1985, pp. 74–77; see also E. P. Sanders, *Jesus and Judaism* (Philadelphia: Fortress Press, 1985).

3. Berakoth 57b, trans. M. Simon, *The Babylonian Talmud*, ed. I. Epstein (London: Soncino Press, 1948), p. 356.

4. The age at which a girl could make her own marital decision was 12-1/2, according to Pharisaic teaching; see Louis Finkelstein, *The Pharisees: The Sociological Background of Their Faith*, 2 Vols. (Philadelphia: The Jewish Publication Society of America, 1962), vol. 1, p. lxxviii.

5. Kuddushin 4:13–14, *The Babylonian Talmud*.

6. C. B. Caird, "Chronology," in *Interpreters' Dictionary of the Bible* (New York: Abingdon Press, 1962), Vol. I, pp. 599–607.

7. "Irenaeus Against Heresies," in *The Apostolic Fathers with Justin Martyr and Irenaeus*, vol. 1 of *The Ante-Nicene Fathers*, ed. Alexander Roberts and James Donaldson (Grand Rapids, MI: Wm. B. Eerdmans Publishing Company, 1950), 2.22.5&6.

8. John 8:57.

9. John 2:20.

10. Matthew 22:23–33; Mark 12:18–27; Luke 20:27–40.

11. Matthew 19:12ff.

12. William Countryman, *Dirt, Greed, and Sex* (Philadelphia: Fortress Press, 1988).

13. Donald Capps, *Jesus: A Psychological Biography* (St. Louis: Chalice Press, 2000).

14. Mark 6:3.

CHAPTER 2

1. Matthew 1:1–17.

2. Luke 3:23–38.

3. Jane Schaberg, *The Illegitimacy of Jesus: A Feminist Theological Interpretation of the Infancy Narratives* (New York: Crossroad, 1990).

4. Luke 10:38–42.

5. John 11:2ff.

6. Luke 7:38.

7. Matthew 26:6ff.; Mark 14:3ff.

8. Luke 7:39.

9. "The Gospel of Philip," *The Nag Hamadi Library in English*, ed. James M. Robinson (San Francisco: Harper & Row, 1988), p. 148.

10. I Corinthians 15:3–8.

11. Raymond J. Lawrence, "The Fish: A Lost Symbol of Sexual Liberation?" *Journal of Religion and Health* 30, no. 4 (Winter 1991): pp. 311–19.

12. Augustine, *The City of God*, Book xviii, Chap. 23, p. 790, trans. Henry Bettenson (New York: Penguin Books, 1981).

13. Tim Butcher, "Earliest Christian Church Found in Israeli Jail," telegraph.co.uk, 7–11–05.

14. J. Harold Ellens, *Sex and the Bible: A New Consideration* (Westport, CT: Praeger, 2006); Raymond J. Lawrence, *The Poisoning of Eros: Sexual Values in Conflict* (New York: Augustine Moore Press, 1989).

CHAPTER 3

1. Bruce Malina, "Does Pornea Mean Fornication?" *Novum Testamentum* XIV (1972): 10–17.

2. On the "eschatological challenge" see Raymond J. Lawrence, *The Poisoning of Eros: Sexual Values in Conflict* (New York: Augustine Moore Press, 1989), pp. 43–49.

3. Lucius Annaeus Seneca, for example, statesman, man of letters, and contemporary of Jesus, referred to sexual desire as "friendship gone mad" in *Letters from a Stoic*, ed. and trans. Robin Campbell (New York: Penguin Books, 1969), p. 50.

4. Acts 16:15, 40.

5. William F. Arndt and F. Wilbur Gingrich, *Greek English Lexicon of the New Testament* (Chicago: University of Chicago Press, 1957), p. 783.

6. Bishop Clement, *On Marriage* 3.6.53, *The Library of Christian Classics, Vol II, Alexandrian Christianity*, ed. J.E.L. Oulton and Henry Chadwick (Philadelphia: Westminster Press, 1954), p. 64.

CHAPTER 4

1. David M. Feldman, *Marital Relations, Birth Control and Abortion in Jewish Law* (New York: Schocken Books, 1974); Louis Finkelstein, *The Pharisees: The Sociological Background of Their Faith*, 2 Vols. (Philadelphia: The Jewish Publication Society of America, 1962); E. P. Sanders, *Jesus and Judaism* (Philadelphia: Fortress Press, 1985).

2. Paul Ricoeur, *The Symbolism of Evil* (Boston: Beacon Press, 1967), pp. 118ff.

3. Sanhedrin 107b, trans. Rabbi Mordecai Schnaidman.

4. H. Friedman and M. Simon, trans., *Midrash Rabbah in Ten Volumes* (London: Soncino Press, 1939), vol. 1, p. 144.

5. Genesis 38:8.

6. Matthew 22:23ff.

7. Joshua 2.

8. Hebrews 11:31.

9. James 2:25.

10. Matthew 1:5.

11. Marvin Pope, *The Anchor Bible Commentary: Song of Songs* (Garden City, NY: Doubleday, 1977).

12. Marvin H. Pope in a review published in *Catholic Biblical Quarterly* 54 (1992): 758–61. The quote is from a review of Roland E. Murphy, *The Song of Songs: A Commentary* ..., ed. S. Dean McBride, Jr. (Minneapolis: Fortress, 1990), pp. xxii and 237.

13. Murphy, *The Song of Songs.* Murphy had pointed out that Thomas Carew wrote of the same *valley* in his poem, "In Praise of his Mistress."

From those hills descends a valley
Where all fall who dare to dally.

14. Marvin H. Pope, *The Anchor Bible Commentary: Song of Songs* (Garden City, NY: Doubleday, 1977), p. 222.

15. Pope, *Catholic Bible Quarterly* 54 (1992):19.

16. Pope, *Anchor Bible Commentary*, p. 19.

17. Ezekiel 16:8.

18. I Kings 1:3.

19. Charles B. Flood, *Hitler: The Path to Power* (Boston: Houghton Mifflin, 1989), pp. 236, 253, 593–94.

20. Herman Wouk, *This Is My God* (Garden City, NY: Doubleday, 1959), p. 155.

CHAPTER 5

1. Strabo, *Geography*, 16.2.39, trans. W. Falconer (London: HG Bohn, 1867).

2. Tacitus, *The Histories*, trans. Kenneth Wellesley (New York: Penguin Books, 1964), pp. 273–74.

3. Celsus is quoted in Raymond J. Lawrence, *The Poisoning of Eros: Sexual Values in Conflict* (New York: Augustine Moore Press, 1989), p. 91.

4. James Carroll, *Constantine's Sword: The Church and the Jews* (New York: Houghton Mifflin, 2001).

5. Stephen Benko, *Pagan Rome and the Early Christians* (Bloomington: Indiana University Press, 1984), p. 98.

6. Stephen Benko, *Pagan Rome and the Early Christians* (Bloomington: Indiana University Press, 1984), p. 98.

7. J. B. Phillips, *The New Testament in Modern English* (New York: Macmillan, 1958).

8. Bishop Clement of Alexandria, "Christ the Educator," 3.11.81, *The Fathers of the Church: Clement of Alexandria*, trans. Simon P. Wood (New York: Fathers of the Church, Inc., 1954), p. 261.

9. Bishop Athenagorus, *Embassy*, trans. Joseph Hugh Crehan (Westminster, MD: Newman Press, 1956), p. 32.

10. M. Cornelius Fronto, *The Octavius of Marcus Minucius Felix*, trans. G. W. Clarke (New York: Newman Press, 1974), pp. 64–65.

11. John Julius Norwich, *Byzantium: The Decline and Fall* (New York: Alfred A. Knopf, 2000), p. 201.

12. Paul Tillich, *The Shaking of the Foundations* (London: SCM Press, 1949), p. 172.

13. Heraclitus is quoted in Leo Steinberg, *The Sexuality of Christ in Renaissance Art and in Modern Oblivion* (New York: Pantheon, 1983), p. 12.

CHAPTER 6

1. Joseph Brodsky, "Reflections," *The New Yorker* (October, 1985): 47.

2. Rowan A. Greer, *Theodore of Mopsuestia: Exegete and Theologian* (London: Faith Press, 1961); Richard. A. Norris, *Manhood and Christ: A Study of the Christology of Theodore of Mopsuestia* (Oxford: Clarendon Press, 1963).

3. *The Letters of the Younger Pliny*, trans. Betty Radice (New York: Penguin Books, 1963), pp. 294–95.

4. For a brilliant study of the early fourth-century church's obsession with sex, see Samuel Laeuchli, *Power and Sexuality* (Philadelphia: Temple University Press, 1972).

5. Charles Freeman, *The Closing of the Western Mind: The Rise of Faith and the Fall of Reason* (New York: Alfred A. Knopf, 2003).

CHAPTER 7

1. *The Letters of St. Jerome*, trans. C. C. Mierow Vol. 1, Letters 1–22 (New York: Newman Press, 1963), p. 152.

2. *St. Jerome: Dogmatic and Polemical Works*, trans. John N. Hritzu (Washington: Catholic University of America Press, 1965), p. 35. But the wording here draws on Pierre de Labriolee's translation from *History and Literature of Christianity from Tertullian to Boethius* (New York: Barnes & Noble, 1968), p. 351.

3. Epistle 107,11.

4. Peter Brown, *Augustine of Hippo* (Berkeley: University of California Press, 1967), pp. 381–92.

5. J.N.D. Kelly, *Jerome: His Life, Writings and Controversies* (New York: Harper & Row, 1975), p. 124.

6. Augustine, *Confessions* 6:15, trans. F. J. Sheed (New York: Sheed & Ward, 1948), p. 126.

7. Donald Capps, "Augustine as Narcissist," *Journal of American Academy of Religion* liii, no. 1 (March 1985): 115–27.

8. Eva Keuls, *The Reign of the Phallus: Sexual Politics in Ancient Athens* (New York: Harper & Row, 1985).

9. Sermon 169:11, cited by Peter Brown, *Religion and Society in the Age of St. Augustine* (New York: Harper & Row, 1972), p. 30.

10. Sermon 151:5. *The Works of St. Augustine*, trans. Edmund Hill, ed. John E. Rotelle (New Rochelle, NY: New City Press, 1992), pp. 43–44. See also Soren Kierkegaard, *Attack on Christendom*, trans. Walter Lowrie (Princeton, NJ: Princeton University Press, 1944).

11. *Contra Julian* 3.14.28.

12. Peter Brown, "Augustine and Sexuality" (Berkeley: University of California Center for Hermeneutical Studies, 1983), p. 12.

CHAPTER 8

1. *The Holy Rule of St. Benedict*, trans. Boniface Verbeyen (Atcheson, KS: St. Benedict's Abbey, 1949), pp. 480–543.

2. St. Gregory the Great, *Pastoral Care*, trans. Henry Davis (Westminster, MD: Newman Press), Part III, Chapter 27, pp. 186–92.

3. Venerable Bede, *A History of the English Church and People*, trans. Leo Shirley-Price (New York: Penguin Books, 1955), p. 80.

4. Ibid.

5. Pierre J. Payer, *Sex and the Penitentials* (Toronto: University of Toronto Press, 1984).

6. Llewellyn Barstow, *Married Priests and the Reforming Papacy: The Eleventh Century Debates* (New York: Edwin Mellen Press, 1982).

7. John Boswell, *Christianity, Social Tolerance, and Homosexuality* (Chicago: University of Chicago Press, 1980).

8. Norman F. Cantor, *Civilization of the Middle Ages* (New York: HarperCollins, 1993).

CHAPTER 9

1. John Julius Norwich, *Byzantium: The Decline and Fall* (New York: Alfred A. Knopf, 2000), p. 93.

2. *Letters of St. Bernard of Clairvaux*, trans. Bruno Scott James (London: Burns Oates, 1953), Letter 244.

3. James Burge, *Heloise and Abelard: A New Biography* (San Francisco: Harper, 2003).

4. *Peter Abelard's Ethics*, trans. D. E. Luscombe (Oxford: Clarendon Press, 1971, p. 21).

5. Joseph Campbell, *The Masks of God: Creative Mythology* (New York: Viking Press, 1968), quoting from Nietzsche, *Thus Spoke Zarathustra: A Book for All and None*, trans. Walter Kaufmann (New York: Viking Press, 1966), p. 38.

6. *The Letters of Abelard and Heloise*, trans. Betty Radice (New York: Penguin Books, 1974), pp. 113–14, 133–35, 138.

7. Ibid.

8. Peter Dronke, *Abelard and Heloise in Medieval Testimonies* (Glasgow: University of Glasgow Press, 1976), p. 15.

9. Giles Constable, ed. *The Letters of Peter the Venerable in Two Volumes* (Cambridge, MA: Harvard University Press, 1967), Vol. 1, Letter 115, pp. 307–8.

10. James Burge, *Heloise and Abelard: A New Biography* (San Francisco: Harper & Row, 2003).

11. Norwich, *Byzantium*, Vol. III, p. 107.

CHAPTER 10

1. Denis deRougement, *Love in the Western World*, trans. Montgomery Belgion (Greenwich, CT: Fawcett, 1956).

2. deRougement, *Love in the Western World*, p. 243.

CHAPTER 11

1. Jasper Ridley, *Statesman and Saint: Cardinal Wolsey, Sir Thomas More, and the Politics of Henry VIII* (New York: Viking Press, 1982), p. 290. See also Richard Marius, *Thomas More: A Biography* (New York: Vintage Books, 1984); G. R. Elton, "The Real Thomas More?" in *Reformation Principle and Practice: Essays in Honor of Arthur Geoffrey Dickens*, ed. Peter Newman Brooks (Scholars Press, 1980), pp. 21–32; Alistair Fox, *Thomas More* (New Haven, CT: Yale University Press, 1983).

2. Peter Ackroyd, *The Life of Thomas More* (New York: Doubleday, 1998), p. 298.

3. Ibid., p. 146.

4. Ibid., p. 230.

5. Ibid., p. 12.

6. Ibid., p. 144.

7. Ibid., p. 143.

8. Ibid., p. 83.

9. Ibid., p. 406.

CHAPTER 12

1. St. Thomas Aquinas, *Summa Theologica* (London: Blackfriars), vol. 13 (Ia 90–102), p. 157.

2. St. Thomas Aquinas citing Augustine's *Solil* 1.10., in *Summa Theologica in Five Volumes*, trans. Fathers of the English Dominican Province (Westminster, MD: Christian Classics, 1981), Vol. II, p. 186.4.

3. Charles Freeman, *The Closing of the Western Mind: The Rise of Faith and the Fall of Reason* (New York: Alfred A. Knopf, 2003), pp. 328ff.

4. L. H. Petitot, *The Life and Spirit of Thomas Aquinas*, trans. Cyprian Burke (Chicago: Priory Press, 1966), pp. 154, 160–66.

5. Heiko Oberman, *Luther: Man between God and the Devil*, trans. Eileen Walliser-Schwarzbart (New Haven, CT: Yale University Press, 1989), p. 310.

6. Leo Steinberg, *The Sexuality of Christ in Renaissance Art and in Modern Oblivion* (New York: Pantheon, 1983), p. 12.

7. William J. Bouwsma, *John Calvin* (New York: Oxford University Press, 1988), p. 53.

8. James Carroll, *Constantine's Sword: The Church and the Jews* (New York: Houghton Mifflin, 2001), p. 425.

9. Oberman, *Luther*, p. 296.

10. Ibid., p. 371.

11. Oberman, *Luther*, p. 296.

12. Erik Erikson, *Young Man Luther* (New York: Norton, 1958).

13. John M. Todd, *Luther* (New York: Crossroad, 1982), p. 320.

14. http://www.spurgeon.org/~phil/history/95theses.htm, accessed October 17, 2006.

15. Susan C. Karant-Nunn and Merry E. Wiesner-Hanks, trans. and eds., *Luther on Women: A Sourcebook* (New York: Cambridge University Press, 2003), p. 141.

16. Theodore G. Tappert and Helmut T. Lehmann, eds, *Luther's Works: Table Talk* (Philadelphia: Fortress Press, 1967), Vol. 54, p. 160.

17. E. G. Schwiebert, *Luther and His Times: The Reformation form a New Perspective* (St. Louis: Concordia Publishing House, 1950), p. 588.

18. Oberman, *Luther*, p. 281.

19. Peter Ackroyd, *The Life of Thomas More* (New York: Doubleday, 1998), p. 248.

20. Ackroyd, *The Life of Thomas More*, p. 278.

21. Ackroyd, *The Life of Thomas More*, p. 276.

22. Martine Brecht, *Martin Luther: Shaping and Defining the Reformation, 1521–1532*, trans. James L. Schaaf (Minneapolis: Fortress Press, 1990), pp. 198, 200.

23. Oberman, *Luther*, p. 287.

24. Tappert and Lehmann, *Luther's Works*, p. 153.

25. Tapper and Lehmann, *Luther's Works*, p. 397.

26. Tapper and Lehmann, *Luther's Works*, p. 177

27. Heiko A. Oberman, "Luther and the Devil," *Lutheran Theological Seminary Bulletin* (Winter 1989): 10.

28. Tappert and Lehmann, *Luther's Works*, p. 65.

29. Tappert and Lehmann, *Luther's Works*, p. 103.

30. Justice Jonas, Michael Coelius, et al. *The Last Days of Luther*, trans. Martin Ebon (Garden City, NY: Doubleday, 1970), p. 21.

31. Oberman, "Luther and the Devil," p. 320.

CHAPTER 13

1. Cathleen Medwick, *Teresa of Avila: The Progress of a Soul* (New York: Doubleday, 1999).

2. Medwick, *Teresa of Avila*, p. ix.

3. Sigmund Freud and Jacob Breuer, *Studies in Hysteria, 1893–1895*, trans. A. A. Brill (Boston: Beacon Press, 1961), p. xv, cited by Medwick, *Teresa of Avila*, pp. xv, 32.

4. Medwick, *Teresa of Avila*, p. 244.

5. Roy Campbell, *The Poems of St. John of the Cross* (London: Harvill, 1951), pp. 11–13.

6. Campbell, *The Poems of St. John of the Cross.*

7. Medwick, *Teresa of Avila*, p. 50.

CHAPTER 14

1. http://www.dioceseofeaston.org. Accessed October 20, 2006.

2. Atavism—the reappearance of a characteristic in an organism after several generations of absence, caused by a recessive gene or complementary genes. Also loosely called "reversion" or "throwback."

3. Hans Kung, *On Being a Christian*, trans. Edward Quinn (Garden City, NY: Doubleday, 1984; orig. published in German, 1974).

4. Jacques Pohier, *God—in Fragments*, trans. John Bowden (New York: Crossroad, 1986), p. 185. See also Jacques Pohier, "Pleasure and Christianity" in *Concilium: Religion in the Seventies*, Vol. 100, *Sexuality in Contemporary Catholicism*, ed. Franz Bockle and Jacques Pohier (New York: Seabury Press, 1976).

5. Pohier, *God—in Fragments*, p. 142

6. Pohier, *God—in Fragments*, p. 183.

7. Pohier, *God—in Fragments*, p. 185.

8. Pohier, "Pleasure and Christianity," p. 104.

9. Mark 2:27.

10. Anton T. Boisen, *The Exploration of the Inner World: A Study of Mental Disorder and Religious Experience* (Philadelphia: University of Pennsylvania Press, 1936); Anton T. Boisen, *Out of the Depths: An Autobiographical Study of Mental Disorder and Religious Experience* (New York: Harper, 1960).

CHAPTER 15

1. The orgone box, or accumulator, was a small closet in which Reich placed his patients for sexually therapeutic purposes. The U.S. Government prosecuted Reich for use of the accumulator and put him in federal prison, where he died. See Orson Bean, *Me and the Orgone* (Princeton, NJ: The American College of Orgonomy, 2000).

2. Personal communication at New York Presbyterian Hospital, January 14, 2005.

3. Anton T. Boisen, *Out of the Depths: An Autobiographical Study of Mental Disorder and Religious Experience* (New York: Harper, 1960), p. 24.

4. Boisen, *Out of the Depths*, p. 25.

5. Boisen, *Out of the Depths*, p. 46.

6. Boisen, *Out of the Depths*, p. 47.

7. Boisen, *Out of the Depths*, p. 131.

8. Boisen, *Out of the Depths*, p. 103.

9. Boisen, *Out of the Depths*, p. 160.

10. Boisen, *Out of the Depths*, p. 169.

11. Boisen, *Out of the Depths*, p. 169.

12. Boisen, *Out of the Depths*, p. 200.

13. Richard A. Schweder, "It's Time to Reinvent Freud," *New York Times*, December 15, 1995, p. A43.

CHAPTER 16

1. John Bowden, *Karl Barth* (London: SCM Press, 1971), p. 11.

2. Personal communication at a meeting at General Theological Seminary, New York City, sometime in the 1980s.

3. The authorized biographies were Eberhard Busch, *Karl Barth*, trans. John Bowden (Philadelphia: Fortress Press, 1976), and Wilhelm and Marion Pauck, *Paul Tillich: His Life and Thought*, 2 Vols. (New York: Harper & Row, 1976).

4. Roland Kleming, ed., *Jews in Germany under Prussian Rule* (Berlin: Bildarchiv Preussischer Kulturbesitz, 1984).

5. Busch, *Karl Barth*, p. 185.

6. Busch, *Karl Barth*, p. 186.

7. Personal communication at a seminar at the School of Theology, at the University of the South, Sewanee, TN, in the 1970s.

8. Busch, *Karl Barth*, p. 472.

9. Busch, *Karl Barth*, p. 472.

10. Karl Barth, *Church Dogmatics*, III/4, ed. G. W. Bromiley and T. F. Torrance (Edinburgh: T&T Clark, 1960), p. 129.

11. Barth, *Church Dogmatics*, p. 228.

12. Barth, *Church Dogmatics*, p. 131.

13. Barth, *Church Dogmatics*, pp. 124, 161.

14. Barth, *Church Dogmatics*, p. 165.

15. Barth, *Church Dogmatics*, p. 239.

16. Barth, *Church Dogmatics*, p. 239.

17. Karl Barth, *Ethics*, ed. Dietrich Brown, trans. G. W. Bromiley (New York: Seabury Press, 1981), p. 227.

18. Barth, *Ethics*, p. 187.

19. Paul Tillich, *Systematic Theology, Vol. II* (Chicago: University of Chicago Press, 1957), p. 41.

20. Tillich, *Systematic Theology*, p. 59.

21. Rollo May, *Paulus* (New York: Harper & Row, 1973), p. 65.

22. Ibid. See also Hannah Tillich, *From Time to Time* (New York: Stein and Day, 1973); Renate Kobler, *In the Shadow of Karl Barth: Charlotte von Kirschbaum*, trans. Keith Crim (Louisville: Westminster/John Knox Press, 1989); Suzanne Selinger, *Charlotte von Kirschbaum and Karl Barth: A Study in Biography and the History of Theology* (University Park: Pennsylvania State University Press, 1998).

23. May, *Paulus*, p. 57.

24. F. Pratt Green, *The Expository Times* 86, no. 352 (August 1975).

25. Personal communication at a lecture at the School of Theology, at the University of the South, Sewanee, TN, in the 1970s.

26. Seward Hiltner, "Tillich, The Person: A Review Article," *Theology Today* 30 (January 1974), p. 352.

27. Hannah Tillich, *From Time to Time* (New York: Stein and Day, 1973).

28. The interviewer is a well-known and highly respected woman writer and biographer, and a personal acquaintance of mine, who in this context prefers to remain anonymous.

CHAPTER 17

1. D. H. Lawrence, *Lady Chatterly's Lover* (The Hague, Netherlands: William Heineman, 1956).

2. Jeffrey Toobin, "Annals of Law: The Trouble with Sex—Why the Law of Sexual Harassment Has Never Worked," *The New Yorker*, February 9, 1998, p. 50.

3. David M. Buss, *The Evolution of Desire: Strategies of Human Mating* (New York: Basic Books, 1994).

4. "Study Finds Sexism in Nature," *The Onion*, March 14–20, 2002, p. 1.

5. Adam Nossiter, "6-Year-Old's Sex Crime: Innocent Peck on Cheek," *New York Times*, September 27, 1996, p. A-14.

6. Myron Madden, Personal communication in Virginia Beach, March 20, 2004.

7. Lloyd DeMause, *The Emotional Life of Nations* (New York: Other Press, 2002), ch. 7; Gillian Gillison, *Between Culture and Fantasy* (New York: The Institute for Psychohistory), http://www.psychohistory.com, accessed October 17, 2006.

8. Robert Anderson, *Tea and Sympathy: A Drama in Three Sets* (New York: Random House, 1953). See also *Summer of '42*, dir. Robert Mulligan, 1971.

9. Jill Bruce, "Geisel Called 'Victim' in Sex Abuse." *The [Schenectady] Daily Gazette*, November 22, 2005, p. 1.

10. Jill Bruce, "Geisel Called 'Victim' in Sex Abuse." *The [Schenectady] Daily Gazette*, November 22, 2005, p. 1.

11. Personal experience, Roanoke, VA, 1990.

12. http://en.wikipedia.org/wiki/branch_davidian.

13. Peter Rutter, *Sex in the Forbidden Zone: When Men in Power—Therapists, Doctors, Clergy & Others Betray Women's* ... (Tarcher, 1989); Jon R. Conte, ed., *Critical Issues in Child Sexual Abuse: Historical, Legal and Psychological Perspectives* (Thousand Oaks, CA: Sage Publications, 2002).

14. Stephen J. Ceci, D. F. Ross, and Michael P. Toglia, *Perspectives on Children's Testimony* (New York: Springer, 1989).

15. Personal observation, Farmville, NC, October 21, 1991.

16. "Innocence Lost," *PBS Frontline TV,* prod. Ofra Bikel, 1993.

17. I was founder and chairman of this committee.

18. Richard A. Gardiner, *True and False Accusations of Child Sex Abuse* (Cresshill, NJ: Creative Therapeutics, 1992); Dorothy Rabinowitz, *No Crueler Tyrannies: Accusations, False Witnesses, and Other Terrors of Our Times* (New York: Wall Street Journal Books, 2003).

19. I was in frequent personal contact with Doug Wiik, owner of Breezy Point.

20. Dr. Lewis Rambo, "Interview with Dr. Peter Rutter, Author ... " *Pastoral Psychology* 39, no. 5 (1991): 332.

21. Rutter, *Sex in the Forbidden Zone*, p. 196.

22. Obituaries, *New York Times*, October 26, 1999, p. B-9.

23. Rustum and Della Roy, in *Honest Sex* (New York: New American Library, 1968), were among the very first of twentieth-century theologians to challenge conventional monogamous Christianity. See also Raymond J. Lawrence, "The Affair as a Redemptive Experience," *Adventures in Loving*, ed. Robert H. Rimmer (New York: New American Library, 1973), pp. 65–69.

24. Marty Klein, "Why There's No Such Thing As Sex Addiction—And Why It Really Matters," http://www.sexed.org/archive/article08.html, accessed November 3, 2006. See also Marty Klein, *America's War on Sex: The Attack on Law, Lust, and Liberty* (Westport, CT: Praeger, 2006).

25. Marjorie Williams, "A Matter of Life and Death," excerpts from *The Woman at the Washington Zoo*: www.vanityfair.com, accessed October 6, 2006. See also Timothy Noah, ed., *The Woman at the Washington Zoo: Writing on Politics, Family and Fate* (Cambridge, MA: Perseus Books, 2005).

CHAPTER 18

1. Donald Capps, "From Masturbation to Homosexuality: A Case of Displaced Moral Disapproval," *Pastoral Psychology* 51, no. 4 (2003): 249–72.

2. "Study: Most Self Abuse Goes Unreported," *The Onion* 40, no. 4 (January 28, 2004).

3. Martin Luther, "Against the Spiritual Estate of Pope and Bishops Falsely So-Called" (1522).

4. Haim G. Ginot, *Between Parent and Teenager* (New York: Macmillan, 1969), p. 169.

5. Capps, 2003, p. 250, citing Samuel Tissot.

6. Thomas Stephen Szasz, *The Therapeutic State: Psychiatry in the Mirror of Current Events* (Buffalo, NY: Prometheus Books, 1984).

7. Capps, 2003, citing Emmanuel Kant.

8. Capps, 2003, p. 256, citing Dr. Timothy Haynes' article published in the *Boston Medical and Surgical Journal* in 1883.

9. William James, *The Varieties of Religious Experience* (New York: Penguin Books, 1982), p. 160.

10. Kim Townsend, *Manhood at Harvard: William James and Others* (New York: W.W. Norton, 1996), p. 53.

11. Capps, 2003, p. 263; Leslie D. Weatherhead, *The Mastery of Sex through Psychology and Religion* (New York: The Macmillan Company, 1947), p. 141.

12. Thomas Szasz, *The Therapeutic State*, p. 351.

13. Thomas Szasz, *The Therapeutic State*, p. 346.

CHAPTER 19

1. John Lehmann, "Grein's Wife Said He Was a Philanderer," *New York Post*, May 14, 2002, cited by virtuosity@listserv.episcopalian.org.

2. "Policy Statement & Protocol on Sexual Misconduct of the Baltimore-Washington Conference of the United Methodist Church," 1993, p. 2.

3. Kimberly Day-Lewis and Wayne E. Gustafson, "Professional Boundaries and Ethics," New York Conference of the United Church of Christ, September 29–30, 2005.

4. Ibid.

5. Ibid.

6. John D. Worrell, "A Basket of Carp: Sexual Conduct in Sydney," in *Nevertheless* (Spring, TX: Pentecost, 2004), p. 11.

7. Ibid.

8. Marie M. Fortune, *Is Nothing Sacred? When Sex Invades a Pastoral Relationship* (San Francisco: Harper and Row, 1989); Marie M. Fortune, *Love Does No Harm: Sexual Ethics for the Rest of Us* (New York: Continuum, 1995).

9. Marie M. Fortune, *Is Nothing Sacred?: When Sex Invades the Pastoral Relationship* (San Francisco: Harper & Row, 1989).

10. Peter Rutter, *Sex in the Forbidden Zone: When Men in Power—Therapists, Doctors, Clergy & Others Betray Women's ...* (New York: Fawcett Crest, 1989), p. 28.

11. "Dear Abby," syndication, March 8, 2004.

12. Genesis 39.

13. Pheromone is "a chemical substance that is produced by an animal and serves especially as a stimulus to other individuals of the same species for one or more behavioral responses." *Miriam Webster's Collegiate Dictionary*, Tenth Edition.

14. Amanda Ripley, "Inside the Church's Closet," *Time Magazine*, May 20, 2002.

15. "Encyclical Letter *Deus Caritas Est* of the Supreme Pontiff Benedict XVI to the Bishops Priests and Deacons Men and Women Religious and All the Lay Faithful on Christian Love," section 5.

POSTSCRIPT

1. I Corinthians 5:1.

2. James Carroll, *op. cit.*, p. 72.

3. Eberhard Busch, *Karl Barth*, pp. 234–35.

Index

About the Author

RAYMOND J. LAWRENCE, JR. is Director of Pastoral Care at New York Presbyterian Hospital, Columbia University Medical Center, General Secretary of the College of Pastoral Supervision and Psychotherapy, and Director of Pastoral Care at the New York Council of Churches. He is the author of *The Poisoning of Eros: Sexual Values in Conflict*, which won the 1989 Book Award from the World Congress for Sexology.

Recent Titles in
Psychology, Religion, and Spirituality
J. Harold Ellens, Series Editor

Married to an Opposite: Making Personality Differences Work for You
Ron Shackelford

Sin against the Innocents: Sexual Abuse by Priests and the Role of the
Catholic Church
Thomas G. Plante, editor

Seeking the Compassionate Life: The Moral Crisis for Psychotherapy and
Society
Carl Goldberg and Virginia Crespo

Psychology and the Bible: A New Way to Read the Scriptures, 4 Volumes
J. Harold Ellens and Wayne E. Rollins, editors

Sex in the Bible: A New Consideration
J. Harold Ellens

Where God and Science Meet: How Brain and Evolutionary Studies
Alter Our Understanding of Religion
Patrick McNamara